D1450854

Literary Wit

Literary
WIT

■ Bruce Michelson

UNIVERSITY OF MASSACHUSETTS PRESS ■ AMHERST

PS430
M48
2000

Printed in the United States of America
LC 00-055179
ISBN 1-55849-273-9 (lib. cloth); 274-7 (paper)

Set in Quadraat and Quadraat Sans by Graphic Composition, Inc.
Designed by Mary Mendell
Printed and bound by Sheridan Books

Library of Congress Cataloging-in-Publication Data
Michelson, Bruce, 1948–
Literary wit / Bruce Michelson.
    p. cm.
Includes bibliographical references and index.
ISBN 1-55849-273-9 (lib. cloth : alk. paper)
ISBN 1-55849-274-7 (pbk. : alk. paper)
1. American wit and humor—History and criticism—
Theory, etc.   2. American literature—History and criticism.
3. English wit and humor—History and criticism—
Theory, etc.   4. English literature—History and criticism.
5. Wit and humor—Philosophy.   I. Title.
PS430 M48 2000   817.009—dc21
00-055179

British Library Cataloguing in Publication data are available.

Permission to reprint the following material is gratefully acknowledged:

Excerpts from Wit by Margaret Edson. Copyright © 1993, 1999 by Margaret
Edson. Reprinted by permission of Faber and Faber Inc., an affiliate of Farrar,
Straus and Giroux, LLC. Wit is published in Britain and Ireland by Nick Hern
Books, and exerpts are reprinted here with permission.

(Permissions to reprint copyrighted material continue on page 183.)

ONCE AGAIN, FOR THERESA

Contents

Acknowledgments

Literary Wit grew in a gale of conversation, and many friends have played a part. With compassionate skepticism, Gregg Camfield, Vic Doyno, Jim Hurt, Herbert Marder, Leon Waldoff, and Julia A. Walker braved early drafts and shared wisdom. As a research assistant, Gardner Rogers has been savvy company on excursions into peculiar ideas; Michael Bérubé, Nancy Blake, Tim Dean, Doug Kibbee, and William Maxwell gave guidance through shoals in critical theory. At the University of Illinois Library, Jo Kibbee, Bill Brockman, and Lynne Rudasill filled in a history of volatile words. Colleagues in the MLA, the American Literature Association, the Mark Twain Circle, and the American Humor Studies Association have

sharpened my speculations, and I am especially grateful for encourage-
ment from Louis Budd, John Bird, Everett Emerson, Susan K. Harris,
Pierre Michel, Tom Quirk, Gretchen Sharlow, Hal Simonson, David E. E.
Sloane, and Kristiaan Versluys. In Delhi, Calcutta, Pondicherry, Hydera-
bad, Mishima, and Tokyo, my colleagues K. K. Anand, Naoki Anzai,
Kousar J. Azam, Pradip De, Carolyn Elliot, Kimiko Gunji, T. S. Kuppus-
wami, Malashri Lal, Nobuaki Nomiki, Emilia Puma, Donna Roginski, and
Pam Sahgal organized cross-cultural discussions which resonate in these
pages. Back home, our sharp, irreverent students in the University of Illinois Campus Honors Program delightfully overthrow every artificial re-
striction on wit and the comic mode. Theresa, Hope, and Sarah Michelson, who know wit to the core and have zero tolerance for evasions, kept
the writing on course and gave back better lessons than I was spooning
out. At the University of Massachusetts Press, Pam Wilkinson has once
again been a brilliant, vigilant copy editor.

In different form, a portion of Chapter 3 appeared in *Christianity and Literature* 42, no. 4, and I am grateful for permission to develop and expand
those ideas here.

B. M.

Literary Wit

If a man had time to study the history
of one word only, wit would perhaps
be the best word he could choose.
—C. S. LEWIS

I dislike arguments of any kind.
They are always vulgar, and often
convincing.
—OSCAR WILDE

I

A Description of Literary Wit

This short book opens a neglected important question. Our conventional descriptions of literary wit have grown archaic and diffuse, and they fail to help us engage well with rich, adventurous texts. Because of deference to values rooted in bygone ideologies and cultural eras, misunderstanding abounds as to what modern literary wit can be, how it can work, and how and why it can matter. For critics and readers, this problem is embarrassing and hurtful, causing us to ignore exciting dimensions of the imaginative art that thrives around us. As a distinct variety of literary discourse—distinct from *wit, humor, comedy,* and *laughter* in nonliterary contexts—literary wit can achieve wonderful intensity, complexity, and resonance. As a quality that can still set the extraordinary above the mundane, literary wit is a fire that keeps our imaginative literature hot, as a cultural practice, even when so much in contemporary experience threatens to smother it or cool it off. For most of a century, however, the same array of assumptions and vague terminology has overshadowed and constricted our capacity to engage with this source of delight and meaning in what we read. If our discussion of modern and contemporary literary wit is to clarify and improve, then it must become contemporary in its own right.[1]

The story of literary wit's loss of importance—not as an enlivening presence in ambitious modern writing but as a subject for recognition and interpretive energy—gives a glimpse into the modern history of ideas and, more precisely, into the modern *idea* of an idea. Obsolete formulations—about consciousness, about literary discourse, about the organization not only of what Georges Bataille referred to generally as l'*expérience intérieure* but also of the external world we must negotiate—have supported this interpretive superficiality. In order to move beyond these assumptions, we have to understand better what they are, where they come from, and why they no longer apply. Such is the intention of this chapter. Subsequent chapters will consider how literary wit, as a practice refreshed and reconstructed in modern and postmodern texts, celebrates and complicates our understanding of the act of reading and the motions of the mind. Modern literary wit can liberate worldly experience and consciousness from false absolutes and suffocating patterns. It can offer "agency" of a special kind, for it can make possible expansion in literary discourse, in aesthetics, in poetics, even in the possibilities of identity. It can adapt superbly to "writing" so much that is changing around us and within us: our cultural, psychological, and moral experience and our understanding of consciousness itself.

The subject here is wit as a central, informing, thematically important presence in literature—in fiction, in poems, in plays, in discourse about literature itself. I am not directly interested in wit as a psychological or social phenomenon or as a substitute term for *humor* or *laughter* or *comedy*, though all these words are commonly (and unfortunately) resorted to as loose synonyms for literary wit. From a discussion of any of these terms, vectors can lead off in many directions: toward comparative cultural anthropology, semiotics and cognitive theory, psychotherapy, politics, gender studies, epistemology, physiology.[2] In the following pages there are brief forays along some of these lines; nonetheless, the continuing intent is to describe and explore literary wit as a significant dimension of serious writing—writing that can alter our understanding of experience and the self. As we shall see, this kind of wit is thoroughly interesting in its own right, as a transformed way of seeing and telling rather than as relief from seriousness, or as digression, or as some other kind of dilution or subversion of intense response.

One corollary: to recover an idea and a description of literary wit, its importance must be demonstrated with significant texts—in other words, in documents that have been thought to matter, texts by writers commonly included in the modern and postmodern literary canon. Nothing would be gained by trying to account for "wit" of every kind or quality, or by categorizing or explaining away everything that might conceivably be construed as literary wit in this fluid multiculture of sit-com, kitsch, camp, and pull-dated bon mots. Conversations about humor, laughter, comedy, and varieties of wit founder when they drift into such universalizing. No useful discussion of modern tragedy or romanticism will classify or dignify every melodrama in the West End or on Broadway or television; good conversations about poetics do not usually waste time with mediocre verse; the most useful thinking about modern satire steers clear of radio shock-jocks and ephemeral lampoons. Since we never lack for degraded versions of every mode, literary and cultural criticism has to be selective, and a revised description of literary wit is important enough to warrant a similar strategy. Moreover, literary wit can be complex and even dangerous, precisely because it can challenge and disrupt paradigms, habits of thought running so deep as to go largely unrecognized even by cultural critics—including habits of thought *about* literary texts, literary modes, and other classifications of discourse.[3]

It might be suggested that over the past thirty years new taxonomies and coinages in literary theory have provided workable substitute expressions for *literary wit*, or that revolutions in methodology have moved the conversation beyond a need for such a phrase. For various reasons, no such coinage has achieved general acceptance in discussions of literary wit in the English-speaking world. Reasons include the instability and controversy regarding the signification of these expressions and their situation (depending on who defines them) within totalizing formulations, which can also seem fundamentally at odds.[4] If a term were to be adapted nonetheless, a likely candidate is *jouissance*, which made its first consequential appearance, with regard to literary analysis, in the work of Roland Barthes and which has also been negotiated by Julia Kristeva, Jacques Lacan, M. H. Abrams, and many others. In each adaptation, however, *jouissance* seems to take on a different signification—looser, in every case, than the terminology we need to engage with this literature, yet also constrictively reflective of the views of specific interpretive communities. In Barthes, the moment of *jouissance* is situated in language and the act of reading, a moment of "crisis" in the reader's "relations with language."[5] Kristeva's *jouissance*, however, extends beyond verbal discourse and its interpretation. Deeply connected to the erotic and to constructions of gender difference, *jouissance* becomes an ecstasy in an inescapably libidinous encounter between the subject and external experience.[6] For Lacan, *jouissance* assumes yet another meaning, intertwining with an essentially Freudian model of human sexuality and also with a Nietzschean will to power.[7] In other words, when any of these competing descriptions of *jouissance*, or several of them together, is imported to negotiate an outbreak of wit in a literary text, the interpretive possibilities, from the outset, may be diluted, preempted, contained, or missed. Literary wit can destabilize our relationship to language, to culturally based patterns of response, to thinking itself—whether or not that thinking is construed as inherently cultural, political, hormonal, gender inflected, or anything else. In recent years literary wit has been mobilized to *détourne* even theoretical constructs like *jouissance*. To engage with this literature more effectively, therefore, we require language that describes, rather than inherently limits, a potentially powerful literary practice.[8]

To achieve a modernized and less-reductive idea of *literary* wit, conventional descriptions of *wit* must be extended, refreshed, qualified—and ultimately left behind. As social discourse in Western English-speaking societies, modern *wit* is distinguished by brevity, eloquence, and surprise. It favors incongruous congruity: quick verbal performances of insight or insights as verbal performance. Either way, wit fosters pleasurable psychological effects, which we commonly refer to as "amusement." With regard to wit of the former sort—where insight, as an intention, seems to surpass verbal performance—the signification, inferences, and other effects can be stronger and more various.

A description of modern literary wit, however, must include several qualities that distinguish it from wit occurring in nonliterary contexts. These qualities are developed and explored in subsequent chapters of this book.

First, the *literary* context is definitive, and in interpretive practice this context should no longer be evaded or ignored. Just as literary criticism now recognizes the significance of the literary context with regard to nearly every other mode of discourse, we must also recognize that literary wit is discourse made distinct, by context, from wit in other varieties of human utterance and other situations. Literary context transforms the utterance, its reception, and its interpretation.

Second, with regard to intention, modern literary wit should not be understood or circumscribed as an opposite of, or a suspension of, thematic seriousness or other varieties of textual or psychological intensity. Not only can literary wit participate in that intensity; it can be a primary source.

Third, within the literary context, modern literary wit can transcend other limitations imposed, or implied, by outmoded descriptions and definitions, among them a premise that literary wit must be merely "intellectual" or merely "cerebral." Because such terms have lost credibility in careful discussions of inner experience, they should no longer be exploited to segregate literary wit in this way, fostering undervaluation of its possibilities.

Fourth, literary wit can challenge paradigms and categories of analysis within which the literary text itself is created and received, not only with regard to the text in which the literary wit occurs and participates but also with regard to all literary texts and paradigmatic expectations on which modern literary discourse is formed and interpreted.

Fifth, literary wit plays a role in the formulation, transmission, and conservation of cultural wisdom and in the acquisition and education of constituencies that sustain "serious" literature as a significant cultural practice. "Witty" literary texts have been crucial to articulation and promulgation of literary and cultural values and to revolutions in aesthetic and intellectual style.

Sixth, in the intellectual life of our culture, paradigms and categories of analysis adapted long ago from Ramian dialectica, classical and Newtonian physics, and Hegelian and Marxian dialectics are being superseded by paradigms more appropriate to a vastly expanded store of knowledge and the consequent reorganization of contemporary experience. In this ongoing revolution in our thinking, modern literary wit plays a significant role.

Touring the Authorities

To develop and situate useful descriptions of modern literary wit, we must consider definitions and authoritative pronouncements now in circulation with regard to wit in literary texts. A brief review will suggest how assumptions have taken shape, how they rely on a small array of older formulations, and how historical and aesthetic situations quite different from our own have figured in their original and lasting popularity. Because glossaries, scholarly dictionaries, and critical guidebooks offer instruction in what to valorize and what to ignore in literary texts, and which descriptive terms to favor and which to avoid in critical discussion, these books have provided an interpretive first line of defense against literary wit, humor, and the comic. After following their definitions back to the rise of authoritative dictionaries in the eighteenth century, we can consider decisive moments in the works of a few canonical intellects, passages that are commonly relied on to settle and contain the problem of wit in literary discourse. It will be seen that the authority of these pronouncements has more to do with the signature on them—in other words, with the renown that these writers achieved in *other* sorts of inquiries and intellectual pursuits—than with the completeness or quality of their formulations about literary wit or humor. Nonetheless, these authors can be helpful, provided we bear in mind the historical and aesthetic predicament in which they wrote—and the differences between those times and ours.

In handbooks published or updated over the past twenty-five years, patterns are clear in the treatment of *wit* and *humor* as candidates for readerly attention. First, these treatments tend to run circular: a paragraph or two addressing *wit* (if there is an entry for the term at all) will commonly refer to a discussion of *humor* somewhere else in the same volume, and the *humor* entry will begin or end with a directive "See also *wit.*" The bothersome terms are thereby negotiated by playing them off against each other. Second, these reference works rarely attempt a distinction between *literary* wit and wit in other cultural contexts, or wit of any other kind. A wisecrack in a café is construed as the same variety of utterance as the witty observation that changes the intention of a lyric poem or the liberating outburst that paradoxically brings a drama to crisis. Mischief arises from this reluctance to make distinctions. Third, reference works specifically about poetry and poetics have been better at describing the practice of wit than most of the all-genre literary guides, perhaps because wit in a poem is assumed to be more complex and consequential than wit that breaks out or intrudes elsewhere in literary and nonliterary discourse. Fourth, in these general literary and cultural guides, language applied to *wit* often exudes suspicion and condescension. "Wit and humor" are presented as varieties of discourse to be acknowledged and then eased out of the way, allowing us to concentrate instead on "serious" dimensions of the literary text.

We can begin with one respected academic glossary from which *wit* is tellingly absent. Still a favorite introduction to cultural studies, Raymond Williams's *Keywords: A Vocabulary of Culture and Society* (1985) intends to cover a "shared body of words and meanings in our most general discussions, in English, of the practices and institutions which we group as culture and society" (15). It also demonstrates a persistence of antiquated paradigms, even in au courant humanist inquiry. As one might expect, *Keywords* often relies on wit to maneuver through this "shared body" of favored cultural expressions; nonetheless, *wit* doesn't appear as one of these keywords. The omission fits a pattern extending far beyond this one glossary: not only are *wit, humor,* and *comedy* passed over as valuable terms for opening modern cultural practices; also absent are *avant garde, counterculture, dadaism, surrealism, situationism, multiculturalism,* and nearly every general-use expression coined in the twentieth-century revolutions in science and technology. *Relativity, cognition, quantum mechanics, unified theory, chaos theory, connectivity, genome, neuroscience, virtual reality*—these are nowhere to be found. Instead, *Keywords* offers substantial entries on *dialectic, imperialism, alienation, masses, aesthetic, socialism, anarchism, communism, realism, naturalism, utilitarian, evolution, materialism,* and other terms that achieved intellectual weight before the reign of Edward VII. If fresher paradigms for imagining literary, psychological, intellectual, and cultural experience have come into their own since then, scant notice seems to be taken. In fact, not even *paradigm* appears as a "keyword"—though *ideology,* a Victorian coinage, is treated extensively. Though *science* is here, the latest source is 1867; the discussion of *aesthetic* names no authorities more current than Walter Pater and Matthew Arnold; the entry on *unconscious* is mostly Coleridge and Freud, and no newer psychological model is mentioned. To sum up: if *wit* does not register as a keyword for Williams, neither do many other terms that could describe or suggest radical renewals of Western culture, of literary practice, and of ways of imagining the self since the fin de siècle. What is valorized here instead is vocabulary suited to keeping literary and cultural analysis within established habits and structures. Like other such guidebooks, *Keywords* demonstrates what Gregg Camfield aptly describes as a lingering preference, among academic humanists, for "outdated models of mind that once had scientific currency, but now persist merely as subterranean footings for a philosophical discourse that refuses to examine its foundations."[9] In negotiating modern cultural experience, we are often coaxed back to vocabularies founded in assumptions about both consciousness and literary practice that date from a long time ago. With regard to literary wit, what results is a containment discourse, which other guides and glossaries have constructed as well.

Also like these others, *Keywords* refers frequently back to the *Oxford English Dictionary* as an indispensable source and an implicit sharer of blame. The current *OED*'s entry on *wit* (as a term describing a variety of discourse) concludes with these two definitions:

> 7. Quickness of intellect or liveliness of fancy, with capacity of apt expression; talent for saying brilliant or sparkling things, esp. in an amusing way. *arch.* (*Cf.* sense 8.)

And "sense 8":

> 8. That quality of speech or writing which consists in the apt association of thought and expression, calculated to surprise and delight by its unexpectedness (for particular applications in 17th and 18th century criticism see esp. quots. 1650, 1677, 1685, 1690, 1704, 1709); later always with reference to the utterance of brilliant or sparkling things in an amusing way.[10]

For the modern *OED*, then, *wit* seems to have lost much of its breadth and dignity—as a word and perhaps also as a cultural and literary practice. The implication here seems to be that as the eighteenth century unfolded, the boulevard farceurs won out, and that modern literary and cultural discourse has split irretrievably (and dialectically, pace Williams) into the "serious" versus the "clever" and the "amusing." In the *OED*'s definition of what *wit* means now, nineteenth-century sentimentalist assumptions about both consciousness and text are implicitly endorsed. Because editions of the *OED* have taken care to be descriptive rather than prescriptive, an inference in this entry—or perhaps it is only a hope that comes to mind while reading it—seems to be that if and when things change for the better in the literary salons and the bookstalls, "wit" as a worthy dimension of written discourse might rise again, to become what it once was—or what Johnson, in his great *Dictionary* of 1755, evidently thought it had been:

> 1. The powers of the mind; the mental faculties; the intellects. This is the original signification. . . .
> 2. Imagination; quickness of fancy. . . . [11]

In Johnson's own time—at least in his view—a degradation of wit as a cultural and literary practice was already under way. With regard to this term, Johnson's faith in definition-by-distinction found support in post-Newtonian models of human mental activity as organized into two processes, which are separate and even at odds. Fancy and imagination, understanding and reason, head and heart, training and education, knowledge and wisdom: though the paradigm of the dialectic had yet to bring such dyads into full cultural ascendance, we can see them embedded in the cautionary paragraph that Johnson situates just after the two opening definitions. This paragraph is the longest citation that Johnson offers for *wit*, and it comes from Locke. It gives another indication that a polarized or contrastive model of intellectual process, wit versus seriousness or wit versus measured, genuine judgment, is catching on, at least in philosophical discourse: "Wit lying most in the assemblage of ideas, and putting those together with quickness and variety, wherein can be found any resemblance, or congruity, thereby to make up pleasant pictures in the fancy. Judgment, on the contrary, lies in separating carefully one from another, ideas, wherein can be found the least difference, thereby to avoid being misled by similitude."

Johnson's moment was of course markedly different from either the English Renaissance, when *wit* was synonymous with "the powers of the mind," or the Romantic and Victorian eras in which *wit* would become something much less. In Johnson's beloved London, cults of sincerity were vying with cerebral Augustanism in the coffee houses, theaters, and reading rooms. Though his *Dictionary's* estimation of *wit* continues to be quoted—in fragments—in modern descriptions of the term, his full sequence of definitions for it is instructive because it suggests that some of the old significations were still viable in his time, although losing importance and strength. Omitting the citations and illustrations, here is the descending order after the opening two:

3. Sentiments produced by quickness of fancy.
4. A man of fancy.
5. A man of genius.
6. Sense; judgment.
7. In the plural. Sound mind; intellect not crazed.
8. Contrivance; stratagem; power of expedients.

In the English Renaissance, Bacon, Shakespeare, and Milton may have assumed no fundamental difference between "wit" and insight or profound intellect,[12] but by the middle of the eighteenth century, conventional thinking *about* thinking has changed.

Following a lead which comes more directly from the OED than from

Johnson, modern literary handbooks and glossaries commonly describe wit (again as discourse requiring no special attention within the literary context) as a diminished practice. With dignified regret and cautious consolation, *The New Princeton Encyclopedia of Poetry and Poetics* describes wit's waning, suggests reasons for it, and considers wit's prospects for recovery as a respectable component of literary discourse:

> A whole new constellation of literary terminology was forming in the earlier 19th c. of which we are the heirs. *Imagination* (q.v.) came to take on the sense of discovery and invention formerly embraced by *w.*, leading to a reduction in the sense of the latter . . . to mere humor, a tendency which became widespread. In the course of the 20th c., notions related to the older meaning of w. have come to the fore, e.g. Freud's psychoanalytic concept of *Witz*, T. S. Eliot's revaluation of "metaphysical" w., C. Brooks' emphasis on irony and paradox . . . as the principal devices of literary complexity and structure, and a persistent strain of parody (q.v.) as a means to what might be called intertextual w., as in Joyce's *Ulysses* and Mann's *Doktor Faustus*. Thus the meaning of w., though it may not have come full circle, has in the 20th c. regained some critical force and, through its literarily serious connection with irony and parody, begun to approach again its old kinship with imagination.[13]

The "old kinship" is summarized: "In its heyday as a critical term, w. referred to the inventive or imaginative faculty and, in particular, to the ability to see similarity in disparates (cf. Aristotle, *Poetics*, 1459A)." In the retrospective offered here, Aristotle establishes ground rules that endured more or less until the nineteenth century, with its cult of imagination, drained the term of meaning; and the best hope for revived critical attention to wit lies in redefining it now in (old) New Critical and (even older) Freudian ways. It may be difficult to see how Brooks and Freud could be teamed for an answer to any postmodern interpretive problem—but literary wit and humor are often responded to in such incongruous ways. The notion that a concept as ungainly as *imagination* usurped wit's fire is also puzzling, requiring us to reconsider paradigms that subtended certain Romantic and Victorian ideas about the mind. Useful, however, is the suggestion that wit, as a literary practice, has indeed suffered some sort of culture-based eclipse, and that it has prospects and justifications for being restored to attention. In contrast to *The New Princeton Encyclopedia*, much of the competition is less thoughtful on the subject.[14] Most of the briefer and more widely circulating dictionaries of literary and cultural terms lock *wit* and humor even more tightly into a contrastive relationship, with humor favored as the kinder, gentler practice.[15] For instance this, from a Concise Dictionary of Literary Terms published by a major producer of American textbooks:

> wit   Acute perception and cleverly appropriate expression of ideas providing amusement and pleasure. Wit is derived from an Old English word (witan) meaning "to know"; hence comes the definition of wit as primarily a matter of sense and understanding. In comparison with *humor, wit is an intellectual display of cleverness and quickness of perception, whereas humor is less obviously mental in its approach to the weaknesses, foibles, and absurd ideas and actions of people generally. Wit is wholly dependent upon apt phrasing; humor rises from situations or incidents and does not rely on sharpness or felicity of expression. Humor involves a sympathetic recognition of humanity and its incongruities; wit plays with words, develops startling contrasts, and appears often in *epigrams and *paradoxes.[16]

There is value in the suggestion that epigrams are worth a visit, to see what modern wit can actually do and whether it can actually be more interesting than facetious wordplay, displays of cleverness, and dependence on apt phrasing. Babette Deutsch's Poetry Handbook does better—again, perhaps because like the New Princeton Encyclopedia it unfolds from an assumption that the discourse of poetry and discourses about poetry are not interchangeable with vocabularies pertaining to other literary genres and modes. On wit, Deutsch is historically grounded, succinct, and distinct— there are no cross-references here to humor, fancy, imagination, or anything else:

> wit   The faculty that makes for metaphor by the perception of likeness in unlike things. To Dryden it was synonymous with imagination, a term that was to have a far narrower meaning in the eighteenth century, with its emphasis on reason and common sense, than it has acquired since. Pope claimed that
> > True Wit is Nature to advantaged dress'd
> > What oft was thought, but ne'er so well express'd. . . .
> Tentatively, but illuminatingly, Eliot defined the wit of certain seventeenth-century poets as "a tough reasonableness beneath the slight lyric grace". As he pointed out, it is present in the work of some twentieth-century poets. Wit is now admired as a sign of the poet's power to relate incongruities, and so give a fresh understanding of complexities that neither Dryden nor Pope took into account.[17]

This definition seems a little combative, perhaps because of Deutsch's advocacy elsewhere for sophisticated, full-minded contemporary verse. This "power to relate incongruities" she does not categorize as sterile, mechanical, or cerebral: profundity is allowed as a possibility, profundity of feeling as well as agility in intellect, word use, and insight. But Deutsch was a contrarian, even a "reactionary" (to borrow a keyword from Williams's neodialectical array), and in the haystack of other glossaries and more restrictive descriptions her needles get lost. In their 1983 *Literary Terms: A Dictionary*, Carl Beckson and Arthur Ganz work forward from Spenser through the Metaphysicals, Thomas Hobbes, and Joseph Addison all the way to Pope, and they quote a full six lines of Pope's *Essay on Criticism*, but ultimately they too favor the OED and conventional wisdom of other handbooks: "In modern times, *wit* is limited to intellectually amusing utterances calculated to delight and surprise. See *humor*" (274–75).

In later chapters I will show that literary wit is not inherently limited in this way, that it is in fact a discourse with the power to transgress and overthrow limits. With regard to the categorical mind and a culture that tries to organize itself into taxonomies, lexicons, directories, and encyclopedias, literary wit can be like the mythical acid that no crucible can contain.

These modern guidebooks reflect consensus in academic literary culture, and we need to understand how that consensus has been constructed. Current definitions grow smoothly from old definitions, and from excerpted words of the eminent. I have said that authorities on literary wit and humor are venerated usually because they reshaped our culture's thinking about matters very different from literary wit and humor, or because they talked about wit, *Witz*, jokes, or laughter in ways that conveniently blur literary situations and intentions with much else—pratfalls, playground ridicule, the Medieval carnival, funny faces, physical deformities, locker-room bawdry, and so on. Addison, Frederich Schiller, Leigh Hunt, George Meredith, Freud, Bergson, Mikhail Bakhtin, Johan Huizinga—it's hard to imagine that we would privilege these commentators on the subject of wit if they hadn't also written so effectively about a great deal more. But before looking into such canonical pronouncements about the nature of wit (literary or otherwise), we need to stay with dictionaries a moment longer to locate moments when these descriptions changed markedly.

By sampling conventional wisdom from the middle of the nineteenth century, and from Johnson's time, and back a bit farther to the end of the Renaissance, we can understand better the context in which stronger or more sophisticated insights about wit took shape, insights that have been exceptionally hard to get rid of. From the peak years of Ruskin and Tennyson and Pre-Raphaelite ritualized sentimentality, the 1853 *Imperial Dictionary, English, Technological, and Scientific, Adapted to the Present State of Literature, Science, and Art* offers a revealing analysis of what *wit* had been in the English tradition, what it now was (in enlightened Victorian times), and why it should be kept in bounds and regarded with suspicion. Johnson's brief remarks about wit's downfall are expanded here into a moral lesson:

> Note—It is difficult to give any strict definition of the term *wit*, its precise boundaries being still too unsettled. It has passed through a greater variety of significations in the course of the last two centuries than most other terms in the English language. Originally, *wit* signified wisdom; and anciently, a man of *witte* was a wise man. In the reign of Elizabeth, a man of pregnant *wit*, or of great *wit*, was a man of vast judgment. In the reign of James I, *wit* was used to signify the intellectual faculties or mental powers collectively. In the time of Cowley it came to signify a superior understanding, and more particularly a quick and brilliant reason. By Dryden it was used as nearly synonymous with talent or ability. According to Locke, it consists in quickness of fancy and imagination. Pope defined *wit* to be a quick conception and an easy delivery; according to which a man of *wit*, or a *wit*, is a man of brilliant fancy; a man of genius. At present, *wit* is used to designate a peculiar faculty of the mind, connected with the more comprehensive faculty of the imagination; and also the effect produced by this faculty, which consists in the display of remote resemblances between dissimilar objects, or an unexpected combination of remote resemblances; in the exhibition or perception of ludicrous points of analogy or resemblance among things in other respects dissimilar. Hence, a man of *wit*, or a *wit*, is considered to be a man in whom a readiness for such exercise of the mind is remarkable. *It is evident that wit excites in the mind an agreeable surprise, and that arising, not from anything marvellous in the subject, but solely from the imagery employed or the strange assemblage of related ideas presented to the mind* [emphasis added]. This end is effected, 1, by debasing things pompous or seemingly grave; 2, by aggrandizing things little and frivolous; or, 3, by setting ordinary objects in a particular and uncommon point of view, by means not only remote, but apparently contrary. . . . Wit is often joined with humor, but not necessarily so; it often displays itself in the keenest satire; *but when it is not kept under proper control, or*

when it becomes the habitual exercise of the mind, it is apt to impair the nobler powers of the understanding, to chill the feelings, to check friendly and social intercourse, and to break down those barriers which have been established by courtesy [emphasis added]. At the same time, when kept within its proper sphere, and judiciously used, it may be rendered very effective in attacking pedantry, pretension, or folly, and also may also be employed as a powerful weapon against error. (1244)[18]

This is essentially where we were a century and a half ago, and essentially where we remain, in spite of upheavals with regard to the interpretation of literary discourse. About twenty years after the *Imperial Dictionary*, Webster's *Dictionary of the English Language*, the authoritative record of the rapidly democratizing American English—an "Academic Edition" of 1867—closes its entry on *wit* with a moralizing paragraph promoting the superior virtues of *humor* and endorsing the same hierarchies with regard to feeling, high seriousness, and proprieties of thought:

Wit formerly meant genius, and now denotes the power of seizing on some thought or occurrence, and, by a sudden turn, presenting it under aspects wholly new and unexpected—apparently natural and admissible, if not perfectly just, and bearing on the subject, or the parties concerned, with a laughable keenness and force. . . . The pleasure we find in *wit* arises from the ingenuity of the turn, the sudden surprise it brings, and the patness of its application to the case, in the new and ludicrous relations thus flashed upon the view. *Humor* is a quality more congenial than *wit* to the English mind. It consists primarily in taking up the peculiarities of a *humorist*, and drawing them out, so that we enjoy a hearty, good-natured laugh at the unconscious development he makes of his whims and oddities. From this original sense, the term has been widened to embrace other sources of kindly mirth of the same general character. (481)

Humor then as a lesser of two evils; wit as distraction, digression, interlude, truancy from the profound, the kindly, the heartfelt, the genuinely serious. If Heathcliff had fresh dictionaries to guide him through his own psychological landscape at Wuthering Heights, this is what they would say—harmonizing with his disposition. For generations after Heathcliff, the pattern continues.[19] But why should this history matter? These are only dictionary entries, for decoding words heard in ordinary discourse or found on the ordinary printed page and not culturally important pronouncements on the ways of the mind.

Nonetheless, an important idea about the intellect, and about its literary output, does subtend John Locke's distinction, Johnson's entry for the word, and these nineteenth- and twentieth-century expansions and variations. At the heart of both Locke's principle and Johnson's development of it is the problematic and vaguely pejorative word *fancy*, a term that Johnson handled thus:

1. Imagination; the power by which the mind forms to itself images and representations of things, persons, or scenes of being.
2. An opinion bred rather by the imagination than the reason.
3. Taste; idea; conception of things.
4. Image; conception; thought.
5. Inclination; liking; fondness.
6. Caprice; humor; whim.
7. Frolick; idle scheme; vagary.
8. Something that pleases or entertains.

For Locke, and subsequently for Johnson, fancy and wit lead the intellect down pleasant pathways, which usually (and at best) go nowhere. Paradigms favored in the Enlightenment—the new scientific method, systems of genus and species, syllogistic reasoning—lead to truer varieties of wisdom, varieties that leave undisturbed the conventional wisdom about what it means to be wise. In the wake of such moralizing, Addison is reverential toward Locke on the subject, but in the famous *Spectator* essays 58 through 63 (1711) he tries to botanize wit into three "species," which he calls *false wit*, *mixt wit*, and *true wit*. Trying in this manner to distinguish interesting and potentially profound literary wit from glibness, gimmick, or facetious performance, Addison offers a taxonomy, which nineteenth- and twentieth-century commentators largely ignored, preferring the various wholesale differentiations between wit (of any sort) and seriousness or humor or feeling or other supposedly higher sensibilities and processes. Addison's *false wit* includes "Anagrams, Chronograms, Lipograms, and Acrosticks: Sometimes of Syllables, as in Ecchoes and Doggerel Rhymes; Sometimes of Words, as in Punns and Quibbles; and sometimes of whole Sentences or Poems, cast into the Figures of *Eggs*, *Axes*, or *Altars*: Nay some carry the Notion of Wit so far, as to ascribe it even to external Mimickry; and to look upon a Man as an ingenious Person, that can resemble the Tone, Posture, or Face of another."[20] *True wit*, he says, "consists in the Resemblance of Ideas" rather than in the resemblance of words, and *mixt wit* is the widespread mingling of the two purer strains. In the *Spectator* essays, Addison has problems defining *true wit*, and he returns repeatedly to the question of how this kind of literary "genius" differs from mere cleverness. Finally, as a true neoclassicist, he resorts to an allegorical dream to describe the noble discourse he has in mind. Essay 63 takes us to a Parnassian or Olympian height, where true connoisseurs of literature can gaze upon ideals that they cannot name:

> I took a full survey of the Persons of WIT and TRUTH, for indeed it was impossible to look upon the first, without seeing the other at the same time. There was behind them a strong and compact Body of Figures. The Genius of *Heroic Poetry* appeared with a Sword in her Hand, and a Lawrel on her Head. *Tragedy* was crowned with Cypress, and covered with Robes dipped in Blood. *Satyr* had Smiles in her Look, and a Dagger under her Garment. *Rhetorick* was known by her Thunderbolt; and *Comedy*, by her Mask. After several other Figures, *Epigram* marched up in the rear, who had been posted there at the beginning of the Expedition, that he might not revolt to the Enemy, whom he was suspected to favour in his Heart. I was very much awed and delighted with the Appearance of the God of Wit; there was something so amiable and yet so piercing in his Looks, as inspired me at once with Love and Terrour. (1:274)

As a tableau to close with, this is touching—for Addison's neoclassical procession is doomed. Perhaps Addison writes with such fervor about wit because in the Age of Reason wit was already losing cachet, losing to new models of reason and of "serious" or "sincere" discourse. Oppositional paradigms were taking hold: *wit* arranged against *judgment, fancy* as opposed to *reason* or *imagination, quickness* and *cleverness,* and *mental agility* against *depth, worth.* When Romanticism, sentimentalism, and the dialectic overswept this cultural landscape, the way was well prepared. A nineteenth-century popular and literary model of consciousness—head versus heart, logic or reason versus intuition, fancy versus imagination, and of course wit (with the attributes that Locke and Johnson and Addison associated with it—"quickness" or "cleverness," a capacity to see or dream up connections where none existed before) versus *seriousness* or *sincerity* or *wisdom.*

This arrangement and evaluation of cultural discourse was obviously gendered. These Romantic, transcendental, and Victorian circumscriptions of literary wit, which continue to influence modern descriptions and assumptions, came almost entirely from literary men (for they were almost always male) promulgating or accepting as absolute a Romantic masculinist poetics. About a century after Addison, Ralph Waldo Emerson was ready (or so he declared in one exuberant essay) to carve the word *whim* onto the doorposts of his comfortable Concord home,[21] celebrating escape from all ordinary ruts and routines and habits of thought and recovering the old powerful connections between "fancy" (or "frolick") and insight. But Emerson seems to have gotten over this whim to be whimsical, for as an essayist and as a poet he rarely practiced what he declared in that memorable and uncharacteristic paragraph. Subsequently, in "The Poet," Emerson would lay out a poetics of conquest and dominion above a poetics that favored free and open-ended play of the mind as it engaged with experience, and, once again, literary wit lost ground.[22] Emerson's bard, whose work it was to call down thunder from the skies and name experience like a latter-day Adam, was not plying a trade in which literary wit could have any great part. Luckily, in the United States, even in Emerson's day, there was an emergent feminist poetics, which in engaging with experience did not abjure literary wit and which in fact did much to keep the discourse alive as Romantic lugubriousness and transcendental sobriety flourished all around.[23] Strong in Margaret Fuller and Emily Dickinson, this alternative poetics resisted the Emersonian premise, celebrated the freedom of the mind, and refused to urge all perceptions, "idle" or wise, onward to some Omega point of high seriousness. The paradox of course was that Fuller and Dickinson, in resisting the masculinist idea of having the "last word," wrote no essays that tried for an Emersonian "last word" about literary wit or anything else. So men had the last word—or at least a lasting word, with regard to marginalizing this freedom from paradigmatic thought and this agile, buoyant, insouciant kind of discourse. Fuller could turn it loose to devastating effect in The Great Lawsuit; Dickinson could break it out in dozens of poems to delight, shock, and turn readerly expectation inside out. With verbal brilliance and transgressions of orthodox thought, they bobbed like vigorous castaways in a Victorian sea.

In contrast to these women, Leigh Hunt was the sort of literary wit that high Victorians could accommodate—diverting and innocuous, although he is rarely read now except by graduate students and people curious about the original for Skimpole in Bleak House. Even so, Hunt's observations about wit, appropriate to the aesthetic of his own time, are exhumed for periodic display in modern treatments of the subject—not as a relic but as something presumably relevant to our own literary discourse. The most durable Hunt excerpt declares that wit in literary texts (and apparently, as usual, in every other context) is the "Arbitrary Juxtaposition of Dissimilar Ideas for some lively purpose of Assimulation or Contrast, generally of both."[24] Arbitrary seems to affirm that such juxtapositions of culturally ordered dissimilarities ought to cause nothing of more consequence than a moment of amusement—no liberated or durably refreshed way of encountering the world. However, in a different essay (one less favored by compilers of wisdom about wit), Hunt does seem to affirm that wit can have much to do with consequence, even with greatness:

> We doubt, indeed, whether on inquiring into the matter, it would not be found that whatever may be the case with minor wits . . . *no very great wit ever existed who had not an equal fund of gravity. His wit itself could not have been subtle and profound without it.* Minor wits discern only the superficial difference of things. Their powers do not pierce to the core, for want of knowledge of the core itself; of the heart of the heart; the *pia mater,* the profound and religious portion, of the brain. Their jests do not hold philosophies, griefs, reformations; are not founded on the cravings of man's weakness for strength, on his regret that he cannot square "the shews of things by the desires of the mind"; *which in certain respects is the greatest of all contrasts, and therefore at once profoundest and most melancholy suggester of wit; the essence of which consists in the combination of remote ideas.*[25]

Ultimately playing larger roles than Hunt in evolving a modern literary criticism, Charles Lamb and William Hazlitt reviewed with rare and breezy attentiveness the English store of literary wit and stage comedy. Regretting that the Romantic mentalities of his own time had devalued this legacy so severely, Lamb celebrated "artificial comedy" as an excursion into intellectual freedom, escape from "the diocese of the strict conscience," which the emerging British moral system seemed to be constructing even in literary discourse:

> All that neutral ground of character, which stood between vice and virtue; or which in fact was indifferent to neither, where neither properly was called in question; that happy breathing-place from the burthen of a perpetual moral questioning . . . is broken up and disenfranchised, as injurious to the interests of society. The privileges of the place are taken away by law. . . .
>
> I confess for myself that . . . I am glad for a season to take an airing . . . —not to live always in the precincts of the law-courts, — but now and then, for a dream-while or so, to imagine a world with no meddling restrictions—to get into the recesses, whither the hunter cannot follow me . . . I wear my shackles more contentedly for having respired the breath of an imaginary freedom.[26]

Ultimately, however, Lamb drafts this celebration of paradigm-jolting freedom into the service of that greater good of his age—the Romantic reverie. Lively assimilations (this is Hunt's term) and inside-out disruptions of the ordinary are the stuff of happy dreams, with no genuine or lasting effect on the way we normally see. Similar in his speculations, Hazlitt builds on Horace Walpole's sentimentalist adage that the world is a comedy to those who think and a tragedy to those who "feel":

> Wit hovers round the borders of the light and trifling, whether in matters of pleasure or pain; for as soon as it describes the serious seriously, it ceases to be wit, and passes into a different form. Wit is, in fact, the eloquence of indifference, or an ingenious and striking exposition of those evanescent and glancing impressions of objects which affect us more from surprise or contrast to the train of our ordinary and literal preconceptions, than from anything in the objects themselves exciting our necessary sympathy or lasting hatred. The favourite employment of wit is to add littleness to littleness, and heap contempt on insignificance by all the arts of petty and incessant warfare.[27]

So wit, literary or otherwise, is a weapon of ridicule, best used in enforcing separations between the lofty and the low—in a cultural moment when lofty and low were much clearer as categories than they might be now. Before Meredith's *An Essay on Comedy* (1877), this was a high-water mark of Romantic and Victorian attention to literary wit, humor, and their cultural work. Half a century on, Meredith's short, freewheeling, impressionistic book intended to describe comedy as a moral and didactic form ("the fountain of sound sense; not the less perfectly sound on account of the sparkle" [227]), rather than to explore anarchic and liberating potentialities of literary wit and humor. Anticipating Freud in describing these as "warlike" discourses, Meredith keeps them in their assigned space as means to an end—the "end" being a promulgation of conventional and sober (if not somber) ethics: that love should prevail and that greed and selfishness should not; that honesty is better than hypocrisy, plainness preferable to affectation, and so on. In Meredith's mind, as in Hazlitt's and Lamb's before him, steady moral progress toward a more-perfect culture was the controlling value, not liberation of consciousness or revolution in aesthetics:

> If you believe that our civilization is founded on common sense (and it is the first condition of sanity to believe it), you will, when

contemplating men, discern a Spirit overhead; not more heavenly than the light flashed upward from glassy surfaces, but luminous and watchful; never shooting beyond them, nor lagging in the rear; so closely attached to them that it may be taken for a slavish reflex, until its features are studied. It has the sage's brows, and the sunny malice of a faun lurks at the corners of the half-closed lips drawn in an idle wariness of half-tension. . . . Its common aspect is one of unsolicitous observation, as if surveying a full field and having leisure to dart on its chosen morsels, without any fluttering eagerness. Men's future upon earth does not attract it; their honesty and shapeliness in the present does; and whenever they wax out of proportion, overblown, affected, pretentious, bombastical, hypocritical, pedantic, fantastically delicate; whenever it sees them self-deceived or hoodwinked, given to run riot in idolatries, drifting into vanities, congregating in absurdities, . . . whenever they offend sound reason, fair justice; are false in humility or mined with conceit, individually or in the bulk; the Spirit overhead will look humanely malign, and cast an oblique light on them, followed by volleys of silvery laughter. That is the Comic Spirit. (82–83)

For Meredith, humor, wit, and comedy, all of which he describes or invokes in language as incantatory as the above, require orderly arrangements adapted from the dialectic. Common sense is on this side, with ourselves; the targets of satire and ridicule, the butts of the jokes, are on the other, and if the humor and the wit are "literary" or "great" or "correct" or "grave" or "Hellenic"—at various moments Meredith tosses all of these adjectives at plays that he likes—then an improving seriousness and an overthrow of Folly are the right outcomes.

Fog abounds here, as it often does in nineteenth-century descriptions of wit or the comic. Formulations grew more sophisticated in the generation after Meredith—the generation that produced authorities whose words still dominate humanist discussions of literary wit.

Bergson, Freud, Bakhtin

With regard to laughter, jokes, wit, and other aspects of the comic, Bergson and Freud have been challenged often over the past half century, so thoroughly that a note about these refutations will save us from covering such ground again.[28] But the work of Bergson and Freud remains canonical about wit and humor; none of these challenges has displaced them. From the perspective of this study, what is most interesting about Freud, Bergson, and Bakhtin is their longevity, the way that their ideas continue to be seen as touchstones in contemporary negotiations with literary wit, which means, usually, efforts to evade it.

All three of these distinguished intellects promulgate models of reality, of the conditions and motions of mind and of text, which operate comfortably within nineteenth-century paradigms, and specifically the paradigm of the dialectic. Though each of these discussions offers new perceptions and alters the available typology, they allow essential structures to remain the same. Also, the two century-old volumes in question, *Le Rire* and *Der Witz und seine Beziehung zum Unbewussten*, are all-encompassing formulations in the classic fin de siècle manner. They are bracing in their generality and inspiring for students who are beginning to theorize about literature and human behavior. But because of this generality they lose or misvalue the special powers and contexts of literary wit, giving it short shrift in a tour through, and description of, nearly every form of merriment, ridicule, or outbreak of the comic.

In psychological and political circles, so many objections have been raised about Freud over the past thirty years that he might now seem hors de combat as a major figure in contemporary humanist theorizing. But because he was a keystone in so many structures of twentieth-century thought, some of his formulations have enormous staying power, especially in subject areas that have been slow to modernize. Bergson may have been neither an experienced clinician nor a trained psychologist nor even an accomplished literary critic, but as a great metaphysician, epistemologist, and avowed antidialectician, he retains intellectual weight, even when he opens a subject as loosely conceived as "laughter," *Le Rire*, every variety of *rire* from every culture and situation, literary and otherwise. Offering what he calls "recipes for manufacturing" the comic, Bergson famously describes laughter as "appealing to intelligence, pure and simple," a nonintuitive, collective, emotionless response to the intrusion of mechanism and rigidity into ordinary experience. Such a description has the virtue of being quotable. On the subject of wit, Bergson looks again for unparadoxical clarity and for categorical definition, which is to say definition that affirms the organization of psychological, literary, and cognitive experience into categories. It's not surprising that Bergson's discussion of *wit* is the weakest section of *Laughter*. He seems to be anticipating trouble as he opens the question:

We now see how it is that writers on wit have perforce confined themselves to commenting on the extraordinary complexity of the things denoted by the term without ever succeeding in defining it. There are many ways of being witty, almost as many as there are of being the reverse. How can we detect what they have in common with one another, unless we first determine the general relationship between the witty and the comic? Once, however, this relationship is cleared up, everything is plain sailing. We then find the same connection between the comic and the witty as exists between a regular scene and the fugitive suggestion of a possible one. Hence, however numerous the forms assumed by the comic, wit will possess an equal number of corresponding varieties. So that the comic, in all its forms, is what should be defined first, by discovering (a task which is already quite difficult enough) the clue that leads from one form to the other. By that very operation wit will have been analysed, and will then appear as nothing more than the comic in a highly volatile state. To follow the opposite plan, however, and attempt directly to evolve a formula for wit, would be courting certain failure. What should we think of a chemist who, having ever so many jars of a certain substance in his laboratory, would prefer getting that substance from the atmosphere, in which merely infinitesimal traces of its vapour are to be found? (110–11)

Bergson's "laboratory" jars happen to be crammed with lines and moments from genteel boulevard comedies—nothing outrageous, certainly nothing from his erstwhile student Alfred Jarry—and the favorite source is the safe, predictable, familiar Molière. Consequently, when Bergson comes around to describing literary wit less vaporously, his description is rooted not only in this kind of comedy but also in traditional categories and dyadic arrangements of consciousness—intelligence and "feeling," head and heart, cleverness and "soul," mental quickness and seriousness, allegro and pensoroso—oppositional arrangements of a sort that Lamb, Johnson, Addison, and even Milton could have taken for granted:

Let us first make a distinction between the two meanings of the word "wit" (*esprit*), the broader one and the more restricted. In the broader meaning of the word, it would seem that what is called wit is a certain *dramatic* way of thinking. Instead of treating his ideas as mere symbols, the wit sees them, he hears them and, above all, makes them converse with one another like persons. He puts them on the stage, and himself, to some extent, into the bargain. A witty nation is, of necessity, a nation enamoured of the theatre. In every wit there is something of a poet—just as in every good reader there is the making of an actor. This comparison is made purposely, because a proportion might easily be established between the four terms. In order to read well we need only the intellectual side of the actor's art; but in order to act well one must be an actor in all one's soul and body. In just the same way, poetic creation calls for some degree of self-forgetfulness, whilst the wit does not usually err in this respect. We always get a glimpse of the latter behind what he says and does. He is not wholly engrossed in the business, because he only brings his intelligence into play.

So any poet may reveal himself as a wit when he pleases. To do this there will be no need for him to acquire anything; it seems rather as though he would have to give up something. He would simply have to let his ideas hold converse with one another "for nothing, for the mere joy of the thing!" [Hugo] He would only have to unfasten the double bond which keeps his ideas in touch with his feelings and his soul in touch with life. In short, he would turn into a wit by simply resolving to be no longer a poet in feeling, but only in intelligence.

But if wit consists, for the most part, in seeing things *sub specie theatri*, it is evidently capable of being specially directed to one variety of dramatic art, namely, comedy. Here we have a more restricted meaning of the term, and, moreover, the only one that interests us from the point of view of the theory of laughter. What is here called *wit* is a gift for dashing off comic scenes in a few strokes—dashing them off, however, so subtly, delicately, and rapidly, that all is over as soon as we begin to notice them. (105–7)

Several generalizations and assumptions in the above passage have been disputed over the years, but not enough to diminish Bergson as the key figure for contemporary discussions of literary wit and humor.[29] With regard to recognizing potentialities of modern literary wit (rather than seventeenth-century French stage wit), there are two major problems in evidence here: (1) the proposition that wit involves or signifies a mind reduced or desensitized rather than intensified and liberated; and (2) that literary wit is, as Bergson says, *sub specie theatri*, one-dimensional and genre-specific discourse rather than discourse adaptable to many genres and modes, and potentially complex (to put it mildly) in its significations. The limitations of these Bergsonian and post-Bergsonian propositions will be shown in subsequent chapters. Other problems, however, may lie deeper. True to its time, *Laughter* advances a general theory with a clear fin de siècle configuration: Bergson's description is offered as applicable across all dimensions of human experience and constructed on clean, balanced oppositions. It also posits models of consciousness and thought akin to Freud's: the mind as essentially bipolar in its structure, linear in its processes, and representable by conventions adapted from Hegelian logic. Bergson's model of the mind is more strongly evident in *The Creative Mind*, which gathers many of his lectures and essays from 1903 until about 1923 and which provides a context for understanding assumptions that underlie *Laughter*. In these non-Saussurian speculations on the interactions of language and thinking, Bergson ultimately arrives at a better rudimentary description of *wit* than is to be found in his *Laughter*. But in *The Creative Mind*, though Bergson comes closer to a plausibly modern idea of cognitive processes, his analogies disclose the bygone scientific moment that produced this discourse and the specific paradigms that both foster it and confine it; in other words, turn-of-the-century cell biology and linear algebra:

> The philosopher does not take pre-existing ideas in order to recast them into a superior synthesis or combine them with a new idea. One might as well believe that in order to speak we go hunting for words that we string together afterwards by means of a thought. The truth is that above the word and above the sentence there is something much more simple than a sentence or even a word: the meaning, which is less a thing thought than a movement of thought, less a movement than a direction. And just as the impulsion given to the embryonic life determines the division of an original cell into cells which in turn divide until the complete organism is formed, so the characteristic movement of each act of thought leads this thought, by an increasing sub-division of itself, to spread out more and more over the successive planes of the mind until it reaches that of speech. Once there it expresses itself by means of a sentence, that is, by a group of pre-existing elements; but it can almost arbitrarily choose the first elements of the group provided that the others are complementary to them; the same thought is translated just as well into diverse sentences composed of entirely different words, provided these words have the same connection between them. Such is the process of speech. And such also is the operation by which philosophy is constituted. The philosopher does not start with pre-existing

ideas; at most one can say that he arrives at them. And when he gets there the idea thus caught up into the movement of his mind, being animated with a new life like the word which receives its meaning from the sentence, is no longer what it was outside the vortex. (121)

The last chapter of this book will consider alternative models for the thinking process and their possible consequences for an updated description of literary wit. The important recognition now, however, is that these models have changed dramatically since Bergson and Freud, that they continue to change rapidly, that they have long since escaped from paradigms on which Bergsonian and Freudian models of wit, laughter, and humor were constructed. A refreshed idea of literary wit needs to draw plausibility and validity from this generalized yet sophisticated uncertainty rather than attach itself to any single, current, provisional model or retreat into the illusory safety of a psychology and an epistemology which, in other fields of intellectual endeavor, we have outgrown.

For a modernized discussion of literary wit, the limitations of Freud's Witz are probably more self-evident than those of Bergson's Le Rire.[30] The first edition of Der Witz und seine Beziehung zum Unbewussten was published in 1905, five years after Laughter and in the same year that saw the first publication of Einstein's general theory of relativity. The coincidence is telling: Freud's venture into Witz was another expression of his faith in dialectical paradigms that had organized Western European thought for generations, while Einstein was exploding the premise (first in the physical sciences and eventually in nearly every other variety of intellectual endeavor except, as yet, the humanities) that reality can be satisfactorily described as some stable arrangement of dualisms and contrasts and oppositions. The fundamentals of Freud's volume are well known, and though they are often challenged or refuted by other psychologists, by anthropologists, by linguists, and by professionals in various other disciplines, his descriptions continue to be trundled out by literary critics when humor and wit turn up inconveniently in interesting texts.[31] The analogies and metaphors that organize Freud's thinking here are familiar ones in Freudian discourse: economics, the release of tension and gratification of the libido, self-exhibition, disguised aggression. Once again, literary context and intention are at best secondary concerns. Wit (ambiguously differentiated from "joke"—Witz has been translated both ways and Freud's vagueness in distinguishing each from the other has caused interpretive problems for most of a century) is presented as pretty much the same psychological urge or predisposition or interpersonal strategy, in all situations, from the library shelf or the salon to the alley behind the bar. The summations are sweeping and categorical:

> The purposes of jokes can easily be reviewed. Where a joke is not an aim in itself—that is, where it is not an innocent one—there are only two purposes that it may serve, and these two can themselves be subsumed under a single heading. It is either a *hostile* joke (serving the purpose of aggressiveness, satire, or defense) or an *obscene* joke (serving the purpose of exposure). It must be repeated in advance that the technical species of the joke—whether it is a verbal or a conceptual joke—bears no relation to these two purposes. (*Jokes and Their Relation to the Unconscious*, 114–15)

It is not surprising, therefore, that when Freud turns to "wit" as a "special capacity" (171), a talent or intellectual predisposition, he finds it pathological:

> The motive force for the production of innocent jokes is not infrequently an ambitious urge to show one's cleverness, to display oneself—an instinct that may be equated with exhibitionism in the sexual field. The presence of numerous inhibited instincts, whose suppression has retained a certain degree of instability, will provide the most favorable disposition for the production of tendentious jokes. Thus individual components of a person's sexual constitution, in particular, can appear as motives for the construction of a joke. A whole class of obscene jokes allows one to infer the presence of a concealed inclination to exhibitionism in their inventors; aggressive tendentious jokes succeed best in people in whose sexuality a powerful sadistic component is demonstrable, which is more or less inhibited in real life. (174–75)

I shall make the case that a literary context is not a "technical species" and that such a context makes a great difference—a "generic" difference, to belabor the Linnaean analogy that Freud and a battalion of literary critics after him have borrowed and belabored. Writers engaged in a special cultural act of *écriture* and keenly aware of peculiarities inherent in printed, published, or enacted texts (in other words, texts edited, crafted, and ultimately negotiated by imagined and genuine audiences of readers who are not just literate but literary) can inspire varieties of *wit* that are inconceivable in these descriptions, which err in lumping the literary, the casual, the vulgar, the antique, the poetic, the dramatic, and so forth, into one ungainly category. This difference can be shown: examples in chapters 2 and 3 of this book will illustrate that modern literary wit can be much more interesting than we have theorized or allowed.

As the last of these three central figures in humanist discussions of wit, humor, and the comic, only Bakhtin was an actual literary critic, and he is the only one for whom the written text and interpretive strategies are distinct and central subjects. The taxonomy that develops Bakhtin's concept of literary discourse, variously called *dialogism* or *the dialogic principle*, now pervades theoretical conversation about textual studies; with four volumes by him now available in English, Bakhtin's prestige as a critic has become comparable to that of Derrida and Barthes. Bakhtin's key meditations on the roots and meaning of wit, humor, and the comic in literature are developed in *Rabelais and His World* (first English translation, 1968). This work, however, is as much a study of "carnival" in the culture of the European Middle Ages as it is a discussion of Rabelais, and once again the student of the comic, the humorous, or the witty in modern Anglo-American literary texts has to extract and extrapolate from Bakhtin's commentary on a French author from four hundred years ago and on an array of folk practices dating back two or three centuries before Rabelais. As a work of cultural anthropology and history, *Rabelais and His World* has drawn its share of fire for exaggerating, generalizing, and misprizing the role and functions of carnival in medieval life.[32] But because his pronouncements on laughter and the comic spirit are offered as ahistorical and applicable (like Bergson's and Freud's) to many levels and modes of human discourse,[33] we must consider these carefully, as they can assist us in arriving at a provisional description of literary wit, a de-limited description that will allow us to reopen and investigate modern texts. Bakhtin can be a genuine help: operating largely free of Freud's libido-based imperatives and Bergson's rather rigid doctrines regarding "rigidity" and mechanism, Bakhtin offers the comic spirit, the anarchic festivity of carnival, as a deeper, wider-ranging sort of escape, an insurrection against any and all varieties of "seriousness," including conventional configurations and motions of "serious" thought. His broad observations about the psychology of the feast day in the Middle Ages are as controversial as broad observations usually are; but Bakhtin's essential drive or aspiration here is for a liberated idea of the liberty of the comic. Readers now must remember that these ideas took shape under the misery of Stalinism, in which an unsanctioned joke or expression of irreverence could be literally fatal:

> All feast day privileges granted by tradition to laughter and jokes were fully accorded to recreation. Not only could the students relax from the official ideological system, from scholarly wisdom and academic rules, but they were allowed to transform these disciplines into gay, degrading games, and jokes. They were first of all freed from the heavy chains of devout seriousness, from the "continual ferment of piety and the fear of God." They were freed from the oppression of such gloomy categories as "eternal," "immovable," "absolute," "unchangeable" and instead were exposed to the gay and free laughing aspect of the world, with its unfinished and open character, with the joy of change and renewal. (83)

A few pages later, Bakhtin moves beyond the Middle Ages and the Feast of Fools, and offers propositions about laughter as a timeless and "serious" human need. Again, though his expansive conclusions about thousands of years of human history are offered without documentation and are open to demolition by careful cultural historians and theorists,[34] the powerful wish implicit here, that laughter and the comic should have this restorative and liberating power, provides evidence, paradoxical or not, that wit is a proposition worth taking "seriously":

> No doubt laughter was in part an external defensive form of truth. It was legalized, it enjoyed privileges, it liberated, to a certain extent, from censorship, oppression, and from the stake. This element should not be underestimated. But it would be inadmissible to reduce the entire meaning of laughter to this aspect alone. Laughter is essentially not an external but an interior form of truth; it cannot be transformed into seriousness without destroying and distorting the very contents of the truth which it unveils. Laughter liberates not only from external censorship but first of all from the great interior censor; it liberates from the fear that developed in man during thousands of years: fear of the sacred, of prohibitions, of the past, of power. It unveils the material bodily principle in its true meaning. Laughter opened men's eyes on that which is new, on the future. This is why it not only permitted the expression of an antifeudal, popular truth; it helped to uncover this truth and to give it an internal form. And this form was achieved and defended during thousands of years in its very depths and in its popular-festive images. Laughter showed

the world anew in its gayest and most sober aspects. Its external privileges are intimately linked with interior forces; they are a recognition of the rights of those forces. This is why laughter could never become an instrument to oppress and blind the people. It always remained a free weapon in their hands. (93–94)

Objecting to Bergson's constrictive emphasis on laughter's "negative functions" (71), Bakhtin approaches a celebration of "laughter" (which in his parlance encompasses nearly everything having to do with the comic) as an ultimate source of intellectual and cultural liberation. Not long after this, Bakhtin reaches a crucial affirmation:

> True ambivalent and universal laughter does not deny seriousness but purifies and completes it. Laughter purifies from dogmatism, from the intolerant and the petrified; it liberates from fanaticism and pedantry, from fear and intimidation, from didacticism, naïveté and illusion, from the single meaning, the single level, from sentimentality. Laughter does not permit seriousness to atrophy and to be torn away from the one being, forever incomplete. It restores this ambivalent wholeness. Such is the function of laughter in the historical development of culture and literature. (122–23)

Here literary historians could take vigorous exception, because this last sweeping generalization—again, without anything like plausible explication or documentation—recalls the bombast of Emerson or Oswald Spengler. But documented or not, and historically accurate or not, Bakhtin, with the weight he now carries as an elder in literary theorizing, has at least expanded the possibilities of the urgent intellectual and cultural work that humor, laughter, wit, and the comic mode might do. By keeping his insights (or hopes) in mind, we retain the potential to see that potentiality—something we would not have if we explored literary wit under the tutelage of Freud and Bergson. Bakhtin thus takes us farther, yet not so far as must be ventured, even in an initial foray into the question. His paean to laughter is loose, impressionistic, a bit extravagant, and certainly without the needed distinctions, especially between modern literary discourse and the noise and riot of his medieval and Rabelaisian carnivalesque, or between wit and other sorts of comic outbreaks. In striking out from here, we need to pursue the possibility that such distinctions are important. A good discussion of literary wit requires that we avoid being short-circuited by reductive overviews of popular cultural practice, omnibus commentaries on varieties of the comic, obsolete psychological theory, nineteenth-century philosophical methodologies, or modern behavioral-science narratives that fail to distinguish literary practice from anything else that human beings might do.

Impossible as perfect empiricism might be, we can develop a more useful description of literary wit by beginning with actual literary texts and observing what we find there rather than by loading up first with procrustean theories. In other words, if refreshed, unencumbered readings of some familiar works demonstrate that literary wit can be more interesting than readerly habits, prejudices, and methodologies commonly allow, then that recognition in itself would be a move in a right direction. If we also recognize that literary wit can be central to "serious" dimensions of the text rather than merely decorative and superficial, then literary wit obviously requires better attention than it normally receives. Moreover, if we approach such texts with a measure of open-mindedness, we can negotiate one key paradox that short-circuits a great deal of commentary. Specifically, we must allow the possibility, at least at the outset, that literary wit is, or can be, an insurrection against conventional and formulaic thinking, that wit can be "clever" enough to make war on cleverness, funny or shocking enough to overturn ordinary assumptions about humor, laughter, and surprise, intellectually or psychologically anarchic enough to jolt, jam, or shatter whatever we thought were absolutes about intellect, the self, and the deep order or disorder of worlds we think we know—or "know" that we don't. We have to let the genie out of the bottle if we want to see how big and powerful it is. We must try not to confine, in any a priori way, a literary practice that may have, as a core and defining "intention," a resistance of all such confinements. In other words, we should initially theorize this discourse only this far: as discourse with potential to disrupt and refresh fundamental assumptions on which theories of discourse are constructed.

In at least one sense, however, this too is loading the dice, because there is no other way to proceed. To evolve a description of literary wit, we have to begin with literary texts, published works that are commonly assumed, in American cultural and academic practice, to lie within a category of discourse that we read and study and teach as "literature." Novels, autobiographical writings and travel books, collections of poems, subversive prefaces to novels, essays of self-conscious "literary criticism," successful plays written for intelligent and cultured modern audiences—these I take to be literary in conventional senses of the term. One can move outward from here in any direction—even to propositions that all utterance is "literary" and that valorizing certain discourses is bourgeois, or hegemonic, or narrow-minded in other ways. My premise for this study is simple: wherever we choose to mark out or transgress borders between literary discourse and other kinds, the peculiarities and powers of wit as a literary practice can be investigated in works that come from the heart of the realm. If that process is going to be worth anyone's time, it ought to start with texts that have made a difference, not as diverting comedy but as moments in the development of modern culture and aesthetics and in the empowerment of literary discourse to engage with modernity, with rapidly transforming experience. To keep the focus as sharp as possible, I also choose to begin with texts that critics and reviewers have unanimously regarded as "witty"—almost always without explanation of what is meant by the term. Mark Twain, Oscar Wilde, Richard Wilbur, and Tom Stoppard are all widely celebrated for their wit—and objected to in some circles because of that same quality. Opening their work, consequently, allows us to describe, deepen, and complicate what everyone seems to take for granted as part of the experience of reading them.

But obviously all the above authors are white males. I have thought about this problem at length, and in various places of this book I offer speculations about literary wit as a gendered practice, a practice that through most of the past century has shown a palpable linkage—like the Modernist sonnet, the neoclassical tragedy, the Poundian epic, or the self-consciously "experimental" novel—to circumstances of privilege afforded on the basis of race, social class, and the Y chromosome. Modern women practitioners of literary wit are very much worth writing about, and minority writers figure strongly in this tradition. Their discourses seem distinct—so much so that they deserve special attention in themselves—not as variations on a literary practice established by and dominated by these or other selected men but as insurrections, perhaps, against that practice, as well as against other forms of literary and intellectual habit.[35] Dorothy Parker's campaign was possibly as complex as Oscar Wilde's—or even more so—because she had to resist not only complacency in the American literary scene in the twenties and thirties but also the often-suffocating Midtown "wit" of Alexander Woollcott and the other white boy-men around the Algonquin Round Table. In those same years, but in a different kind of America, Zora Neale Hurston had to negotiate both an Anglo-Saxon male literary establishment and a male-dominated Harlem Renaissance, which could misunderstand experimentation and comic reflexivity in her narratives and personal style. Recent Native American writers seem energized by an intricately reflexive wit, often aimed at stereotypes—of Native Americans and also of the emergent Native American literary voice.

The literary wit here may provide special power to a community of writers engaging with white culture yet resisting inundation, but those are interpretive challenges beyond my reach.[36] If we can succinctly describe literary wit as a modern subversive practice, we may understand better a complex literary wit of resistance as a discourse of American minority and women writers. A young scientist named Valentine, in a wonderland of speculation, observes wistfully in Tom Stoppard's *Arcadia* that "there's an order that things can't happen in. You can't open a door until there's a house." This book tries to begin that kind of construction—a "starter home," which others can extend, modify, or pull down.

Epigrams

I throw probability out of the window for the sake of a phrase, and the chance of an epigram makes me desert truth. Still I do aim at making a work of art.
—Oscar Wilde

It is more trouble to make a maxim than it is to do right.
—Samuel Clemens (as Mark Twain, as Pudd'nhead Wilson)

As has been observed, lexicons and encyclopedias of modern literary terms, poetics, and literary theory have little to say about wit as an interesting and thematic dimension of modern discourse, and sustained address to literary wit in published criticism is sparse. The prevailing assumption seems to be that while so much else has changed with regard to authorship, audiences, historical situations, and cultural and philosophical contexts, literary wit has kept essentially the same patterns and significations since the days of William Congreve and Pope, and that latter-day readers and critics have learned to devalue it as a distraction. I suggested that we can rebuild this conversation by visiting canonical texts. Within these texts we can find firm, manageable, interesting distillations of literary wit to discuss carefully. These are epigrams—catchy, "clever," "amusing," and aphoristic brief utterances that have done much to make the reputation of these authors; though like *wit* in its modern sense, the descriptors available to us—words like *catchy, clever, amusing*—come with an aura of impatience and condescension. The next three chapters will show some of the harm these terms do in describing certain intense, complex utterances in literary contexts, utterances that cannot only change the signification of everything around them in a given text but can also signify unexplored complexity within the self that speaks, writes, listens, or

reads. Published scholarship is also scarce about modern epigrams, aphorisms, and maxims as modes of utterance[37]—in lexicons such terms are
also treated briefly and interchangeably, and modern literary scholarship
has given them little attention. The collective academic and popular wisdom about epigrams is usually expressed Pope style—with recourse to a
few other well-remembered epigrams. My basic assumptions about epigrams follow Pope and glossaries that cite him: epigrams are concise,
amusing (alas!), clever, memorable utterances, moments where "wit"
(again, by commonplace definitions) shines through. This much will get
us started. Kenneth Clark liked to say that, although he couldn't define
civilization, he could know it when he saw it. If we can begin by assuming
that people who read literature usually know an epigram or an adage or a
maxim when they see one, then we can look carefully at a few of these
and evolve a better description of what they are and can do, and what
wit is and can do, in a novel, a poem, a play, or some other recognizably
literary context.

Obviously, epigrams are sometimes amusing and sometimes not, just
as laughter sometimes signifies profound liberation of the mind, and
sometimes (perhaps most times) signifies nothing of the sort. But additional preliminary observations are possible about epigrams that express
or demonstrate literary wit. They often seem like utterances apart, unadulterated by whatever else might be going on in the surrounding text—if
indeed there is a surrounding text. In fact they are frequently laid out sepa-
rately on the printed page, with open space above and below. Sometimes
that blank space is only implicit, in the thematic or rhetorical separateness
of the epigram from the prose around it. These inkless lines can signify,
in their silence, as textual moments in which Western-style habits of exposition are suspended or ignored—habits of clarification, illustration, development, limitation, words and more words to adjust and justify other
words. Set off explicitly or otherwise in this way, epigrams can celebrate
a human power to see, connect, and think in leaps and flashes, just as
they can defy the acquired processes and rituals for "thinking," with ink,
paper, thick paragraphs, and school-learned logic. To formal analysis and
to conventions of intellectual critique, the cultural work of epigrams can
be what Max Weber called an inconvenient fact—especially when one considers what epigrams have done to make the fabric of Western reason,
consciousness, and spirituality.

Nonetheless, on such a printed page, the empty space after the epigram
can be dangerous territory. A witty observation floating there, adrift from

structures of logic and doctrine and normal habits of represented thought, can also intend doubt as readily as defiance. Epigrams can suggest turmoil, a large and fluid uncertainty that, like a river in a wilderness, tosses up now and then these bright flakes of discrete insight, of ostensibly serene liberation from consequences of insight. This is an additional way in which epigrams can strike home as "true," as utterances to take deeply into the mind. For within the intellectual repose of an epigram, two "minds," different and yet the same, can be implied—a mind that somehow knows and a mind that does not; a consciousness risen above tides and rituals of modern literary reasoning; and a self resisting, if for only that moment, its own confusion. Out of intellectual or psychological nowhere an epigram can seem to flash, and then onward we go, into—what? The next paragraph, the next encounter with experience, the next crisis of the mind.

For an epigram in a literary context, other qualities and effects need recognition. Such epigrams can embarrass even as they delight, and not simply because (to debase Pope's great epigram about epigrams) they say what oft was thought but ne'er so well expressed by anyone else. For at least an instant, a literary epigram can shame an entire apparatus of thought, complicate or disrupt some unexamined system by which one may roll complacently through literary texts or worldly experience, failing to countenance twists and contradictions that can make literature and life more interesting. Such an epigram can inherently admonish not just dull everyday thinking but also the very regularity of everyday thought. It can tug at the threads of an ideological fabric normally taken for granted, and open a possibility that all can come undone. A little empty space after the epigram, therefore, can be salutary as well as subversive. If the utterance itself defies habits of intellect and argumentation, then at the end of the utterance there can be a kind of cease-fire, in which listeners or readers might get away from the implications or make whatever psychological bargain they prefer with dangerously disruptive perceptions. To sum up: if literary epigrams can defy habits that pass for logic and reasoning in our culture, they also can affirm the intellectual liberty of the reader, affirm it as relentless *écriture* rarely can.

The end of the nineteenth century saw outpourings of this species of literary wit, and two of the authors considered at length in this book, Mark Twain and Oscar Wilde, led a fashionable practice, which also included George Bernard Shaw, Ambrose Bierce, Nietzsche, Alfred Jarry, Arthur Symons, Edith Wharton, George Ade, J. M. Barrie, and other fin de siècle personalities. Nietzsche's epigrams in the middle of *Beyond Good and Evil* were crucial in changing the direction and the discourse of modern moral philosophy; Twain's great outburst of one-line vortices of thought fueled the restoration of his status as an American social philosopher, and they remain so synonymous with the Mark Twain myth that Twain epigrams are still being counterfeited. As a preface retrofitted to a gothic novel, one sequence of Oscar Wilde's bon mots helped trigger the most important Anglo-American aesthetic revolution since the Preface to *Lyrical Ballads* and lay the groundwork for many contemplations associated with the post-modern ethos and style. My suggestion about the possible importance of epigrammatic discourse is simple: conveniently or not for the systematic reader and careful analyst, the cultural magnitude and reach of religious, philosophical, political, and literary texts can lie precisely there, in their epigrams, proverbs, maxims, adages—compact, supremely memorable, quotable observations and imperatives. In comparison to these, from the perspective of cultures out beyond academe, those reams of meticulous inquiry that such utterances inspire may be only what Wallace Stevens brackets and dismisses as "(Pages of illustrations)." Expository prose, like this page you are reading, may be the normal and necessary slo-mo of our literary culture. Now and then, however, a few epigrams and maxims have altered the foundations of our moral, aesthetic, and imaginative life. Matthew 5 through 7 is probably the best example in Western history but there are many modern instances of much being changed, with very few words.

Which is one more reason why epigrams—witty ones especially—can be a nuisance in the literary landscape. To the logician or ideologue, they can suggest a bothersome mental capacity to operate both within and beyond conventional processes for interpreting experience. In a modern context, besotted with systematic philosophy, categorical imperatives, and elaborate rhetorical etiquette, an epigram can be an act of vast refusal, of intellectual insurrection. For if it really is "clever," such an epigram has a way of elevating the sayer, for at least the instant of the utterance, to parity with canonical sages, prophets, philosophers—and this kind of turbulence cannot be tolerated except as a sort of "time-out," a bit of levity followed by an abrupt (and perhaps unconscionable) reassertion of a status quo. Consequential artists and literary authors who dish out epigrams can be especially troublesome, in part because their meteoric utterances may not keep their place as trivial amusements or "light" observations. Self-contained and damnably memorable, they escape into the streets beyond the theater or the reading room, possibly to foul up the predictable, exclusionary, and possibly irrelevant dialogues of a reasonably literate culture with itself.

Epigrams say, and surprise, and refuse to explain.

Western conventions of thought, however—which means our conventions for the recording and reenactment of thought—favor long, long streams of distinctions and connections and explications: as far back as Plato this has been standard practice when we want to signify (to each other, to ourselves) that consequential thinking is underway, even when it is not. Epigrams might be inconvenient "free radicals" in the aging body of Western humanistic and social thought or a calyx left behind when the encompassing argument has burnt and purged away. But they can be dangerous, challenging an etiquette of written thoughtful discourse and deeply rooted, culturally constructed frameworks for thinking itself. An outbreak of literary wit may be more than a shortcut through longer cognitive sequences; it can disrupt assumptions that the mind "in its freest play" flies by any pattern even vaguely resembling an iterated algorithm, or a Euclidean or Newtonian proof, or a screed of university-bred expository prose. With our cognitive sciences evolving so rapidly, a plausible description of literary wit cannot and should not be affixed to any ephemeral theory of intelligence or cluster of fresh hypotheses about how the mind operates. In fact, literary wit has clues of its own to share about those operations. For the moment, we need to recognize that in practically every dimension, neuroscience and theories of cognition have been changing drastically since the various conventions about wit and humor were laid down. Though literary wit is complex discourse, we have deepened and complicated our theorizing about nearly every other form of discourse except this. Engaging the problem with borrowed or prefabricated theory will yield only contradictions, absurd paradoxes, and more embarrassment. The alternative is to look carefully, and with an open mind, at some well-regarded authors, and see what they can show us. We can start with one extraordinarily rich modern historical moment, in which the most famous and durable wit in American literary history and the best author of literary wit that Great Britain has produced in two hundred years were changing the art of the epigram, authorship itself, and aesthetics, and modern ideas of written utterance and identity.

There are two ways of disliking art. . . .
One is to dislike it.
The other is to like it rationally.
—OSCAR WILDE

Truth is the most valuable thing we have.
Let us economize it.
—PUDD'NHEAD WILSON

11

A Calendar and a Preface

Mark Twain, Oscar Wilde, and the art of the epigram: there are good reasons to pair these two authors in a closer look at modern literary wit. As epigrammarians they reached their prime in the 1890s, and together they led a resurgence of aphorisms, maxims, and bon mots in Anglo-American letters and popular culture. Although they were friends only in a superficial American sense of the word, Mark Twain and Oscar Wilde studied and learned from each other in the arts of literary wit and the cultivation of international celebrity.[1] As the 1890s began, both of these writers had achieved fame with tactics that new information technologies were making possible: photo opportunities; widely reprinted press interviews spiced with catchy quotations; press-covered speaking tours to town halls and opera houses in big cities and the outback; worldwide copyrights; and relentless general public relations.[2] As brilliant literary artists, these two were also masters of self-promotion and already famous on a scale that living writers in the English-speaking world had rarely achieved before. If Byron can be said to have invented Anglo-American literary stardom at the opening of the nineteenth century, then Mark Twain and Oscar Wilde had taken it to new heights by the close. While still a young man, Wilde had led a notorious aesthetic exodus from Victorian shades of brown and black, in both deportment and discourse. He had attracted downtown and dockside crowds (and publicity, always publicity) with his plumb-colored knee breeches and green greatcoats, his turbans and his sky-blue neckties, with leash-led lobsters and sunflowers in Piccadilly, and with his gold-tipped cigarettes, shoulder-length hair, outlandish boutonnieres, sing-song intonations—and with his tides of amazing and hilarious aphorisms.[3] On Mark Twain's home turf, the Wilde show had gone all the way out to Leadville, Colorado, in an 1882 lecture tour that crisscrossed the heartland for months. That tour had been suggested, bankrolled, and managed by Richard D'Oyly Carte, who hoped to build American audiences for the Gilbert and Sullivan operetta *Patience*, a London hit satirizing the Wilde craze. The ramifying ironies of modern-style culture hype had already grown big as Wildean sunflowers.[4] Thoroughly aware of Wilde's celebrity and the stunts, costumes, and manipulations that advanced it, Samuel Clemens put more hard work into his own public look and manner, the performative oddities that still figure in the Mark Twain legend: the light-toned suits, floppy cravats, cigars and corncob pipes, the exaggerated backcountry drawl, the grand entrances, the wild hair.[5] For both these authors, witty epigrams played an important part in the act. They were essential to the show-business side of the art and the career.

As the nineties opened, however, Mark Twain and Oscar Wilde were each engaged in perilous self-transformations as literary artists. Their hard-won and precious public identities, which paid the bills, were also closing in, threatening to circumscribe them as types, and thereby diminishing their possibilities for growth and change as writers and public voices. Twain in 1890 was a literary comedian with travel books and humorous-sketch collections to his credit, and popular novels, mostly for sale by the dubious subscription trade and mostly about young boys. Thanks to profligate spending and bad investments, his finances were coming apart, and as a writer he was fighting a dry spell.[6] The famous Oscar Wilde of that year was (still) an amusing talker, reviewer, and all-around West End attraction, but he had proved a washout as editor of a magazine called *The Woman's World*, and he was as yet an undistinguished poet and a dramatist manqué with several failed plays.[7] Mark Twain wanted desperately to move in new directions, to take on social and moral issues that he had never faced effectively before, and to write narratives that resembled nothing that he had ever done.[8] Oscar Wilde's crisis was every bit as serious as Twain's: for Wilde had to become, at last, the kind of artist that his own charming heretical monologues had been promising his public for more than ten years.

For both of these writers, there was an emergency need to escape or transcend their own celebrity without destroying it. By the end of 1894 they had both succeeded, and literary wit made possible this revolution in cultural identity. One of the paradoxes of literary wit is that it can represent a free play of consciousness, a mind operating beyond any conventional constructions of intellect, or ethos, or even personality—yet its moments of escape *also* represent the self as something more complete and "real." Exploiting that paradox, Mark Twain and Oscar Wilde took their admiring readers with them on the most important aesthetic and epistemological adventures of their respective careers. Wilde assembled and transformed his epigrams into the most eloquent and durable literary manifesto of the modern era, creating a brief document that has outfaced thousands of pages of closely reasoned, densely worded revolutionary aesthetics coming before and after. Meanwhile, with *Pudd'nhead Wilson's Calendar*, Mark Twain created the first really interesting "Man without Qualities" in American fiction, and transformed and modernized the relationship between sayer and saying, the sage and the wisdom, the self and its own spoken and written words.

In June 1890, when *The Picture of Dorian Gray* first appeared (without a preface) in the American *Lippincott's Magazine*, Wilde was taking chances as a performer, an artist, a reinventor of literary modes and forms and trying to wend his way out of the theater stalls and up past the footlights into genuine artistic prominence. In that same year, Mark Twain was fighting bankruptcies of more than the monetary kind. *Huckleberry Finn* was six years behind him; *A Connecticut Yankee in King Arthur's Court* (1889) had ended in thematic confusion and gratuitous gore. The Paige Typesetter was threatening his once-considerable fortune and his wife Olivia's inheritance as well. A seductive and dangerous media revolution was under way, and literary fossilhood, about which he had once teased Emerson and John Greenleaf Whittier and Oliver Wendell Holmes (at the famous Whittier birthday dinner more than a decade earlier) was looming now for him too. The literary wit of *Pudd'nhead Wilson's Calendar*, spread over two major books that Mark Twain published in the nineties, proved to be his most important act of resistance and self-reinvention at the end of the century. The *Calendar* presents a radical experiment in creating a literary character and re-creating an author. It refreshed and complicated the Mark Twain persona; it broke down boundaries between the comedian and the prophet; and it unleashed epigrams, maxims, and aphorisms that extended Twain's fame and his cultural impact far beyond the audience for his narratives.

For Oscar Wilde, the art of the epigram worked a transformation even more basic and radical. Though Wilde had spent years scattering bon mots here and there regarding art, culture, and other renegade geniuses from Cellini through Whistler, his aestheticism did not evolve from a pose into a revolutionary principle until "Preface," which Wilde published in the *Fortnightly Review* six months after *Dorian Gray*'s first appearance. While answering some nasty criticism in the London press, this preface reinvented the art, context, and implications of the Wildean literary epigram. Before this, the Wilde bon mot had reached his public as words embedded like inlaid jewels, in paragraphs that chatted on and on until the best lines and the subversive propositions were lost in welters of diverting language. Here instead was a document terse, cool, and defiant in its very compactness.

The poetics, as it were, of this retrofitted preface made the Wildean epigram new and powerful. Challenging or dismissing outright a literary culture's Arnoldian values and Ruskinian aesthetics, this preface also defies fundamental habits of critical discourse. Only two or three pages long in published editions, the preface was an unprecedented modern literary moment, enriching and complicating the Wilde presence on the Anglo-American literary scene. Even so, the preface also works as a splendid performance of Wildean *wit*: it was—and is—surprising, amusing, clever, even light-hearted and self-parodic. Wilde's public style, like Mark Twain's, had always included self-parody, and the sidelong smile and the dismissive, playful wave of the cigarette are enacted even here in these pages, which read, from some perspectives, as a literary manifesto. Similarly *Pudd'nhead Wilson's* much quoted calendar maxims could be understood as a meditation on identity, and as such they helped Mark Twain achieve new status as a pundit and a quotable American elder; they also showcased his comic genius, and they transformed a meandering detective story into a narrative that can be interpreted as both "serious" fiction and classic outrageous American humor. While *The Tragedy of Pudd'nhead*

Wilson might not qualify at all as a tragedy, much has been said about weighty subjects the novel does try to raise: race prejudice, class, materialism, the psyche, the law, social ethics, the biological prison house, and so on.[9] Some of David Wilson's maxims and epigrams seem to be directly about such dark matters—and sadly or wonderfully, some of them evade or refuse high seriousness altogether. Either way, these calendar moments further complicate a novel whose structure, characterization, and plot resist interpretation more thoroughly than any previous Mark Twain narrative. They challenge the ideology and significations of calendars, proverbs, epigrams; they also defamiliarize the relationship among Sam Clemens, Mark Twain, and the printed word.[10]

Nonetheless, this amazing *Calendar* has had no palpable effect on modern conversations about aesthetics. Wilde's preface, however, changed not only the literary and cultural persona of Oscar Wilde but also the literary culture itself, even after that culture had decided, at least for a time, to try to forget about the unspeakable Oscar Wilde. Nearly every well-known twentieth-century Anglo-American or Continental manifesto—about art, imaginative literature, film, or even rock music—owes a debt to these two or three sparsely printed pages.[11] The *Calendar* transformed forever the cultural entity we know as Mark Twain; the novel in which the *Calendar* first appeared participates in a radical reinvention of the novel, thanks in great part to these epigrams. The preface to *Dorian Gray* presents a key document in the modern reinvention of criticism. And literary wit lies at the core of both these powerful discourses.

Contexts, Voices, False Leads

When Mark Twain took up the mass production of "amusing" maxims in the nineties, he carried the practice further than most readers now recognize. *Century Magazine*'s 1893 serialization of *Pudd'nhead Wilson* included calendar entries, which were not reprinted in the American Publishing Company's first edition a year later or in the 1894 British edition from Chatto and Windus.[12] *More Tramps Abroad*, the British version of *Following the Equator*, included calendar epigraphs absent from American imprints in Clemens's lifetime, and there were other calendar outbreaks in incongruous places as late as 1902 in a story called "The Belated Russian Passport." Apparently with Twain's blessings, *Calendar* did appear twice as a separate published document: in 1894 and 1897 *Century Magazine* published it as a spin-off from the novel's serialization, and in the last decade of his life Twain authorized the sale of post cards with favorite calendar lines, sometimes along with photographs of himself, a fact that could have some bearing on the problem of who is speaking, whose voice and personality we should ascribe to these witticisms.[13] The habit, or effort, of churning out apothegms or maxims or epigrams seems to have taken on a life of its own for Mark Twain, and although we have no clear indications about what literary models, if any, he was emulating when he took to dropping or carving out these utterances, they established him as a leader in a select and urbane company of writers and public figures whose quick, modulated word performances appealed strongly to a modern audience.

Nonetheless, a somebody or a something called Pudd'nhead Wilson supposedly speaks or writes the first words in the novel which bears his name, and he (or it) does so even before the text of Mark Twain's "Whisper to the Reader." "Whisper" itself presents an antipreface, which self-destructs in a long joke about (of all things) the back streets of Florence and Dante and Beatrice, offering no clue as to what this book is going to be about, or what mode or modes it intends to explore or exploit or merely visit. Right from the top of the opening page, then, this Wilson-voice comes disembodied—for Wilson has not been introduced yet, nor even glimpsed, and there are no opening hints of when, where, and how he lives or of what imaginative dimension to locate him in, even tentatively. Wilde's preface mystified, or at least provoked, in a different sort of way. *Dorian Gray* was published as an actual and expanded book (with seven more chapters, and this preface) in April 1891, a month after "Preface" had appeared, in a slightly different form, in Frank Harris's *Fortnightly Review*.[14] Positioned now at the front of this novel and printed in italics, it can seem to float, like a cloud or smoke-screen of gnomic wisdom, especially because Wilde's magisterial "I" shows up nowhere within these epigrams. "OSCAR WILDE" does appear as an ascription after the last, but subsequent editions have sometimes dropped the name or lost the italics.[15] Still, regardless of signatures and fonts, any mystery about who really speaks here is moot. For surrounding *Dorian Gray* was, and is, the cultural event of Oscar Wilde, the star-level personality constructed (especially at that moment) of witticisms and pronouncements that sounded so much like these—and that in turn made this a preface not just for a gothic novel but also for that long-awaited "real" literary career. The opening three lines—

> The artist is the creator of beautiful things.
>
> To reveal art and conceal the artist is art's aim.
>
> The critic is he who can translate into another manner or a new material his impression of beautiful things.

—sum up breezily what the whole public show has been about: cultural contexts, voices, motives. Actually, the preface that unfolds from here has a respectable pedigree. It seems to expand a famous passage in the *Meditations* of Marcus Aurelius, a work Wilde probably knew from his Oxford schooling in the classics and one that since 1862 had been available in George Long's elegant English translation. The passage in question, as rendered by Long, exudes the magisterial *helas* that a fin de siècle aesthete could adore:

> Everything that is in any way beautiful is beautiful in itself and terminates in itself, not having praise as part of itself since a thing is neither better nor worse for having been praised. I affirm this also of the things that are called beautiful by the vulgar, for example, material things and works of art. That which is really beautiful has no need of anything; not more than law, not more than truth, not more than benevolence or modesty. Which of those things is beautiful because it is praised, or spoiled by being blamed? Is such a thing as an emerald made worse than it was, if it is not praised? Or gold, ivory, purple, a lyre, a little knife, a flower, a shrub?[16]

Like Wilde's preface, the busy emperor lays out pithily all we need to know about beauty, art, and the redundancy of more commentary on either subject. So much for that: *Meditations* moves on to graver matters. Unpacking these ancient premises as Wilde does, and spreading them out like proverbs, the preface achieves a difference in tone: a kind of idling, a distinctly anti-Stoic repose. The small spaces of empty paper between one utterance and the next become part of the utterance, subverting the agitation that caused the Victorian critical mind (including Wilde's, before this moment in his career) to pour itself into endless sweaty paragraphs and chapters. Oscar Wilde came on the scene in an age of treatises, authoritative compendia, all-encompassing histories by Thomas Carlyle, Thomas Macaulay, John Ruskin, Benjamin Jowett, Henry Adams, Edmund Gosse, James Frazer, Oswald Spengler, and Arnold Toynbee. Amid that tide of relentless explication, each of these discrete sentences in the preface seems to radiate a wish or a threat to say nothing further. Together, they give an impression of an aesthetic sage having to bestir from a bearskin-draped settee to dispense, yet again, in another way and then another, principles that quicker and less-Victorian listeners would have grasped from the first; or, if we were sufficiently aesthetic or Aurelian, from no utterance at all.

This use of the flat word *things* to finish the three opening declarations, however, is still a puzzler, coming as the word does from the imagined pen or voice of the first wit of literary London. Not "The artist is a creator of beauty" or "The artist is the creator of the beautiful," or anything comparably (and conventionally) classical in its sound—instead, *things*, suggesting an artisan rather than an *artiste*, someone merely decorative in his or her intentions rather than transcendental or moral. Compared to these opening lines, Keats's intertwined postulates about beauty and truth at the close of the great Grecian urn ode seem more firmly "aesthetic" than this from the leader of the aesthetes. Yet if Wilde's lines are more prosaic than Keats's, they are also more cryptic. In the preface, "things" is a thing with connotative weight, invoking certain mysteries even while dismissing others, connecting to a classical heritage yet achieving for these lines a resonant mundanity that sets them apart from any single declaration in Aristotle, Horace, Longinus, or other quotable authorities on the nature of art and beauty.

The Wildean manner, along with the nascent cultural movements of aestheticism and decadence, were "things" that could be known with little trouble. Moreover, in such a landscape the preface could be immediately situated. A public who knew Oscar Wilde could begin to navigate this mass of epigrams and to hear a distinct voice among them. In contrast, the opening maxims of *The Tragedy of Pudd'nhead Wilson*, and "Whisper," which serves as Twain's preface to this novel, seem to derail such understanding or confidence that with this array of epigrams we can think that we know where we are. "Whisper to the Reader" is discourse that would be called dadaist twenty years after, for "Whisper" subverts everything: travel reportage, certifications of authenticity or truth in the printed word, and the pretensions not only of literary realism but also of sanity or sense in "Tragedy" or prose fiction. From a mysterious source, the epigraph that comes before "Whisper" defends the ass—

> There is no character, howsoever good and fine, but it can be destroyed by ridicule, howsoever poor and witless. Observe the ass, for instance: his character is about perfect, he is the choicest spirit among all the humbler animals, yet see what ridicule has brought him to. Instead of feeling complimented when we are called an ass, we are left in doubt.—*Pudd'nhead Wilson's Calendar*. (15)

—yet "Whisper" itself sounds asinine or counterfeits writerly insanity. Where you are, when you are, what you affirm, and what you are—these all become nonsense. The epigraph that follows, atop the first chapter of the actual novel, "Tell the truth or trump, but get the trick," sounds like sound advice—but about what? In what contexts must you "get the trick," whether you tell the truth or trump, whatever that means? Does this gamesmanship include the game of storytelling, or some quality of Pudd'nhead Wilson or *Pudd'nhead Wilson*, or the construction and maintenance of a public self? Sounding like wisdom, the opening pair of calendar entries also could be gibberish, *détournement* of the very idea of the proverb, the adage, the epigram.

Unless . . .

. . . unless the genial Mark Twain persona, as brilliantly marketed as Oscar Wilde's but in Twain's case synonymous with common sense and a good heart rather than hypertrophic sophistication, offers a comfortable glide through such enigmas. In other words, if as readers we believe we already know Mark Twain, and we already like what we know, then we can accept serenely a few odd maxims until something identifiable as David or Pudd'nhead Wilson takes shape among them, or from them, to serve as their imagined "author," a Someone Else to credit them to or to blame them on.

Performance, Masquerade, Disappearance

Wilde's lines in the preface also come with personality and notoriety attached to them—but with regard to interpretation, the comfort level is less. Are these declarations of Wilde's (or of somebody just like him) "serious" somehow, a manifesto in skeletal form, a crucial change of mood or intensity in the advancement of Wilde's aesthetic system or antisystem? Has the foppish entertainer transmogrified, right here, into the aesthetic revolutionary? If that is so, then what about that second epigram, this one about the concealment of the artist? If Wilde values concealment, then is this maxim a gesture of self-erasure—or is it Oscar Wilde caught again in another act of self-exhibition, showing off by means of this coy gesture of self-erasure? After all, when the actual novel begins on the pages following, Wilde will enact the artist and give us "Art." Therefore this is self-evidently a preface to a novel by an ecstatically public man. What can such concealment be then, but another paradox, and an advisory that the more we think we know the mind and motives of the artist, the less we really do; and the more the artist parades before the public, the more inscrutable he or she becomes? And if any of that is so, then what of particular epigrams in the preface that might draw attention and of the strings of epigrams running before and after? Revelations all, of artistic motives and the Truth of Beauty and all that? Yet if to reveal is to conceal, then what is the preface but flamboyant concealment?

Is this overreading? That hardly seems possible, for the next maxim in the series is another Cheshire cat utterance which vanishes when looked at steadily, leaving an enigmatic grin suspended in the air:

> The critic is he who can translate into another manner or a new material his impression of beautiful things.

If Wilde's consummately Wildean maxims in the preface suggest a grin without a face, then Pudd'nhead Wilson's calendar entries suggest a voice without color or tone—without connection to facial expression of any sort. We have someone (we are apparently to suppose) named Wilson ("Pudd'nhead" at this point may or may not be a name that this Wilson person has assumed gratefully or grudgingly) behind which lurks a well-known unknown named Mark Twain, behind which lurks Samuel Clemens. And in the preface we have a complex of profundities or truisms (depending on how we read them—and, in terms of modern aesthetic history, when)[17] dropped by the famous but supposedly frivolous (at that moment) and supposedly profound (at our moment) Oscar Wilde: an Irish Oxonian homosexual masquerading (as long as he could) as a London family man and an aesthete of mysterious political and moral convictions. Obviously this Wilde fellow delivers in a single dose more epigrams than Twain-Wilson, and with lulling cadences the preface moves through a sequence that seems to float above oceans of ambiguity like a fresh and gorgeous clump of seaweed. But with Twain's novel, if we "read through" from the first page to the last, an entire chapter intrudes between each small sampling of Wilson's calendar wisdom, a chapter that may or may not (and usually won't) tell much about Wilson except perhaps that he is still there in Dawson's Landing, doing little, lying fallow as an attorney and puttering with finger-prints and calendars, on the margins of what is supposedly a novel about himself.

If the preface obviously contains literary wit, David Wilson's quirky *Calendar* is also a literary act, in multiple and somewhat stranger ways. The novel does mention Wilson writing his *Calendar* and passing it to Judge Driscoll to read. While it would be a stretch to say that *Pudd'nhead Wilson* is therefore plausibly a book about a man writing a book, it is a novel (of sorts) in which a character who is supposed to be central (but isn't) is supposedly engaged in writing witticisms, which are (again, supposedly) thereafter commandeered by Mark Twain (whoever he is) as epigraphs for a morally consequential book about events that never happened in a made-up place called Dawson's Landing. The remark that ruins Wilson as a freshly arrived local lawyer, about wishing that he owned half of one obnoxious local dog, is dropped orally to strangers on the street; in other words, it is the kind of offhand wisecrack that Bergson and Freud treated as indistinguishable from wit in literary discourse. But because his *Calendar* is alluded to and presented as a text that Wilson has labored over and written out—a book by an imaginary character who isn't even "there" in either the fictional town or the "real" novel that is named for him—the *Calendar*, in its epistemological and textual strangeness, underscores the inherent strangeness of epigrams as advice, or wisdom, or amusements, or all or none of these at once. It also shows us the compounded strangeness of the epigram or witticism in print, floating on a white page with no one credited, no author nearby, only (at best) a name on a title page, a name signifying a human being and a psychological and existential moment that—again, at best—might be imagined by a reader but never really known. Epigrams in such dubious contexts can slip free—from author, from context, from any given moment in cultural history.

And epigrams set apart like this, or by intervening and possibly irrelevant chapters, can break free even from the context of other epigrams.

Epigram as Epigraph

But there is an undertow. If the scattering of the Wilson calendar entries makes possible this kind of liberation, the recurring signature on them, this "Pudd'nhead Wilson," hieroglyphic as it is, works in an opposite way. *Somebody* seems to be speaking, and as readers we may want, or even need, to imagine him, even if he is a character who in his own novel isn't there. Even this opening entry, therefore, can achieve a retrospective poignancy, for it too is signed "Pudd'nhead Wilson," and there is an implication— albeit vague—not only that he has accepted this ridiculing nickname but also that he has not turned it to advantage. There is an implication, inherent in the epigram itself, that Wilson may never have come to grips, psychologically, with the implications of this alias. The joke at the end of the first calendar excerpt is a joke of understatement: "we are left in doubt" means, or at least might mean, that we readers instinctively or culturally know that being called an ass is insulting, despite the animal's virtues, which are summarized to set up the closing line. But since we don't know who Pudd'nhead is, or whether he is a genuine fool, and since we cannot know until several page gatherings have passed that he is at least in some dimensions a thoughtful man, we are "left in doubt" as to whether this calendar maker is really left in doubt. In other words, in one instant we enjoy this utterance, this dubious witticism, and are bewildered by it. By 1894 most readers of Mark Twain knew very well his skill and reputation for deadpan comedy, and by sidestepping this foggy business of Wilson and who he is and how sharp he might be and what this tragedy of his might be about, we can hear Twain on the platform playing his "muggins" role, the deadpan idiot-savant delivery followed by the amazed stare to stretch the joke and the laughter. But if we follow our reader conditioning to attribute a character's words in some measure to the character himself, we can laugh at Wilson as well as with him, sensing the truth in his comment as well as its exquisite stupidity. The novel hasn't begun yet, but this epigram-epigraph opens the questions of what sort of consciousness we are hearing from and what constitutes wisdom and foolishness in the world that this possibly wise, possibly pudd'nheaded individual watches from the sidelines.

The record is clear that Pudd'nhead Wilson was written in haste and clumsily edited.[18] But the "jack-leg" plot does develop a central theme: the absurd social conventions regarding race and identity and the unnerving possibilities that the self is informed and damned by the bigotries of the culture, the mysterious chemistry of the blood, the capricious whorls on the fingertips. Similar is the shock wave of the novel's wit, which is mostly (supposedly) David Wilson's wit. After chapter 10 the epigrams seem scattershot, variable in compression and resonance and weak in their imaginable connection to Wilson, who by this point in the narrative has become at least translucently visible as the lawyer without money, family, anything resembling worldly success. There are witty comments about Thanksgiving, about investing in stocks, and about women as pencil sharpeners—all from a man who has neither money nor wife nor family to feast with on any holiday. The only Wilson wisecrack we can come close to placing in a psychological season or story of a life is Wilson's pre-Pudd'nhead "I wish I owned half that dog" remark when he first appears in the streets of Dawson's Landing. Of that we know only this much: that he mutters that line and its fatal follow-up, "Because I'd kill my half," half to himself, and half to the half-witted townsmen who ask this stranger what he means. Something like meditation or conversation might be taking place here, and we can perhaps "know" that Wilson is a pudd'nhead for not sensing the pudd'nheadedness of the folk he now lives among. Still, there is plenty of murk here with regard to Wilson's motives. Does he speak from anxiousness to amuse others and to display his wit? Out of contempt

for dogs, people, the normal niceties and caveats of interpersonal communication among strangers? From some other inclination or from a mix of
them all? Mystery. Nonetheless, we know at least the when, the where,
and part of the why of one witty and socially fatal utterance. The others
float in as if from another dimension—and that other dimension needs
to be distinguished and described.

The action of Pudd'nhead Wilson unfolds over more than twenty years. If
Wilson's brief observations and maxims can be read as his way of bearing
witness to that passage of time, then could the entire Calendar also be read
as the text of a human drama? Chapter 1 presents Wilson as a man in
social and professional eclipse, suffering obscurity and ridicule as a consequence of one utterance that went afoul—his first wisecrack in this town.
Thereafter, if the calendar wit can be understood as coming from the pen
of a man ostracized because of his wit, then each epigram has a shadow
of failure on it. For epigram is performance: in expression it achieves perfection not exclusively for the self but also for appreciation by others. In
Wilson's case, those others are evidently not listening, at least not carefully, because epigrams have made him the "pudd'nhead." By this name
the town he has chosen chooses to call him, and possibly it is even what
he calls himself, perhaps with irony or resignation. Pudd'nhead Wilson's Calendar, always in italics, is the text, the supposed publication, that Mark
Twain cites whenever he quotes from it. But chapter 5 of Twain's novel
offers the only mention of this calendar being circulated at all:

> For some years Wilson had been privately at work on a whimsical
> almanac, for his amusement—a calendar, with a little dab of osten-
> sible philosophy, usually in ironical form, appended to each date; and
> the Judge thought that these quips and fancies of Wilson's were neatly
> turned and cute; so he carried a handful of them around, one day,
> and read them to some of the chief citizens. But irony was not for
> those people; their mental vision was not focussed for it. They read
> those playful trifles in the solidest earnest, and decided without hesi-
> tancy that if there had been any doubt that Dave Wilson was a pudd'n-
> head—which there had n't—this revelation removed that doubt for
> good and all. (70–71)[19]

So much for Wilson's literary success. The general opinion of the citizens
of Dawson's Landing seems to cast a permanent shadow on the value of
Wilson's brand of literary wit. Should his complete Calendar be understood
then as a twenty-year crumb-trail of one gifted lonely mind, one slow-
evolving record of a private moral education? If this is one interpretive

option, it leads to another paradox, for to know more about this "text" and to contextualize it in this way, is to dim the implications these epigrams carry, individually and together, regarding the inherent strangeness of all epigrams as guidance about human experience or insight into even one human mind. To put it another way, part of the "context" of the calendar entries is that they are situated within a novel that has breathtakingly little to do with them. A self-conscious reader cannot escape the literary-ness of this wit, which means the boundaries between this kind of discourse, this predicament of print, and other, simpler, more-respectable modes and contexts wherein a culture parlays with itself. In our own time, and certainly in Mark Twain's, novels are exquisitely dubious vehicles for communication about anything of importance; *caveat lector* remains a warning for all persons seeking morals in such peculiar places or (as the famous epigraph to *Huck Finn* continues) seeking even a motive or a plot.

To sum up: even if the maxims from this doubly imaginary book called *Pudd'nhead Wilson's Calendar* can be read as "from" a nobody named David or Pudd'nhead Wilson, there are no indications how they come to be here at the top of these chapters of a *real* book, or what connections between epigram and narrative we ought to countenance, hope for, or refuse. They "whisper" that off in the shadows there is an acerbic consciousness ticking away, an extra in his own drama but intensely here as an interpreter of the human condition, and not just in Dawson's Landing but everywhere and anytime. These calendar entries can sketch an outline where an interesting character ought to be, but isn't.

In *Following the Equator* this silhouetting continues. Actually there are more Pudd'nhead Wilson maxims here than in *Pudd'nhead Wilson*, though Wilson is never mentioned in this long account of Mark Twain's world tour. With no clues in *Following the Equator* as to who Pudd'nhead is and where these maxims are coming from, readers of this fat travelogue who have not read *Pudd'nhead Wilson* can enjoy a more extenuated uncertainty about them. "Wit and wisdom" sprinkled by an almost-anonymous Somebody Else in a Mark Twain book of travels: there may be no way to solve interpretive problems there except intuitively, and one epigram at a time, with the commonplace that a maxim speaks truth because it strikes us that way, catching some small recognition that has occurred to us before, in our own dubious and ordinary ill-worded reckonings with the world.

About ten years after *Following the Equator*, in another avalanche of literary wit from a nearly anonymous source, Ambrose Bierce's *Devil's Dictionary* offered an adage about adages, that they are "boned wisdom for weak teeth."[20] *Aphorism* he defined much the same way, as "predigested wisdom" (196). And then *epigram*: "A short, sharp saying in prose or verse, frequently characterized by acidity or acerbity and sometimes by wisdom" (232). Bierce's word choice is consistent and cagey, disparaging yet paradoxical, coming as it does from a writer best remembered now for his own aphorisms and adages. The *Devil's Dictionary* skips clear of suggesting that such utterances are groundless or counterfeit as "wisdom." Perhaps they do grind to hominy some varieties of truth, but it doesn't follow—not even to the cynical Bierce—that they provide no nourishment. "Predigested" implies that epigrams tend to close out conversations, with other people or only within the self, rather than start them or keep them fueled. And of Wilson's epigrams this dynamic seems to be true: they do have an aura of being conversation stoppers, last words in some process of rumination. They differ from the maxims of Wilde's preface, in that Wilson's often seem to imply that this or that subject is not (or no longer) worth thinking about. Wilde's, in contrast, seem to draw attention to matters that require review from a fresh perspective. A few examples of the Wilsonian last word from *The Tragedy of Pudd'nhead Wilson*:

> Why is it that we rejoice at a birth and grieve at a funeral? It is because we are not the person involved. (111)

> As to the Adjective: when in doubt, strike it out. (130)

> When I reflect upon the number of disagreeable people who I know have gone to a better world, I am moved to lead a different life. (166)

> Nothing so needs reforming as other people's habits. (197)

> If you pick up a starving dog and make him prosperous, he will not bite you. This is the principal difference between a dog and a man. (214)

> Even popularity can be overdone. In Rome, along at first, you are full of regrets that Michelangelo died; but by and by you only regret that you did n't see him do it. (221)

> Gratitude and treachery are merely the two extremities of the same procession. You have seen all of it that is worth staying for when the bad and the gaudy officials have gone by. (225)

A reader in a sour mood can decide that in *Pudd'nhead Wilson* the epigrams are a kind of cheating, an illusion that characterization is taking place when it really isn't. Since there are already options for damning this novel, epigrammatic sleight of hand can be part of the inventory, especially if this literary wit tallies up to no ethos, no personality, nothing resembling a "round" character or even a flat one with clear outlines. *Calendar* has much about what the British used to call "Lifemanship"—yet Wilson's "career," when he finally gets one, comes to him through a fluke matchup of fingerprints in a murder case: the first time that Wilson's hobby has ever done him or local justice any good. If a case could be made that David Wilson is in some way a "round" character, it requires acceptance that his radical interrogation of identity, by means of his *Calendar* and his interest in fingerprints, is a sufficient, vaguely Kierkegaardian surrogate for identity of some more conventional sort. In Pudd'nhead's wit there is commentary on worldly experience, commentary on the self that evaluates and interprets experience, commentary on wit and its consequences and worth. His epigrams in the novel often break out in at least three directions, subverting assumptions about the order and sense of the world, subverting our sense of Wilson himself as a "sensible" man, subverting also our sense of sense, of the logic by which experience, culture, and the mind itself proceed. Wilson's calendar making warrants only that one paragraph in his novel, a paragraph ending in an adage not his own, about the fate of people who dare to make "whimsical" adages and "quips" and "fancies." The problem, or so the novel's narrator half-lucidly tells us, is that irony hasn't arrived in the outback yet, that Wilson is somehow again in the wrong place intellectually or ahead of his time.

But in that closing, what exactly is meant by *irony*? If the intention is that Wilson does not, in some dimension, actually mean what he says and writes—about God, about the patterns and burdens of life, about friendship and all the rest—then are readers of this text like the Dawson's Landing townsfolk, although a bit more tactful about the interpretive confusion? In other words, does sophistication, with regard to Wilson's calendar entries and "quips," amount only to holding one's peace, and avoiding the question as to whether, in any sense, David Wilson really "means it"—that is, means what he says? The kind of irony so scarce in Dawson's Landing, then, may be willingness to accept quips and maxims and epigrams and even discrete ideas as contingent, provisional, a synthetic fuel to propel the self along when creeds and systematic formulations lose power to convince. Pudd'nhead's maxims convey no truth, no guidance about the ethics of the man who writes them (and who writes them as Emily Dickinson wrote her epigrammatic and changeful poetry: surely for herself; indeterminately for others). The individual calendar entries may convey not a moral premise or a social outlook, but rather a season of the mind in which such premises take shape. We have "fingerprints" of David Wilson's moments and moods, but not of Wilson's philosophy, and it might be absurd to string epigrams together into some kind of cogent perspective or to assume that in such a string the identity of an interesting human being is revealed. Mistaking the one for the other—mood and moment for philosophical thought—Dawson's Landing dreams and mistakenly preserves the Pudd'nhead Wilson that it wants, pinning him to the scaffold of one circulated joke. Insofar as the novel is about Wilson at all (and in many ways it isn't), it is about David Wilson as a wit, and about the social, textual, and interpretive predicament and consequences of wit. If the calendar entries are forays into understanding, then they are something quite different from conclusions. So with Wilson's *Calendar* and the personality suggested by it, the darker side of wit, its dangerous possibilities and its moral and social liabilities, comes clearer. In other words, the *Calendar* could and perhaps should be read as the hop-scotching philosophical adventure of one scattered modern (and perhaps consummately modern) American man.

If that is so, then what Wilson might exemplify, albeit crudely, is a relation that Mark Twain implicitly apprehended, around this point in his career, between wit of a writerly and conversational sort—the wit that diverts and amuses—and a more powerful sort of creative intelligence and self-realization. The same consciousness that compelled Wilson into twenty years of misunderstanding and social and professional exclusion opens him to new descriptions of the self, of individuality, of identity. Commentary on the novel usually sidesteps the detail that this forward-looking, science-minded amateur in fingerprints and criminal forensics also dabbles in palm reading and seems to believe in it for no good or half-way plausible scientific reason at all. Chapter 11, in which Wilson, looking at the lines in Luigi's palm, determines that the twin has "killed some one, but whether man, woman, or child, I do not make out," stands out in the narrative, presenting a gothic strategy for implicating the twins, soon after, as suspects in the murder of Judge Driscoll. The narrative supplies no explanation of Wilson's peculiar expertise or clairvoyance, and Tom's charge that it is "rank sorcery" is answered only by Luigi's revelation that Wilson has guessed right. Science and claptrap: Wilson's guileless inquiries into both realms do not make him either a scientist manqué or a charlatan stumbling into great discoveries and local fame. Wilson's free-floating, innocent curiosity might, however, be seen as matching, and in some measure explaining, his penchant for incongruous observations about life and The Way Things Are.

Starting Fresh with the Calendar

Twain's "tragedy" of David Wilson, therefore, could amount to this: that his philosophical caprices and water treadings make him a dilettante in an older, more precise, yet less-pejorative sense of the word. Pudd'nhead's freewheeling thoughts, home-grown adages, and unrestricted curiosity seem to carry him wherever they will, and what they seem to signify, as they accumulate, is a contingent, self-amused, scattered identity. The figure in this carpet of epigrams remains an ethical mystery except for his puzzling conformity with backcountry American social life—and also except for his professionally and socially fatal habit of saying exactly what he thinks, when he thinks it, and to whomever he happens to be with— or to whomever this *Calendar* might circulate.

Once more: to look for David Wilson in his *Calendar* is to find nothing, or to find contradictions or a critique of the Western cultural habit of seeking the self within the written words. We can take our pick, or we can begin again from a fundamentally different interpretive direction—starting and staying with what we actually have and know. What we have is an array of many short passages, self-evidently epigrams or attempts in that vein, printed singly or in pairs on this page and that one, and set off from the paragraphic world of expository prose by blank space, and sometimes by a little illustration, which usually has nothing to do with the calendar entry. This time, let us *not* leap over these intervening spaces or construct dubious connections to Wilson's politics or soul, or to Mark Twain's religious convictions, or to the political crises of the 1890s, or to anything else so grand.

Another dimension of the printed epigram, after all, is that it does not enforce, require, or even in a strict sense permit linear connections between one utterance and any other. So here we are—at the top of a given page, above a heading that says Chapter so-and-so, with a brief extract from a calendar supposedly written and either published by someone we never come to know, or (we are perhaps to imagine) recovered and published here at some later date by Mark Twain. We also "know" that this "composing somebody" is a character in a fiction—perhaps based on someone real, perhaps not. Each utterance therefore occurs with very few interpretive tethers trailing behind. What, then, if we construe disconnectedness as a strength or value of each excerpt and of the whole balloon cluster of witticisms and minitexts that accumulate over the course of this larger text, the novel, which is itself so minimally related to any or all of them? Why should readers even care who Pudd'nhead Wilson is? Mark

Twain evidently did not, and there may be no point in our carrying worries about Wilson's identity or moral life further than Twain himself took them. The pleasure and profundity of these calendar entries could be that they constitute quite a different sort of discourse altogether—provocation and "wisdom" without source, without reference, without sustaining personality or ideology or any like complication. Cast aside prejudicial assumptions about what such discourse is and where it comes from, and a refreshed creative relationship can exist with these islands of print on the page.

And to go a step even further in this direction: the peculiar strength of these witticisms and epigrams is that they allow, or encourage, the entertaining of unorthodox thought and heretical possibility, without entanglement in the usual hazards: instances, proofs, counterarguments, extenuating circumstances, exceptions, elaborations, ethos, or probes into the intellectual, religious circulatory system of whoever it is that we imagine is speaking. These terse propositions and utterances simply appear; they do not call for rebuttal or offer evidence; they carry their own force and polish, and their evident wit and verbal tightness convince as ordinary prose and argumentation might not. We are also liberated from homage to or even mere acquiescence with any sage or allegiance to any mode of rebellion against any dominant formulation. And there is this too: we become liberated, for at least a moment, from an imperative that such entertained possibilities must be drafted into something larger, the construction of some new or inherently suspicious system.

With pockets thus emptied, one can turn to that calendar quip that is potentially the most dangerously erosive, an epigram, as it were, to end all epigrams. It opens chapter 2 of The Tragedy of Pudd'nhead Wilson:

> Adam was but human—this explains it all. He did not want the apple for the apple's sake, he wanted it only because it was forbidden. The mistake was in not forbidding the serpent; then he would have eaten the serpent. (27)

Interpretations, in ascending order of perilousness: this epigram could be a nudge or a blow first, at half-remembered Sunday school lessons and at the Anglo-American practice of calling on dull parishioners to explain scripture and divine will to inattentive children; or second, at the hopelessly inadequate human imagination, especially when faced with great mysteries; or third, at Divine stupidity, if indeed the world was begun and managed as Genesis tells it; or last, at the very idea of a "divinity" or sensible primum mobile of any sort. Each and all of these interpretations,

however, must recognize that the utterance in question, benign or outlandish as it might be, hangs in space, up in the printerly air, away from
elaboration or explication, above everything, alone, polished, final. Further, if readers go looking for implications in that silence, that refusal,
then they must recognize that any such implications are opposed. In other
words, if the silence that comes after this all-doubting epigram is a refusal
to explain, a dismissive gesture of some sort, an implication that there is
really nothing more to say, then that silence is also a weakening of the
foregoing utterance, a failure to explain, qualify, support, or risk saying
more. The blank space after a good modern epigram—especially an anonymous one or, in this case, an ambiguously anonymous one—constitutes
both a moment of victory and a moment of evasion, or even of aphasia.
When bound into your family Bible or some book of wise sayings by the
greats (or at least the famous) of the Western world, perhaps the wordless
interludes are spaces for readerly reverence, admiration, or acquiescent
appreciation. Most secular epigrams, however, cannot exude such con-
trails of authority, and the evasions behind and around David Wilson's
Calendar should put conventional "authority" out of the question.

In addition, evasions in this Genesis observation are not merely situational but also internal, especially in the key circumlocution: "The mistake
was in not forbidding. . . ." This roundabout verb choice ducks the question of agency and responsibility—allowing the "mistake" to lie practically anywhere—with the Sunday school teachers, or the transcribers or
translators of Genesis, or the author of the Pentateuch (Moses perhaps,
or Moses & Co.), or the Old Testament Yahweh, or the unnameable forces
that began and sustain it all, or the legions of scholars and theologians
who keep such narratives refurbished and rolling along. Absurdities are
observed and they seem to be cosmic—but exactly where are they and
who must take the blame? Similar evasions are evident in other calendar
entries dealing (loosely) with things scriptural and theological, particu-
larly the scattered quartet of Adam-and-Eve observations. If the first two
can be read from some perspective as dark exegesis, the two that follow
seem to ridicule the compulsion to be exegetical about Scripture or anything else.

Since there is so little in the way of connection between each epigraph
and the chapter it accompanies, we are free to look at the small group of
Adam-and-Eve observations together, to see if in some manner they gloss
each other and provide guidance out of the interpretive maze. These other
Adam-and-Eve ruminations (or ruminations, rather, from Clemens-as-
Twain-as-Wilson) would cancel each other out if the whole sequence and

context weren't so effective in disrupting the work of decoding them and assigning weight and value. The remark about Adam as our benefactor, for bringing death into the world, sounds like a calendar-ender, a last word of despair or world refusal, an affirmation that there is "nothing more to say," as Edwin Arlington Robinson, within a few years of Twain's novel, said over and over in his profound absurd poem "The House on the Hill." Robinson kept saying more, and so does Twain-as-Wilson and Clemens-as-Twain. But if the first two of these Adam observations can be read as dark exegesis, the two that come afterward seem to ridicule the compulsion to be exegetical about Scripture, or about anything else. The teething comment atop chapter 4:

> Adam and Eve had many advantages, but the principal one was, that they escaped teething. (52)

jolts the already-compromised solemnity of the Adam-as-benefactor remark. If we are wondering on what ground the gift of mortality and the escape from worldly care is being celebrated, then the answer somehow seems to include "teething"—and so Wilson's (or Mark Twain's) contemplation of Adam's grave or Yorick's skull becomes either a comic nonmemory of being an uncomfortable infant, or (more likely) a lugubrious memory of inconvenience in parenting or babysitting—though of course Wilson never fathers anyone and never is seen caring for a small child. Clip out the Adam-as-benefactor epigram and move it somewhere far away—for example, to a C. S. Lewis meditation on Christian mythology and modern imperatives to believe—and it changes utterly. But leave it where Mark Twain placed it, and the cross-talk from the other Adam lines, and about matters as diverse and worldly as stock buying and pencil sharpening, makes it a moment that readers who have come looking for a novel can take or leave, or rather take *and* leave, at the ambivalence-charged instant of encounter and response. Leave Genesis behind in the onward flow of this novel, and the last glimpse of Scripture has to do with watermelons:

> The true Southern watermelon is a boon apart, and not to be mentioned with commoner things. It is chief of this world's luxuries, king by the grace of God over all the fruits of the earth. When one has tasted it, he knows what the angels eat. It was not a Southern watermelon that Eve took: we know it because she repented. (179)

Here is another joke about Genesis—also perhaps a joke about the preceding jokes about Genesis—and unmistakably also a celebration of life, as something good that comes in the stretch of time between teething and death. If we are reading the novel front to back or the culled-out epigraphs in sequence, then this epigraph takes us clear out of the dark patch into which some of the earlier calendar entries may have led. If Genesis and the divine plan and the value of being alive are all suspect, then suspicion about any or all of these is also suspect.

Mazes of meanings, then, in the scattered wit of a title character who isn't there, at least not as conceivable citizen-by-choice in this backwater or as round imaginative construct in the narrative proper. Wilson's non-presence in his own novel may not even seem like competent storytelling. Even so, attaching epigrams to such a noncharacter advances a project that may have mattered to Mark Twain as much as giving readers a more complete protagonist. In fact such intentions inherently conflict: if David Wilson were a convincing character, then his sayings would "say" less, as readers would know more (or believe they knew more) about how to contextualize and interpret this calendar. Heresies may lurk in these voice-less lines about Adam and Eve and Genesis, but they can exude banality as well as common sense. David Wilson's scriptural observations, floating free of ascription to a plausible David Wilson, also float beyond analysis and sink beneath it, being at once too profound and too absurd for re-sponse. And if we read each such epigram as an epigraph and consult the main body of the given chapter for elaboration, little of relevance can be found, which only compounds the problem of valorizing a Pudd'nhead Wilson bon mot.

Thus an ultimate conundrum to which the Calendar leads us—the prob-lem of determining what to do, as readers, with the printed word, wisdom supposedly set down by someone we really don't know, or someone we think we do know (Mark Twain, for instance, or Samuel Clemens) but whose thinking and worldly and spiritual and psychological experience and expertise can never "truly" be fathomed. People are always printing up things that they evidently intend for others to believe, and for our part, we would sometimes like to know that such proffered wisdom is founded on something solid, an experiential substrate, which as Thoreau says (in his own print-laden pages about a strange man alone with Brahma or merely his own ego in the Concord woods) allows us to say "This is, and no mistake." Print stabilizes a thought, arranging it (or some fragment of it) in black type, which can (supposedly) be decoded later and (perhaps) remembered and taken to heart. In other ways, print deepens mystery, especially when the individual utterance is a thing set apart and when attention is drawn to the fact that about this soothsaying wit a reader knows only surfaces or myths or shadows—or nothing at all.

In the discourse of literary wit, much of the pleasure consists of not knowing where in the readerly world you are. This principle runs counter to prevailing rules and habits of engaging with literary texts. Sensible or not, the scholastic American way is to read to decipher—which (we assume) requires some understanding of the historical situation of the text and various pressures on the given utterance. Epigrams and literary wit, however, are often let off the hook. If we don't know who this Wilson is or was, and if we don't really know who Mark Twain was when he wrote epigrams as Pudd'nhead Wilson, then we also don't know who is speaking in Proverbs or Ecclesiastes either or what specific personal or cultural experience and received wisdom might underlie each such perception, many of which have found their way to the core of the Western ethos. Out of disembodied voices we create wisdom: for good or ill, that is a philosophical and theological practice of the West. In fact, it seems that the more we know about who is speaking, the less we are likely to believe what he or she has to say. Any attempt to clarify situations, contexts, or motives that underlie Pudd'nhead Wilson's calendar entries can have, therefore, two effects, neither of them comforting: they can foster a delusion of knowing the person who constructs these utterances, and they can disrupt the independent response of readers who encounter such explications.

Calendar: "any concise and systematic arrangement of facts, observances, etc; a register; a list; a schedule, as of pending court cases."[21] All these calendar entries are actually by Mark Twain; except that Mark Twain was a public personality made up by Samuel Clemens—not a homogenized fiction but rather a misplacing, displacing, and muddling of the truth. This is the context and the substance of the Calendar: dis-connection rather than connection; disruption, complication, even ridicule of the habits and rituals for assigning voices and personalities to printed words or attributing authority or intention to received ideas. "Tell us who wrote the line," we might want to protest, "and we will know how wise or witty it is!" No such luck here. Therefore, if for a moment (the moment of the epigram) we can stop wondering who is speaking, or at least stop trying to answer such questions, we can experience a liberation that might be the real and deepest intention of these epigrams. Because they remain mysterious, words out of the old Southwest sky that stretches over Dawson's Landing and the story, they remain free of any limiting assignment to a personality, a worldly experience, an ethos, or anything like.

In *Following the Equator*, where the agency is even further removed and indefinite, a landslide majority of David Wilson's words are scattered. There are seventy chapters in Mark Twain's last travel book, compared to the twenty-one chapters (and "Whisper" and the conclusion) in the novel; and four of *Equator*'s chapters (15, 36, 59, and 69) have two maxims apiece, for a total of seventy-four, or almost twice as many as in *Pudd'nhead Wilson*.

But the difference extends into quality. For David Wilson, or whoever or whatever he is, as character, mask, proverb-writing ghost does notably better work in *Following the Equator*. The supposed source of these new epigraphs, *Pudd'nhead Wilson's New Calendar*, shows a new stage, a refinement, in the craft of the witty maxim. The entries here are generally leaner, quicker, more varied in subject and in tonal range than those of the first *Calendar*. More important, here and there we can see genuine connection between these epigraphs and the subject matter of the chapters they open. The *New Calendar* actually refers to the equator (!), to the Queen's English, to other gods in other cultures, and when Twain reaches South Africa, even to the Boer War—which timeliness poses problems if we persist in connecting this and the other epigrams to a Wilson, who in the novel supposedly reached full-grown active manhood about sixty years before Twain's world tour and the Boer troubles and who must therefore be imagined as cranking out his *New Calendar* as a man of ninety. The closing calendar entry in the *Following the Equator* opens with the line "I have traveled more than anyone else," a boast that seems a dropping of the Wilson facade. Even so, the persona of New Calendarist David Wilson is kept up persistently if half-heartedly, like a disposable Halloween costume, put on as a license to say anything one likes but essentially disconnected from supposedly informative discourse that might be offered in actual chapters of this thick and newsy book. The lines of the *New Calendar* are breezy, sometimes ominous, and bubbling with contradictions. Consider the following pairings that are possible when these epigrams are gathered together:

> Pity is for the living, envy is for the dead. (Chapter 19)
> Man will do many things to get himself loved, he will do all things to get himself envied. (Chapter 21)

> Be careless in your dress if you must, but keep a tidy soul. (Chapter 23)
> Everyone is a moon, and has a dark side which he never shows to anybody. (Chapter 66)

Everything human is pathetic. The secret source of Humor itself is not joy but sorrow. There is no humor in heaven. (Chapter 10)

Don't part with your illusions. When they are gone you may still exist but you have ceased to live. (Chapter 59)

Read these lines as fragments of some plausible ethos or body of wisdom, and more maxims will be needed to negotiate conflicts among these maxims. The *New Calendar* offers amusing and provocative insights, but it also offers glimpses of a mind moving freely from one perception to the next, with delightful and even amazing disregard for relations among them, for connections between the last disruptive thought and the next one. In *Following the Equator*, Twain is on the move as never before, and when he self-evidently breaks away from the Pudd'nhead facade for that final epigraph about having traveled more than anyone else, a self-congratulatory tone radiates through this playfully solipsistic remark about how everybody else speaks Mark Twain's English with some sort of accent. Translation? Does it mean that we all talk funny, and everybody (including of course whoever we decide is speaking) speaks in and from a place, a moment, a particular intersection of dubious experience and wool-gathered wisdom?

The only way to construe that Wilson, or even Mark Twain, has "traveled more than anyone else" is to understand such travels as imaginative, intellectual, or even (dare we say it?) spiritual. Whether Mark Twain had traveled farther than anyone else, over the physical face of the earth, is open to easy rebuttal. By the time this last of his travel books reached the public, Joseph Conrad and Rudyard Kipling had certainly roamed more, and had done so from earlier days in their respective lives. True, Mark Twain's words had certainly traveled as far as anyone else's, or at least any other writer's words of his own generation, and he had also been traveling far in a perilous intellectual and spiritual journey, through a forest of new experience, questioning the nature and the prospects of the self, his culture, the entire *condition humaine*. Totalizing formulations and deadly seriousness were closing in on the fin de siècle artist and intellectual from every imaginable side—if escape and psychological survival meant escape from the old habits of thought and discourse, then so be it. In *Calendar* and *New Calendar*, Sam as Mark as David as Pudd'nhead goes on a lark, and if we join him, we ourselves escape ourselves, at least for an instant, and from the psychological and doctrinal encumbrances on the Western identity. The epigraphs offer a quick holiday from rules and encumbrances out of which the Western self is made.

In the Harper editions of *Following the Equator* there is a famous illustration of Mark Twain making his Great Man's Progress through India, walking with his hands free in his white waistcoat pockets but with a dozen or so native porters queued up behind him, matching his stroll pace for pace, ready to follow him wherever he dodges. Thus the Mark Twain predicament in a snapshot: gone are the days when a younger Sam Clemens could wander the world with light baggage (of any sort, including the flimsy baggage of public identity) and with some measure of solitude, anonymity, and freedom. *Following the Equator*, after all, thinly conceals the story of a distinguished lecturer tramping not from one town and temple and tourist spot to the next, but really from one paying audience to another, a succession of houses packed with audiences who thought they knew who he was and knew what they wanted him to be. Fame and public identity and a chance to pay down his crushing debts waited on every dais from Vancouver to Bombay. For both Mark Twain and his readers at the century's end, certain new "isms" were also dogging their tracks, gathering to explain everything, and in the process diminish the consequentiality of the individual mind and soul. A baggage train of inescapable big ideas was beginning to shadow us all. Wisdom without system, literary wit without obligation to explain or play the game of making sense: these offered escape—or at least an interlude of perfect, amoral, prelogical peace, before the impedimenta of systematic thought and exhaustive explication, borne by those same "trippers and askers" who bothered Walt Whitman, tripped back onto Mark Twain's very own heels.

Antipreface, Metapreface, Détournement

When he wrote his preface to *Dorian Gray*—the preface that eventually became so important to a revolution in the very idea of art—Oscar Wilde, like Mark Twain, was responding to the power and the burden of his own notoriety and to the pieties and oppressive logic of decades of Anglo-American literary moralizing. At that point in Wilde's career, these few pages were a compaction of, and an escape from, the noodling of Wilde's diverting but meandering monologues on art, criticism, culture, and the intellect. He was also responding to a personal need to make his pot really boil, and to give this late-Victorian gothic tale an extra measure of aesthetic and intellectual heat. The semi-isolated, tight utterances of the preface played a game, therefore, but they refused to play the traditional game of prefaces. No disclaimers here or apologies or laboriously clever arguments; no gestures of fealty or indebtedness; no snuggling into any tradition or claiming of a cultural legacy. None of that at all. The opening line condescends in its simplicity. It does not enunciate a timeless truth so much as begin a retelling of the ABCs of art, apparently for an audience who has talked so much and read so much about art that the primordial truth (as Oscar Wilde construes it) might be forgotten.

In most reliable editions, the preface to *Dorian Gray* is italicized—setting it off not only from the novel proper but also perhaps from the controlling consciousness of the novel proper, or from its "intentions," or from its potentialities as a demonstration of whatever it is that the preface is asserting. These italicized lines also take on the aura of a quotation, intuition, or received wisdom: they imply that these observations are part of an assertion of great importance. Yet what, finally, are they asserting? Do these postulates add up or do they compress (with a little intellectual violence) into a reasoned argument or at least a logically associated sequence? Because they come all in a bunch, we have more motive and cue to read them this way than Wilson's *Calendar*. However, to follow that inclination is again to risk essay-izing an array of statements that is patently not presented as an essay. In fact, the preface looks more like a poem or a gathering of overheard utterances or journal entries than like argumentative prose.

If we have no idea when or why or how an imaginary David Wilson "wrote" his *Calendar*, the circumstances of the preface to *Dorian Gray* are clearer. When *The Picture of Dorian Gray* finally reached the public in *Lippincott's Magazine*, the *St. James Gazette* lost no time in drubbing the tale, and when Wilde replied in four letters published in the last week of June 1890, they were subverted with aggressive editorial notes accompanying the appearance of Wilde's letters. Later that year, Wilde had wasted time and ink going back and forth with the hostile *Scots Observer*, whose anonymous reviewer had called *Dorian Gray* a "perverted" exercise in "grubbing in muck heaps."[22] When months of wordy apologias accomplished nothing, the time was ripe for another rhetorical strategy. The preface therefore came about as a sort of afterword. It was published first all by itself in the *Fortnightly Review*—an ex post facto "preface" reheating a controversy that had been around for most of a year and promoting the revised and expanded *Dorian Gray*, which was set for hardcover release a month after. When the W. H. Smith bookshops in London announced their refusal to stock it because it was a "filthy" and notorious work, hot sales were virtually assured, and "Preface" proved a smart move in one of the cleverest literary campaigns at the century's end.

However, the preface obviously stands taller now than as a lasting last

word in a multimonth flurry of now-forgotten argument. It proved to be
a breakthrough, or a breakout, in the practice of literary manifestos, popping the gas-filled balloon of pietistic and reasonable genteel Victorian
disputation. For what is under attack here is aesthetic and literary argument itself, argument according to Queensbury Rules that had evolved
over generations of essays and earnest letters to *Blackwood's* and the *Atlantic*
and *Harper's, Scots Observer, Century Magazine, Saturday Review,* and all the rest.
Wilde's preface refuses outright those forms, civilities, and methodologies, and in their stead we have declaration after declaration, dropped and
left for readers to take or leave as they choose. The sovereignty of the
artist, which this is supposedly about, becomes implicitly a celebration
of the sovereignty of the reader as well. The little spaces between these
postulates or observations are also breathing places for ourselves, opportunities to digest, reject, or strike whatever bargain we wish with these
offerings.

If these are read then as autonomous maxims and not as another argumentative Victorian essay, and if logic and labored argument are actually
part of the cultural problem addressed by them all, then why not stand
the preface on its head as a way of entering it, looking at the last two
epigrams by themselves, and considering what manner of document
they conclude?

> We can forgive a man for making a useful thing as long as he does not admire
> it. The only excuse for making a useless thing is that one admires it intensely.
>   All art is quite useless.

If these paired declarations aren't a conclusion or a punch line for the
preface, they are at least a point of arrival, and the empty space after the
final period of the final epigram suggests a firm refusal to explain further.
That doesn't turn out to be true in a broad sense, for in the novel that
immediately follows the preface (or rather in the novel to which the preface was retroactively added), Sir Henry Wotton, as a Wildean mouthpiece,
has much more to say about art and its uselessness, and both preface and
novel roll forward on a tide of additional maxims about those subjects.
Still, these two closing epigrams have an explicit link to each other and
an aura of completion, and because they have become axioms in modern
critical discourse, it is worth wondering exactly what they mean, exactly
who it is that means them, and when.

To focus on the two last words: they are elegantly simple as a closing,
but why *quite* useless? Should we pay attention to the inserted *quite,* or is
it only an aesthetic "beat" or breath place, like the "utterly utter" noises

that Gilbert and Sullivan in *Patience* and other promoter-satirizers of aestheticism heard as the babble of effete young men gathered worshipfully
around the younger Oscar Wilde? One can experiment with readings in
which this *quite* carries meaning rather than merely sound. Might it signify
that there are varying degrees of seriousness, that "art" is not always and
absolutely useless but nonetheless more "useless" than various other
human *things* (the word keeps turning up in the preface) or pursuits? This
is not tail-chasing: the *quite* adds a whiff of uncertainty to this last flat
and certain-sounding declaration, deconstructing the culminating state-
ment, and even turning it inside out. Something is either useless or it
isn't—at least in the usual pathways of logic. The *quite* here is not just
emphasis but also a suggestion that uselessness is another "thing" fraught
with paradox, that a truly useless "thing" has a psychological and spiritual,
aesthetic, and (dare it be ventured) a social and moral "use" in its very
refusal of paradigms by which usefulness and worth are measured. In
other words, that "all art is quite useless" is more serious than an assertion
that "all art is serious." This is so because the observation—Wilde's observation—opens "serious" speculation and implications rather than closes
them down and leads to open-ended complications rather than dead-end
simplisms. The *all* in the closing adage is just as provocative—dangerous,
magisterial, and suggestive of those stage-performance witticisms and
newspaper wisecracks that Wilde's popularity rested on—absurdly vast
generalities that delighted and provoked a public rather than instructed or
enraged them. This preface-closing postulate about "all art" followed on
the heels of Wilde's funny, disruptive pronouncements about all education, all the upper classes, all America—and in the immediate context of
this preface, all the English and American middle classes and all Anglo-
American romanticism and realism. The last line of the preface obviously
settles nothing; rather it opens up everything to speculation, to possibilities, to new fields of perception, distinction, tautology, and empowering
disconnection from all the established rules with which the fin de siècle
decade had begun.

Nonetheless, the closing line of the preface also resonates with the
other "all art" pronouncement in the preface, the eighteenth such in this
sequence of twenty-four—and when we set these two "all art" observations against each other, interpretive troubles can compound.

All art is at once surface and symbol.

And to read either surface or symbol is perilous. Well, if symbols can be
expected to symbolize something, and if surfaces are a point of interaction

between art and ordinary experience, then either reading strategy would seem to lead inevitably to meaning, or to "use." The "peril," then, is to fall victim to notions that art signifies? That art does teach, or tells or at least observes with some measure of value? If these readings do not add up, so much the better, for adding up is self-evidently not an intention of the preface.

But having looked selectively at epigrams from the beginning, middle, and end of Wilde's preface, we must also consider the effect of the entire brief document. This preface is a sequence of about two dozen declarations, some of them comprising more than one sentence. Eight of them begin flush left; others are indented a few spaces, and no group is set off with skipped lines in a separate section or stanza from the rest. If the overall look, therefore, suggests a poem by Algernon Swinburne or Arthur Symons or perhaps something from the early works of Ezra Pound, then is this a poem of some sort, masquerading as a preface, or a preface with poetic pretensions, or some evasion of either mode of discourse and of others as well?

This can be debated—and if disagreement results, then (as Wilde's twenty-third observation in the sequence declares) the critic as artist is "in accord with himself"—whatever that means. And since there are no paragraphs in the preface, can we not read the whole thing any way we like, even backward? Actually, the preface runs in a circle, for the last observation is essentially the same as the first, wrapping around in a Mobius strip of continuity, paradox, and escape from conventional logic.

Taken as a whole, then, the preface sets a trap—especially for one who ventures into it to put its assertions into logical order, or to impute an order, or to reconcile them with modern critical praxis as a logic-based activity. The preface seems to spin around on itself—but if we go looking for an axis, somewhere in the middle (a comparatively still point in this whirling circle) we find two double-assertions, dead center:

> No artist desires to prove anything. Even things that are true can be proved.
> No artist has ethical sympathies. An ethical sympathy in an artist is an
> unpardonable mannerism of style.

So the opening assertion in each set collides with an immovable fact about literary and visual arts in Wilde's own day—and each outlandish opener is rear-ended, as it were, by one that immediately follows. "Even things that are true can be proved" reads like a parlor-game paradox, a line out of a Wildean farce, but if it means that the usual habit in our culture is for untrue "things" (that word again) to be "proved," then the implication is that our school-learned logic takes us "truly" nowhere and that the artist is therefore exonerated with regard to making sense, because (as Algernon says dismissively at the end of act 1 of *The Importance of Being Earnest*) "Nobody ever does." Denying the moral earnestness that saturated the literary world of his time, Wilde covers himself with an urbane nihilistic shrug and a quick shift to the next proposition, which turns out to be as history-denying as the one about didactic art.

But why so many sweeping refusals in such a short space? "Ethical sympathies," after all, were rife in the salons, the literary magazines, the boulevards of Wilde's London, Howells's Boston, Henry James and Emile Zola and Paul Bourget's Paris. They humidified the cultural air from Kate Chopin's Grand Isle to Sarah Orne Jewett's Maine Coast. If artists of some purer, ethically unsympathetic breed were in short supply, they had been scarce for a long time. What then of these earnest, ethical-sympathied London literary folk, including many with whom Wilde regularly and lavishly dined—at their expense? Do they all qualify as unpardonable mannerists too?

If the above summation has Wildean airs of finality to it, then it is time to uncage another paradox of this preface. If it is about art, can it be also a work of literary art in and of itself? Is it interpretive violence to shake the preface so hard to divulge its meaning, or its contradictions and paradoxes, which are also a kind of meaning? In its form and in its component maxims, this preface seems to scorn the clumsy practice of interpretation—and at some point we may have to stop interpreting the preface as an oddly written critical essay and contemplate it as something else. Then what about the possibility mentioned above, of the preface as aesthetic or decadent poetry? When listening to it, rather than decoding it, one can hear cadences suggesting an overall metrical pattern, and for tonal or thematic unity it is awash with repetends, of a sort that would have pleased Symons and Swinburne and possibly even Thomas Hardy, Robinson, and William Vaughn Moody. The preface runs about 380 words and within it we have *the artist* eleven times, *art* ten times, the phrase *beautiful things* five times, and several other weighty and sonorous words and phrases occurring twice, thrice, or four times. *Ethical sympathy, face in a glass, surface, symbol, peril*—these recurrences cross the preface like flagstones positioned tastefully in a Millais painting of a mountain stream. *Author, novel, literature, story, text*—such terms as these never occur. The nearest address to narrative fiction and to the generic and modal experiments that this preface prefaces are these dismissive lines about "books," narrative or no:

> There is no such thing as a moral or an immoral book. Books are well written, or badly written. That is all.

But again, what is "all?" Meaning almost nothing, Wilde's three-word tag line is a shrug, evading or refusing further talk about that huge subject, the ethical or moral intention of literary works. That is all. And the intention of these two short lines cannot be to settle this or any other great matter with regard to literature or "art." Wilde will not "prove" his point because as he says magisterially a little farther down the page, "Even things that are true can be proved"—which does not prove anything either and which leads back into the familiar mystery (familiar to Wilde readers) of what Wilde intends when he uses words like *true* or *truth*. The point (if it can be called that) to the comment about the morality and immorality of books is not that style and structure are all but that moral intentions and moral readings are not enough and that we need to be broader and more supple as readers and artists than Victorian values typically permit. Terms like *well written* and *badly written* can obviously encompass moral intentions, a perilous realm of potentially moral symbols below surfaces.

Several lines that come after the dismissal of moral readings and "ethical sympathies" seem to gloss those dismissals, allowing some accord between aesthetic admiration and the unglamorous carpentry of moral engagement:

> All art is at once surface and symbol.
> Those who go beneath the surface do so at their peril.
> Those who read the symbol do so at their peril.
> It is the spectator, and not life, that art really mirrors.

So paradox again—and contradiction again. Very well; if this preface contains multitudes, it also judges multitudes. The paired observations below are roundhouse blows against the age:

> The nineteenth century dislike of Realism is the rage of Caliban seeing his own face in a glass.
> The nineteenth century dislike of Romanticism is the rage of Caliban not seeing his own face in a glass.

So at the fin de siècle, is the siècle now unmasked as Caliban, one way or another—and not just the always-blamed bourgeoisie or the stodgy

Oxbridge dons and Fleet Street reviewers? All of them evidently have expected too much or the wrong thing from art, and the two dominant aesthetic formulations of the nineteenth century (before the appearance in England of Wilde's aestheticism) have contradicted each other beyond the point of absurdity. Or perhaps these lines refer to pockets of "rage" within a broader and more benign context instead of to one hundred years of unadulterated raging to and fro. As usual, there is no way of telling for sure, perhaps because telling for sure is what this preface stands firmly and consistently against, not only in its discrete declarations but also, and more important, in their volatile interaction, their contradictions, and most remarkably in the cadence, the tonalities, the prosody of the complete text.

But even so, this is only more interpretation, more of the plodding craft that brings art down. Step back from the preface several paces more: these words of Wilde's are also carefully chosen sounds, part of an incantation as much as they are part of any critical treatise. The preface suggests rhythms and recirclings of a Mallarmé poem more than it does a discourse on aesthetic values—and more, actually, than do Stéphane Mallarmé's own prefaces and manifestos, which in comparison to Wilde's seem talky and defensive.

We have known for a long time that Mallarmé was a source for Wilde's thinking about art. But for decades an argument has smoldered with regard to what Wilde meant by truth and true when he used these words in his epigrams. From a pattern of utterance in the preface and from other epigram-gatherings, we can guess that truth is whatever is left—which is apparently much—when logic and fact collecting leave off. The rhythm of the language here, its syllabic repetitions, its familiarity as words that both explain and evade explanation in ordinary discourse—all these qualities combine to subvert interpretation of any Victorian or modern academic variety and induce instead the kind of reading that allows some affirmations to pass without scrutiny and some varieties of "truth" to be uttered or invoked without murderous or trivializing explication.

It is possible, therefore, that Wilde's great preface, like the art of which it speaks, is offered as a beautiful thing—to be contemplated, and intuitively (rather than logically or even rationally) understood, and admired intensely, without the usual interpretive mayhem. Nonetheless, in an exploration of literary wit, and with regard to a preface that may look like an aesthetic or decadent poem but that finally is not, this supposition cannot be a point of arrival. There is at least one more option to experiment with, and that is the possibility of countenancing all these options at once and allowing them perhaps to cancel each other out. It can be fun, it can be liberating, to be lost in a maze or to have the marked-out trail vanish behind you and in front of you.

Two more short sets of epigrams from the preface, which seem to celebrate that kind of psychological and aesthetic liberation:

> Those who find ugly meanings in beautiful things are corrupt without being charming. This is a fault.
>> Those who find beautiful meanings in beautiful things are the cultivated. For these there is hope.
> They are the elect to whom beautiful things mean only Beauty.

>> All art is at once surface and symbol.
> Those who go beneath the surface do so at their peril.
> Those who read the symbol do so at their peril.

In Anglo-American religious-political parlance the word *elect* is dangerous, and Wilde knew it. This first trio of maxims has heretical overtones, as it echoes cadences from the King James translation of the Sermon on the Mount and culminates with this bizarre mock-Calvinist doctrine of aesthetic salvation. The second set also makes beatitudinal noise: blessed are the surface readers; blessed are the symbol readers, in unspecified "peril" as they venture beneath surfaces. Part of the peril, perhaps, is that "symbol" leads to signification—and thus to that Caliban-confrontation with the "glass." That confrontation subjects not only ourselves, who are Calibans, but also art itself to the "peril" of readerly rage of one form or another. In other words, the second set of observations could destabilize any reading of the first—as if this first set of observations weren't already fraught with interpretive troubles.

We can close this contemplation by turning to another of Oscar Wilde's most-dangerous words. We shall never know for sure what he meant by *truth* and *true* as he tossed those terms around in essays and plays or in this preface, which eventually became the implicit preface for everything he wrote:

> The English are always degrading truths into facts. When a truth becomes a fact it loses all its intellectual value.[23]

> Religions die when they are proved to be true.[24]

> If one tells the truth, one is sure, sooner or later, to be found out.[25]

And so on. Truth, whatever it is, turns out to be one of Wilde's pet subjects, and one of his targets, in the free play of his literary wit. And the preface's culminating line, *All art is quite useless,* offers both a challenge and a surrender. The sentence refuses the pieties of the Victorian period, denies the use in any dimension of the novel that follows, denies the use of this preface, this arty response to artless criticism that attacked *Dorian Gray* as bad art, immoral art, art against decency and culture.

As the omega-point of Wilde's manifesto, the final epigram carries its own negation. This witty preface becomes a poem, a rejoinder, a deposition on poetics, aesthetics, the art of reading, the predicament of the artist, the futility of argument—and the uselessness of applying logic, or conventional print representations of logic, to art and the delightful motions of the mind. Theorizing gives way to intuition; paragraphs give way to postulates; laborious critique and defense yield to paradox—in other words, to a condition of mind in which art, artist, and reader can thrive. "All art is quite useless," he says. Does he mean it? What does it "mean" to mean it? Is Wilde in one quick phrase embracing and dismissing "all art"? Does he "mean" that Ruskin was wrong all the time, about every tomb image and Blessed Virgin statue from the eleventh century to the present? Does he "mean" that the Pre-Raphaelites were wasting their time with earnest Early Church symbolism? A face of youth, of startling youth, is represented here—a portrait of Wilde, and perhaps of ourselves, before the moralizing of middle age and distinctions and paradoxes overwhelm the observing "educated" mind. We can talk of Oscar Wilde's literary wit as a celebration, as both a preservation and a recovery of psychological and intellectual innocence. Still, these are elegant, crafted epigrams set carefully in a literary context and not mere transcriptions of Wilde-speech, the oral wit that seemed so spontaneous and that amused and puzzled reporters and *saloniers.* Like Mark Twain's (or Pudd'nhead Wilson's or Sam Clemens's) richly enigmatic *Calendar,* Oscar Wilde's literary wit, situated here in this preface to *Dorian Gray,* is not a vehicle for aesthetic or intellectual high seriousness or a sugar coating to make it palatable and popular. It *is* the seriousness, in its very essence. The possibilities of signification within every epigram, and among them all, affirm possibility—for art, for truth, for belief, for the intellect, for the self.

Mind in its purest play is like some bat
That beats about in caverns all alone,
Contriving by a kind of senseless wit
Not to conclude against a wall of stone.
—RICHARD WILBUR

It's the best possible time to be alive,
when almost everything you thought
you knew is wrong.
—TOM STOPPARD, ARCADIA

Witty Plays, Witty Poems

A recent course description by a colleague, good friend, and accomplished teacher lays out "coverage" for a fourteen-session graduate seminar in American poetry since 1920.

> Issues for discussion include: the development of personae and poetic impersonation; the connection between emerging psychological theories of personality and modernist doctrines of impersonality; occult techniques of voicing in the context of channeling, mesmerism, spiritualism, demonic possession, and multiple personality disorder; connections between poetic influence and hypnotic influence;

gender-switching and vocal transvestism; the disjunction between
voice and subjectivity; occultism, secrecy, privacy, and the closet;
modernist commitments to poetic "difficulty," problems of authorship and authority introduced by the impersonalist aesthetic, such
as collective authorship, appropriation, and the investing of absolute
authority in the state (as in fascism) . . .

How to unpack verse in a new millennium. Compared to this, exploring
Mark Twain's literary wit, or Oscar Wilde's, seems so simple: a matter of
looking with fresh eyes and a few modernized basic premises about premises. Since Twain and Wilde are certified comic geniuses, a better understanding of their literary wit only adds dignity and interest to their writings, and heightens appreciation of their sense of humor. There is no need
to push their literary works across epistemological borders, overhaul
meaning or canonical valuation, or disrupt conventional understanding
of those genres or modes in which they were written. Talking about literary wit as an important (and misunderstood) presence in contemporary
drama and verse is riskier, as certain prevalent tastes have to be ques-
tioned.

   According to one canon wrangler (summarizing American Poetry since
World War II in a top-selling anthology), literary wit is a discourse of comfortable detachment, fashionable in the 1950s when rising poets supposedly wanted to play it safe:

   Avoiding the first person, poets would find an object, a landscape, or
   an observed encounter that epitomized and clarified their feelings.
   A poem was the product of retrospection, a gesture of composure
   following the initial shock or stimulus that provided the occasion for
   writing. Often composed in intricate stanzas and skillfully rhymed,
   such a poem deployed its mastery of verse form as one sign of the
   civilized mind's power to explore, tame, and distill raw experience. . . . It was a time of renewed travel in Europe; there were Ful-
   bright fellowships for American students to study abroad, prizes for
   writers who wanted to travel and write in Europe. Wilbur and others
   wrote poems about European art and artifacts and landscapes. . . .
   Unlike the pessimistic Eliot of The Waste Land, such poets found the
   treasures of the past . . . nourishing in poems whose chief pleasure
   was that of evaluation and balancing, of weighing such alternatives
   as spirituality and worldliness.[1]

In a rival anthology the summarizing language is more loaded, but the assumption underneath seems the same. *Witty* means superficial; *clever* means low-risk mannered, light:

> The accepted poetry of the immediate post-war period was also distant from reality as students knew it. Carefully stylized and usually formal, 1950s poems were drawn from "meaningful" observation of life, their message crystallized in an image or symbol that the educated reader would find allusively succinct. The prevalent critical practices of close reading, of explication of a text, shaped the poems that were written at the start of this contemporary period. . . . Whatever was ironic, allusive, and concise—and remained distant from both the poet and the poet's world—was considered "good."[2]

With regard to contemporary drama, similar interpretive habits turn up. Among reviewers and anthologists, the quality and seriousness of a given drama often seem inversely proportional to the number of good laughs per act. More than two or three signify comedy; less than that, and there might be a *drama* here worth thinking about, when Tonys, Pulitzers, and Oliviers are decided and the year's important plays are winnowed from the rest. In a "good" drama the final act shouldn't rate a cracked smile.

If Shakespeare and Mozart and Beckett were rarely as serious as this, then perhaps the culture has grown wisely grimmer. In the 1999 New York theater season, a dedicated weekender could put together (with doubleheaders and a credit card) a relentless tour of prize-winning drama: revivals of Eugene O'Neill's bleak *The Iceman Cometh* and Arthur Miller's equally relentless *Death of a Salesman*, Conor McPherson's *The Weir* (Olivier Award for Best Play: guilt, grief, loneliness, alcoholism, and wasted lives in the Irish outback), David Hare's *Amy's View* (actress loses daughter, lover, money, youth, fame, everything); and Margaret Edson's *Wit* (the 1999 Pulitzer prize winner: lonely English professor with terminal cancer, a play that the final chapter of this book will discuss at length). Though a good Knicks game might be needed after such a tour, there are mother lodes here for academic discussion, with scarce literary wit to get in the way.

Interpretive mistakes that only dull readings of Twain or Wilde—distinctions ignored between wit in a modern literary context and wit as discourse in other interactions—can wreck an engagement with "witty" verse that is not light, or witty drama that is neither farce nor comedy. With regard to plays and poems, the needed discriminations are subtle and grounded in contingencies special to those varieties of discourse. If discussion of such values has been scarce, there are excuses available: interclass politics, conflicted arrays of cultural signifiers, tricks of marketing, contemporary academic tastes and interventions; and, perhaps above all, the sheer haste with which we must negotiate the gale of telling, saving only a few precious texts here and there from all the discourse we tack through every day.

As readers or watchers, paddling fast to make any headway, we respond intuitively to obscure, peculiar, and obvious cues from many directions. Much has been said about the impact of context and historical moment on interpretive process. In constructing better descriptions of literary wit in modern verse and drama, however, we should note resemblances between the mental agility associated with literary wit and the intellectual velocity with which as readers or audience we evaluate miscellaneous and incongruous signifiers of the sort mentioned above. With regard to whatever we might begin to read or witness, our calculations can be instantaneous, as we try to decide (fairly or otherwise) just how weighty an encounter with this new text ought to be and what kind of attention we should be paying. Are we browsing a well-reviewed "serious" tome from a distinguished publisher? Is there an ardent shirtless buccaneer on the front cover? Are we watching actors at the Royal National or the Guthrie? Or young unknowns in old plaid shirts, and possibly drunk, at a poetry slam in the Canadian Rockies? Subtle or not, the clues abound, and most of us can screen them in an intuitive flash. Some might be arguably within the fabric of the discourse; others lurk in hunches or prejudices brought along with us to the moment of engagement. Either way, however, this kind of mental agility, which figures so often in achieving first impressions of a literary text, arouses suspicion when overt in the text itself. For many learned and clever American readers, conspicuous wit in verse is a fault, because it signifies learning and cleverness. A long, crafted discourse that opens like Richard Wilbur's 1987 poem "Lying," with mention of a party in a sedate garden, and comfortable well-beveraged people making small talk about, oh, grackles, and with lots of word-play—

> To claim, at a dead party, to have spotted a grackle,
> When in fact you haven't of late, can do no harm.
> Your reputation for saying things of interest
> Will not be marred, if you hasten to other topics,
> Nor will the delicate web of human trust
> Be ruptured by that airy fabrication.
> Later, however, talking with toxic zest

Of golf, or taxes, or the rest of it
Where the beaked ladle plies the chuckling ice,
You may enjoy a chill of severance, hearing
Above your head the shrug of unreal wings.[3]

—should not presume, after this, to the intensity foreshadowed in a garden poem like Adrienne Rich's "The Middle-Aged," which signals depth and sobriety by opening this way:

Their faces, safe as an interior
Of Holland tiles and Oriental carpet,
Where the fruit-bowl, always filled, stood in a light
Of placid afternoon—their voices' measure,
Their figures moving in the Sunday garden
To lay the tea outdoors or trim the borders,
Afflicted, haunted us. For to be young
Was always to live in other people's houses
Whose peace, if we sought it, had been made by others,
Was ours at second-hand and not for long, . . . [4]

Likewise, a play that begins with gorgeous English aristocrats in a sunlit parlor of a "stately home" (this is from Tom's Stoppard's stage directions to *Arcadia*) on a country estate cannot hope to contend in the same thematic weight class as a play that opens with dejected drunks in a dead-end bar, with a defeated, deluded salesman coming home to his tiny hemmed-in house, or with a faithless woman, disillusioned with her own profession and career, dying alone in a hospital ward. From some perspectives, such hierarchies of literary seriousness might be valid. The point is that when they are assigned without scrutiny, they foster misvaluation of much that is interesting in contemporary theater and verse.

As with Twain's *Calendar* and Wilde's preface, a way to disturb the status quo is through attention to a few exceptional works and to the resonance of the literary wit that distinguishes them. At the outset of any intervention against contemporary prejudice, however, and as another step toward a better description of modern literary wit, something must be said about the "literary-ness" of these specific texts—Tom Stoppard's 1993 play *Arcadia* and a few poems of Richard Wilbur's—and how these contexts can inflect and transform the wit that transforms them. Although each text, each moment in the drama or the given poem, offers guidance as to where we are (as readers and witnesses) and what sort of cognitive and interpretative situation we might be in, the specialness of the experience is made clear in several ways even before the first poem is opened or the house lights dim. Seminar predicaments notwithstanding, we tend to sit up straighter, as it were, to attend plays and read poems. Though the poet or the dramatist may seem to have left ceremony and even civility behind, psychological civilities still need to be active for us to accept being packed in rows in a theater or placed in that unnatural state of readerly consciousness with which poems are often engaged. To the play we come cleanly if not tastefully attired; crowding, bad ventilation, and jostling are accepted with less protest than might be true on the underground or the bus or even at the movies; we will probably not vocalize unless others around us do so; we try not to rattle the playbill or make other noises; and polite playgoers will risk thoracic lesions rather than succumb to a cough when the lights are down and actors are busy.

Watching a play is still a ceremony; opening a book of poems begins a psychological and cognitive process more ceremonial than beginning, say, a mass-market paperback to kill time on an airliner. When we hit a poem while thumbing through prose in a literary magazine, many of us seem to shift gears, reading slower, "shields up," perhaps trying to recall what we think we know about the supposedly urgent aesthetic and moral practice of reading poems. This may be in part an aftereffect of tedious or mis-remembered class sessions, overbearing teachers, pompous intervening critics, the Poet's Corner basalt slabs of a solemn literary heritage, but regardless of cause, amid such settings and expectations outbreaks of literary wit cause trouble. In the poem or the serious play, wit threatens to disrupt or profane a text and undercut passionate attention to it. Or, as we have seen with Mark Twain and Oscar Wilde, literary wit can intensify and deepen certain possible significations and pleasures of a rich text. In modern or postmodern literary contexts, in fact, it must do either one or the other.

Like the little joke that opens the homily in liberal American churches, an outbreak of wit in a literary text can be respectable, at least among critics, only if it keeps its place and gives way to unamusing contemplations that come after. Richard Wilbur and Tom Stoppard violate this expectation all the time. Some of Wilbur's poems are notoriously witty—and defiantly facetious. Some of them are witty and intense, dangerous and profound. Over a span of three decades, Tom Stoppard has turned out breezy cerebral comedies for BBC Radio and exuberant screenplays; his literary wit can be, and has been, a sound-and-light show, which diverts like an evening of holiday fireworks. But Tom Stoppard's famous wit has also created some of the most thoughtful (as opposed to programmatically intellectual) and psychologically searching drama written in English since the Second World War.

The Literary Wit of Arcadia

In *Arcadia*, at least two narratives are braided together.[5] In 1809, a precocious thirteen-year-old girl named Thomasina Coverly and her handsome tutor, Septimus Hodge, fresh from his degree at Trinity College, Cambridge, are in residence at the expansive estate of Sidley Park in Derbyshire; also at the house is Lady Croom (mistress of the house and Thomasina's mother) who is having second thoughts about restyling her orderly neoclassical gardens into the wild gothic-Romantic mode. A Richard Noakes (a latter-day and second-rate Capability Brown) is masterminding this operation, complete with a noisy new steam engine, and taking abuse from his employer for literally muddying-up the beauty of the park. Thomasina has a fifteen-year-old brother named Augustus, who does not share his sister's intellectual curiosity. There are also several guests: a comically bad poet named Ezra Chater; his comically promiscuous wife, who never appears on stage; Lady Croom's brother, one Captain Brice of the Royal Navy, and Lord Byron, a college chum of Septimus's who also never appears on stage but who is alluded to frequently and becomes a focus of *Arcadia*'s other story. A guileless young genius who can make leaps in theoretical physics and mathematics, Thomasina has a crush on Septimus Hodge, and the witty, acerbic young tutor returns the affection—but all that sentiment is Platonic, at least at the outset. Hodge has remained cool and professional by expending his sexual vigor in various locales on the grounds with Mrs. Chater. As the play opens, one of these barnyard-style trysts has just been observed; gossip is flying about and a few minutes later a suitably outraged Chater blusters in to challenge Septimus to a duel. What follows is a deliciously Wildean and Congrevean exchange in which Septimus, with his young pupil out of the room, spins Chater like a top, knowing that Chater's vanity as an author outweighs his outrage as a cuckold. Flattered and baffled by a flurry of double entendres, then by hilarious misunderstandings when Lady Croom, Captain Brice, and Mr. Noakes enter (the aesthetic "rape" of the Sidley Park gardens tangles up verbally with the alleged copulations al fresco). Chater is thrown off his quest for the kind of satisfaction he had been demanding. By the end of scene 3, however, Septimus is no longer amused by the hypocrisy and banality of Chater and Captain Brice and by the easy sport of confounding them both. A duel is set for the following morning, with Lord Byron standing in as Septimus's second. At the close of act 1, Thomasina, on a whim, doodles a hermit onto Noakes's drawings for the transformed grounds, "for what is a hermitage without a hermit?" This small act of vandalism reverberates for a couple of centuries and sets up the detective story that is the other half of the plot of *Arcadia.*

Meanwhile . . . in the same room about two hundred years after (the scenes and stories are craftily interwoven) Hannah Jarvis, an amateur cultural historian, single, and (as the Characters list specifies) in her late thirties, is doing some landscape archaeology as a resident guest of the unseen modern mistress of Sidley Park. Also in residence now is Valentine, elder son in the family and a graduate student in biology at Oxford, who turns out to be infatuated with Hannah; his teenaged sister Chloë (breezy and no intellectual match for Thomasina); and a silent, possibly brilliant younger brother named Gus (played by the same actor who plays Thomasina's brother, Augustus). Having published a good-selling but nastily reviewed book about Shelley, Hannah is studying the transformation of Sidley Park back in the days of Septimus and Thomasina and working the place up as a metaphor for the ills of the Romantic sensibility. The transformed gardens (so she supposes, in part because of Thomasina's cartoon) had a hermit in residence—a false lead at first, which keeps the moderns guessing and which, with a classic Stoppard twist, turns out to be true—and Hannah wants to know who it was and whether she can draft him into her study as a "perfect symbol." "Of what?" asks a visiting academic—of whom more in a moment—and his question hits a trip wire:

> HANNAH: The whole Romantic sham, Bernard! It's what happened to the Enlightenment, isn't it? A century of intellectual rigour turned in on itself. A mind in chaos suspected of genius. In a setting of cheap thrills and false emotion. The history of the garden says it all, beautifully. There's an engraving of Sidley Park in 1730 that makes you want to weep. Paradise in the age of reason. By 1760 everything had gone—the topiary, pools and terraces, fountains, an avenue of limes—the whole sublime geometry was ploughed under by Capability Brown. . . . And then Richard Noakes came in to bring God up to date. By the time he'd finished it looked like this (*the sketch book*). The decline from thinking to feeling, you see. (27)

Here and shortly after, Hannah establishes herself as the intellectual and emotional center of *Arcadia*'s modern story. Her dislike of ritualized, bogus "feeling" and her nostalgia for order and reason and "intellectual rigor" begin to resonate. If *Arcadia* might turn out to be a play about gardens, it might also become a play about plays, about modern literary devaluations of science, about contrived wildness, faked spontaneity, and the loss of what previous Ages of Reason valued as wit—and the implications are dangerous. Hannah is talking here to an English literature professor named Bernard Nightingale, who does not listen to her. A self-important don from the University of Sussex who can resist no opportunity to one-up and condescend, Bernard is following false leads of his own, inklings (based on brief notes, which he has found in a copy of Chater's bad epic poem *The Couch of Eros*, that go back and forth among Chater, Mrs. Chater, and Septimus) that Byron himself actually fought the threatened duel here in 1809, killed Ezra Chater, and thereafter fled to the Continent. Hannah, catching on that Bernard has savaged her book in a review, nonetheless cautions him about jumping to such conclusions, but Bernard will not hear that either, and their squabbling detective work leads eventually to the Sidley Park game books, diaries, sheaves of letters, and wispy indications about what really happened. Meanwhile, the math student Valentine shows Hannah what he has found out about Thomasina from her own journals: that this young girl, who had died in a fire in this house on the eve of her seventeenth birthday (an event we are told of late in the play but do not see) had precocious and amazing insights into chaos theory, principles of entropy, and quantum physics, insights that put her a century ahead of her time.

So—two tales of suspense, thoroughly aerated with conversational wit, structural ingeniousness, and laughter—one narrative in the Romantic heyday, with Byron himself out in the bushes somewhere, and one at the millennium's end, with professional and amateur humanists and a young scientist (people perhaps like ourselves) trying to figure out what transpired, and why, and what it might signify. Did Byron step up for Septimus and shoot Ezra Chater? Did Septimus? Does one of the characters ultimately become the mad hermit of Sidley Park; can we learn or guess the reason? Will the obnoxious Bernard win the paltry and parasitic sort of fame that he wants from all this, or will he get instead his just deserts? Will Hannah arrive at a momentous truth and win a reputation for herself? Will she go to bed with Valentine? With Bernard? Will the aphasic Gus Coverly say something at last? Will Byron show up on stage at all? The solutions to some of these matinee-style mysteries turn out to be both clever and touching, and if you have not yet read or seen the play and want the suspense to be spoiled, you can consult the note appended to this sentence.[6] Beyond the plot beguilements of *Arcadia*, however, the play creates literary suspense, reaching further than the structural question of whether all this can weave together as an elegant contrivance in the tradition of those entertainments that came to be known in the middle of the nineteenth century as well-made plays. With all these plot threads in *Arcadia*, there is plenty to keep a modern audience awake and guessing; but the most compelling "plot" has been broached in the opening scene. Thomasina has stumbled on a mathematical strategy for modeling the natural world and also on several disconcerting principles having to do with time and the physical universe. What shall she do with these—and what might they in turn do to her? In our own time, Valentine picks up Thomasina's intellectual trail by finding her lesson book while searching through the old manuscripts at Sidley Park. Where did this girl's discovery and its implications lead her psychologically and spiritually, and where might they lead *him*? Is Thomasina's brief life a story of forbidden and fatal knowledge, of a new sort of Fall? And is this a dream that will open treacherously in a costumed Wildean drawing-room farce only to leave us "alone on an empty shore," as Septimus calls our ultimate condition in *Arcadia*'s closing scene? This latter sort of suspense draws attention because the stakes are so high: beyond, or rather before, the "existential crisis" material that the play opens up—quite surprisingly, after the caprice of the opening ten minutes—there are problems about drama, about literary modes and discourses and our own culturally conditioned expectations of them. Can a play like this, which flaunts contrivances and occasionally breaks into farce and which parades the kind of literary wit that is associated, in our time, with the lightest varieties of stage entertainment, negotiate matters of this scope and consequence? And with literary wit erupting nearly everywhere within the play—there are bon mots, great comebacks, epigrams, verbal clevernesses, neat plot twists and time shifts and other telltale signs of witty entertainment in almost every minute of *Arcadia*—could it imaginably achieve or sustain that kind of intense high-seriousness, even if an audience were to allow it to try?

Another paradox straightaway, then, with regard to Stoppard's play and its interpretation: because Tom Stoppard has been famous for thirty years as a playwright who goes his own peculiar way, and because the term *wit* (vague and loaded as ever) has been applied to his plays as regularly as it has to the poems of Richard Wilbur, an "unconditioned" audience for his work may be impossible. A veteran Stoppard audience will harbor suspicions that in each new play something of elaborate consequence might be going on, that clever comedy and outright farce will eventually mingle with something else, something bigger. It's well known that Stoppard's plays have often been about the foolishness of thinking by methods or outmoded algorithms, of allowing tradition and mindlessly followed procedures to organize experience. If a Stoppard play begins in nonsense, it will move onward from that, will try to make sense, and will try in surprising new ways. So—in the opening seconds of what looks to be a costume comedy, a bright, attractive upper-class girl asks a risky question; a handsome tutor, also upper class, answers with a witty evasion, which, as it turns out, evades not at all, since Thomasina sees through the response immediately; and a teasing game begins in which the pupil tries to corner her teacher into telling the truth:

THOMASINA: Septimus, what is carnal embrace?

SEPTIMUS: Carnal embrace is the practice of throwing one's arms around a side of beef.

THOMASINA: Is that all?

SEPTIMUS: No . . . a shoulder of mutton, a haunch of venison well hugged, an embrace of grouse . . . *caro, carnis*; feminine; flesh.

THOMASINA: Is it a sin?

SEPTIMUS: Not necessarily, my lady, but when carnal embrace is sinful it is a sin of the flesh, QED. We had *caro* in our Gallic Wars—'The Britons live on milk and meat'—'*lacte et carne vivunt*'. I am sorry that the seed fell on stony ground.

THOMASINA: That was the sin of Onan, wasn't it, Septimus?

SEPTIMUS: Yes. He was giving his brother's wife a Latin lesson and she was hardly the wiser after it than before. I thought you were finding a proof for Fermat's last theorem. (1–2)

The Platonic relationship between pupil and teacher, freewheeling and full of good-natured play and mutual respect, remains for the moment undisrupted, yet also uneasy. The exchange complicates a tutor-pupil relationship in the instant of introducing it. As an audience we are still decoding the conventions of the setting, the apparently conventional relationship within it—and something important is already jeopardized. The play is off with a comic rush—but in what imaginable direction? Sex is evidently in this Romantic pastoral air—but Septimus is twenty-seven and Thomasina is thirteen, and we cannot know where her lively curiosity and his apparently vigorous manhood will take them. In the world of drama and the world beyond the theater, sex is chaos; if this play is going to open with talk like this between a grown man and a young girl, where can it go from here? It is something of a relief to see that Thomasina does know more about "carnal embrace" than she lets on at first. Teasing and interrogating Septimus and relaying gossip about trysts, which later turn out to be his own with Mrs. Chater, she takes the play in the safer direction of bedroom farce, or at least sex-in-the-gazebo farce. For the next minute or so Septimus and Thomasina go back and forth with conventional (or cliché) confusion as to who in the household saw whom do what and with whom and where and when. Septimus has dodged the dangerous question with a reply of conspicuously literary wit, an answer with uncommon rhetorical elegance and even a Latin gloss: his lines are extravagantly writerly, not oral or offhand, drawing attention to this scene as a *scene*, a perfect opening moment in a play, if that play (or at least this half of this double-plotted play) is an excursion into reflexivity, a meditation, flippant or otherwise, not on English social history but rather on an English literary dream. And in that dreamworld, the most dangerous question, for a proper young lady, for a tutor of that young lady, and for the idyllic gentility of this setting, has been parried with wordplay. Bravura mental agility and a good English university schooling in the antique arts of wit have kept the devil at bay, and Arcadia is preserved—in this room, if not outside on the Romantically ravaged grounds of Sidley Park. Thomasina, responding with wit of her own (once again, wit with a literary grounding) steers the conversation back to sex, which is what she already knows "carnal embrace" refers to. In the midst of all that, Fermat's last theorem pops up, as one of the standing enigmas of modern mathematics, and shortly after, the two lines of patter, about sex and about mathematics, interbraid like converging dimensions in some clash of realities:

THOMASINA: Is carnal embrace kissing?

SEPTIMUS: Yes

THOMASINA: And throwing one's arms around Mrs. Chater?

SEPTIMUS: Yes. Now, Fermat's last theorem—

THOMASINA: I thought as much. I hope you are ashamed.

SEPTIMUS: I, my lady?

THOMASINA: If *you* do not teach me the true meaning of things, who will?

SEPTIMUS: Ah. Yes, I am ashamed. Carnal embrace is sexual congress, which is the insertion of the male genital organ into the female genital organ for purposes of procreation and pleasure. Fermat's last theorem, by contrast, asserts that when x, y and z are whole numbers each raised to the power of n, the sum of the first two can never equal the third when n is greater than 2.

(*Pause*)

THOMASINA: Eurghhh!

SEPTIMUS: Nevertheless, that is the theorem.

THOMASINA: It is disgusting and incomprehensible. Now when I am grown to practise it myself I shall never do so without thinking of you. (3)

If this is spontaneous conversation overheard, then this is delightful and risky play of two young free minds. But of course this is also *not* an overheard moment of conversation; there are cues throughout that this too is an ostentatiously literary moment, a crafted exposition (of some sort) in a brazenly play-ish play.

From that perspective, what have these exchanges been about? First, the inadequacy of language, even of precise and scholarly definitions (*caro, carnis*), to explain anything worth knowing. Septimus's definition of *carnal embrace* is perfectly accurate and hilariously incomplete; Ezra Chater's dreadful love epic, *The Couch of Eros*, has, in Septimus's view, less carnality in it than does Thomasina's algebra. Second, they have been about the absurdity of trying to keep the subject of sex out of the schoolroom or off the estate when young women and young men are involved; third (but by no means finally), they have raised the "disgusting and incomprehensible" truth lurking out there, waiting for the young—not just the truth of sexuality but also the truth of mathematics, of physics, of all real or illusory models of where and what we are. In the latter exchange, Thomasina isn't talking about sexual intercourse; like a true wit, she is talking about several things at once, crafting a remark that encompasses everything that has been touched on by the two of them since the opening second of the play. Sex she finds disgusting and incomprehensible; so too, in her view, is the kind of math-logical universe that Fermat opened or constructed; and when she has grown to "practice it" herself (practice what? sex? mathematics? both?) she will always think of Septimus, which means precisely what? That Septimus has divulged to her, at a tender age, the forbidden, unappetizing, un-Romantic truth about sex? About mathematics? Does she mean that she loves him and cannot imagine "carnal embrace" without him? Ultimately the answer to all these possibilities turns out to be "yes"—and we find that out soon enough because in one sense we do know where we are and where we are going. We are in the text of a play, in a literary work where hidden dimensions of witty utterance are customarily revealed in the course of one evening in the theater or in a few dozen pages of a published script.

I have said that *Arcadia* is flamboyantly literary, and that this literary-ness is everywhere, not just in the allusions to Byron and Peacock and Thackeray and in the familiar Stoppard gambit of having a detestable English professor or foolish critic wandering through, getting everything wrong. This opening scene has conspicuous ancestry; part of the pleasure and suspense of watching Arcadia begin lies in sensing that kinship and wondering how this drama might develop and escape that legacy. A modern literary audience has happily visited here before: a spirited and apparently innocent young woman, in a parklike English country setting, doing her lessons with fierce and charming reluctance; a tutor trying to edit the truth and evade the consequences of telling it. Sound familiar? So too does the repartee, drawing attention to the absurdities of language, of writing, of learning from books:

> CECILY: I keep a diary in order to enter the wonderful secrets of my life. If I didn't write them down, I should probably forget all about them.
>
> MISS PRISM: Memory, my dear Cecily, is the diary that we all carry about with us.
>
> CECILY: Yes, but it usually chronicles the things that have never happened, and couldn't possibly have happened. I believe that Memory is responsible for nearly all the three-volume novels that Mudie sends us.
>
> MISS PRISM: Do not speak slightingly of the three-volume novel, Cecily. I wrote one myself in earlier days.
>
> CECILY: Did you really, Miss Prism? How wonderfully clever you are! I hope it did not end happily? I don't like novels that end happily. They depress me so much.
>
> MISS PRISM: The good ended happily, and the bad unhappily. That is what Fiction means.
>
> [a moment later]
>
> MISS PRISM: Cecily, you will read your political economy in my absence. The chapter on the Fall of the Rupee you may omit. It is somewhat too sensational. Even these metallic problems have their melodramatic side.
>
> CECILY: (picks up books and throws them back on the table) Horrid political economy! Horrid geography! Horrid, horrid German! (443, 494)[7]

The Importance of Being Earnest reverberates in act 1 of Arcadia not simply because Wilde's play is the archetypal modern comedy about young aristocrats and romantic mix-ups in a manicured countryside. The echoes are more interesting than that, for Earnest is also distinguished for its blithe but mordant skepticism about knowing, discovering, and saying. Throughout Wilde's play there are pronouncements on these subjects, by Lady Bracknell (Lady Croom's ancestor; or perhaps her grandchild, depending on which chronology is favored—the historical setting of each play or the date of its publication), by Miss Prism, and sometimes by Algy and Cecily and Gwendolyn. There are constant wisecracks and epigrams and paradoxes about the distinctions (or lack of them) between saying and being understood, between innocence and ignorance, between an "educated" mind and the kind of happy barbarism that can sail without a shiver straight into absurdity, or profundity, or both at the same instant, obliterating the borders between the one and the other.

Even so, Arcadia isn't The Importance of Being Earnest updated or warmed over. Cecily never moves from girlish crush to womanly love, and she never breaks into genius; Thomasina does both—to genius right away, to womanly love at the end of Arcadia on the night of her death. In the never-land of Earnest nobody dies, except offstage to make room for the blissful young. Loneliness and the empty shore are never glimpsed, not even by earnest Ernest. Nonetheless, the echoes of the classic play ring within the first act of the new one:

> LADY CROOM: Something has occurred with the girl since I saw her last, and surely that was yesterday. How old are you this morning?
>
> THOMASINA: Thirteen years and ten months, mama.
>
> LADY CROOM: Thirteen years and ten months. She is not due to be pert for six months at the earliest, or to have notions of taste for much longer. Mr. Hodge, I hold you accountable. (12)

Late in Arcadia, a reprise of the scene above:

> LADY CROOM: How old are you today?
>
> THOMASINA: Sixteen years and eleven months, mama, and three weeks.
>
> LADY CROOM: Sixteen years and eleven months. We must have you married before you are educated beyond eligibility. (84)

From act 1 of Earnest:

> LADY BRACKNELL: How old are you?
>
> JACK: Twenty-nine
>
> LADY BRACKNELL: A very good age to be married at. I have always been of the opinion that a man who desires to get married should know either everything or nothing. Which do you know?
>
> JACK: (after some hesitation) I know nothing, Lady Bracknell.
>
> LADY BRACKNELL: I am pleased to hear it. I do not approve of anything that tampers with natural ignorance. Ignorance is like a delicate exotic fruit; touch it and the bloom is gone. The whole theory of modern education is radically unsound. Fortunately in England, at any rate, education produces no effect whatsoever. (434)

Also from act 1:

JACK: That, my dear Algy, is the whole truth pure and simple.

ALGERNON: The truth is rarely pure and never simple. Modern life would be very tedious if it were either, and modern literature a complete impossibility!

JACK: That wouldn't be at all a bad thing.

ALGERNON: Literary criticism is not your forte, my dear fellow. Don't try it. You should leave that to people who haven't been at a University. They do it so well in the daily papers. (427)

From scene 1 of *Arcadia*:

THOMASINA: (*To* SEPTIMUS) How is a ruined child different from a ruined castle?

SEPTIMUS: On such questions I defer to Mr. Noakes.

NOAKES: (*Out of his depth*) A ruined castle is picturesque, certainly.

SEPTIMUS: That is the main difference. (*To Brice*) I teach the classical authors. If I do not elucidate their meaning, who will?

BRICE: As her tutor you have a duty to keep her in ignorance.

LADY CROOM: Do not dabble in paradox, Edward, it puts you in danger of fortuitous wit. Thomasina, wait in your bedroom.

THOMASINA: (*Retiring*) Yes, mama, I did not intend to get you into trouble, Septimus. I am very sorry for it. It is plain that there are some things a girl is allowed to understand, and these include the whole of algebra, but there are others, such as embracing a side of beef, that must be kept from her until she is old enough to have a carcass of her own. (11)

Earnest is also present as the archetype of form—or rather of one of the forms that *Arcadia* emulates and transfigures. As literary wit in excelsis, *Earnest* is a sequence of brilliant ripostes; which delight the ear and the mind of the audience but which tell us next to nothing about the character of the characters who speak them. Is Algy imaginably capable of loving Cecily Cardew? Could a marriage between Gwendolyn and Jack-Earnest Worthing last fifteen minutes beyond the ceremony? Could a plausible human being speak and think like any of these characters without being in some strict sense an idiot? Such questions are as absurd as the characters we might ask them about, for *Earnest* is not a comedy or a farce but inherently an antiplay, resisting at nearly every turn the conditioned suspension of disbelief, the educated will to see figures on a stage as representations of complete human beings. Also about stagecraft and disbelief of many sorts, *Arcadia* looks into the dark behind the bright footlights of

Earnest. The ignorance that all the major characters of *Earnest* embody and profess, the delicate fruit, as Lady Bracknell calls it, of knowing nothing (thanks to the failures of British education), becomes the human condition: education of the late-twentieth-century sort, if it has any effect whatsoever, leads to recognition of our immense unknowing. Hannah Jarvis sums up the predicament in a duet with Valentine—the resolution of the love exchange that he has begun two scenes previous. She warns her young admirer not to despair of not knowing and not to hope that answers will ever be forthcoming:

> HANNAH: Oh, that. It's *all* trivial—your grouse, my hermit, Bernard's Byron. Comparing what we're looking for misses the point. It's wanting to know that makes us matter. Otherwise we're going out the way we came in. That's why you can't believe in the afterlife, Valentine. Believe in the after, by all means, but not the life. Believe in God, the soul, the spirit, the infinite, believe in angels if you like, but not in the great celestial get-together for an exchange of views. If the answers are in the back of the book I can wait, but what a drag. Better to struggle on knowing that failure is final. *(She looks over* Valentine's *shoulder at the computer screen. Reacting)* Oh!, but . . . how beautiful! (75–76)

Septimus's declamation on disorder into disorder and the absurdity of the idea of free will stops with a joke-instruction to a tortoise, a joke about the tortoise's "free fill" and the delusion that human beings actually instruct and control anything. Hannah's stoic declamation on the finality of failure ends with her marveling at the lovely pattern that Valentine's chaos-numbers make on the screen. The pattern of the two speeches is the same, and beautiful, and in a sense true: to honest explorers of the cosmos and the human condition, no QED is final; no theory is ever more than a step in an endless process. When Stoppard is at his best, his plays explore these saving graces of indeterminacy; of being psychologically out beyond the shadow of both belief and unbelief; of countenancing the possibility of consolations and perceptions beyond anything that we can acquire from human culture and its various faiths—intellectual, aesthetic, political, spiritual—or from reason as reason is culturally inflected, reason of the if-then, true-false, subject-verb-object configuration; of the dancer always solid and still and distinct from the dance. Literary wit in a Stoppard play draws attention to the artificiality and contingency of theater, the delightful strangeness of seeing people we don't know play people we don't know, actors speaking lines of characters that are not lines of characters but lines written by this Tom Stoppard and not assigned to a character but presented *as* the character.

All of which is to say that the literary wit observed thus far in *Arcadia* draws attention to its artificiality—which means that suspense is real and rising with regard to the structure and the prospects of this "drama." Flashy comedy of manners and conversational wit; Wildean conspicuous artifice; cadenza speeches (also conspicuously eloquent and artificial) here and there like this one by Hannah, addressing a weighty problem—really *the* problem—of the human condition: Is *Arcadia* then a play that transcends modes, or is it a comedy with occasional dissonant moments of overweening pretentiousness? If the literary wit here is not decorative, not sugarcoating on a pill of serious or presumptuous philosophizing, then there must be moments in this play in which wit and insight become one, in which bon mot and imaginative breakthrough are perceived as having something important in common. In other words, if *Arcadia* is going to be a work of flamboyant artifice and a play about wit, about intelligence, about the psychological and moral consequences of adventurous thinking, then an old and broken connection has to be reestablished, an understanding that thought and "feeling," cleverness and genius, wit and penetrating intelligence are connected—connected more deeply than holdover assumptions about the mind allow them to be. That moment of connection in *Arcadia* comes early and suddenly, in the middle of the parlor repartee that has set the play spinning in the direction of light entertainment:

SEPTIMUS: Well, so much for Mr. Noakes. He puts himself forward as a gentleman, a philosopher of the picturesque, a visionary who can move mountains and cause lakes, but in the scheme of the garden he is as the serpent.

THOMASINA: When you stir your rice pudding, Septimus, the spoonful of jam spreads itself round making red trails like the picture of a meteor in my astronomical atlas. But if you stir backward, the jam will not come together again. Indeed, the pudding does not notice and continues to turn pink just as before. Do you think this is odd?

SEPTIMUS: No.

THOMASINA: Well, I do. You cannot stir things apart.

SEPTIMUS: No more you can, time must needs run backward, and since it will not, we must stir our way onward mixing as we go, disorder out of disorder into disorder until pink is complete, unchanging and unchangeable, and we are done with it forever. This is known as free will or self-determination.

(He picks up the tortoise and moves it a few inches as though it had strayed, on top of some loose papers, and admonishes it.) Sit! (4–5)

As the first of Thomasina's breezy breakthroughs, this slips away from the comforting stage world of Wilde, and also from the familiar (if not so inherently comforting) setting and cast of a Jane Austen novel. *Arcadia's* Romantic-era Derbyshire seems to be morphing into Cal Tech and opening contemplations beyond the education and experience of typical Anglo-American theatergoers—beyond the species of "reality" (Newtonian, naturalistic, Marxian, Romantic, etc.), which contemporary plays by Harold Pinter or David Mamet or Wendy Wasserstein or David Hare or most other authors normally presume. But before getting lost in theories of entropy or iterated algorithms or Thomasina's quantum universe *avant la lettre*, it is crucial to observe that *Arcadia* still, and to the end, remains a play about characters, and that the human interest of this dialogue is not that world-shaking ideas are being woven into it but that it remains throughout a dialogue that is very much Thomasina and Septimus—in cadence, in intimacy, and in kind and quality of intelligence. The wit (literary or otherwise) that student and tutor share at the outset is quite the same as the wit (in the classic sense of the word) that takes Thomasina on this profound intellectual caprice and that also allows Septimus to follow her, with understanding, playfulness, and intellectual and emotional support. His closing comment about "free will" is a handful of word-dust tossed playfully and ruefully into the air of that Sidley Park room and into the air of the theater-space that contains it. Septimus's words catch neatly the untidy, entropic universe that the Romantic world was only beginning to negotiate, a universe that a modern audience might believe it understands, though the great problem remains as unresolved now as it was then: what all that has to do with the human condition. If we laugh at his evasive closing, we laugh at his evasion and at our own as well—the ongoing evasion and collective, unsteady, life-conserving delusion that brings us to this text or to this theater in the first place.

The Thomasina-Septimus story in *Arcadia* is set in April 1809 in Derbyshire; in that year, about two hundred miles due south, another young woman decades ahead of her time was at work on *Sense and Sensibility*, and somewhere in that house were the rejected drafts of *First Impressions*, the story that eventually became *Pride and Prejudice*. Because these two novels would create the mythology of Thomasina Coverly's decade, as an Arcadia of country houses, of spirited, accomplished young women, and of handsome English gentlemen struggling to understand them, our own first impressions of *Arcadia* have solid English literary credentials. The 1809 date allows Stoppard to half-adapt and half-contrive the Byron mystery, the literary-celebrity murder case that puts Hannah and Valentine and Bernard and, ultimately, the speechless boy Gus all on Thomasina's trail. But this Jane Austen setting, though shivered in an early moment by Thomasina's quantum leap into a quantum-physics universe, provides nonetheless an imaginative familiarity. In this vigorously literary narrative, an audience observing the dress and bric-a-brac of Napoleon's world, and hearing and seeing a social discourse from Austen's, can know in a sense where it is and understand this setting and these characters better and faster, paradoxically enough, than it could quickly know two characters in a late-twentieth-century context—for example, Hannah or Bernard or Valentine. Happily or otherwise, Anglo-American imaginative literature has stylized the world and the values of the Romantic English gentry. And Septimus and Thomasina provide Stoppard's postmodern audience—which is to say an audience wandering in the wilderness of postmodern science and human behavior—a cultural and psychological refuge from which to explore the less-familiar world that we actually live in. As imaginative constructs in a text, all these people at the old Sidley Park are, to a modern audience, old friends: a brilliant young woman who must work to win respect, and ultimately love, from a handsome, witty, and free-thinking aristocrat; a comically overbearing but good-hearted upper-class mother; a pretentious but innocuous bad poet and his lascivious country-bourgeois wife; and some humorous types from the period (an all-knowing butler, a stiff RN captain, an incompetent hired artiste) bustling through the scenes now and then. Trysts and abscondings; Love, Honor, and Duty; comic dames and ladies: thanks to Jane Austen, *this is home*. She is our Blue Guide to this historical-imaginary world, and when Stoppard takes us playfully and nostalgically back to it from time to time, the paradoxical, inside-out, and witty (again in the classic sense) arrangement of *Arcadia* grows clearer. Our own world, the postmodern world, is the uncharted territory. In the contemporary Sidley Park, the young unkempt mathematician, who doesn't read Byron or care at all for the Romantics, is the true Romantic poet; the certified Romantic (or rather the professional and salaried Romanticist) is a charlatan and a bigger vulgarian than the scientists whom he hates for their vulgarity. The amateur historian is a better explorer of the past because she brings to that contemplation the fresh (and even scientific) wisdom of the present and the comforted uncertainty that puts her sublimely in tune with the ghosts of Septimus Hodge and Thomasina.

But Valentine first, as a poet of chaos theory and mathematics. Hardly a blue-jeaned update of either Algy or Jack, he is a seer, like Byron before him, of great, dark, compelling patterns in the world he studies. His opening line is an inarticulate "Sod, sod, sod, sod, sod . . ." as many as it takes (according to the stage directions) to cross the scene and ignore Bernard; but by the end of the first act he has emerged as a poet of the contemporary story, speaking of love and worldly wonder and offering the exhilaration of imaginative life made new by the countenancing of new possibilities. He is talking to Hannah Jarvis here, making love to her after a fashion, though Hannah is much older than he. But at this point in the drama he is also responding to the words of Septimus, which still hang in the room from two centuries before, the words of romantic *tristesse* closing with the "free-will" joke, as Septimus gazed over the implications of what Thomasina had cheerfully thought up. To Hannah now and to Septimus then, Valentine's longest and best speech is full of an enthusiasm that Thomasina would have understood:

It makes me so happy. To be at the beginning again, knowing almost nothing. People were talking about the end of physics. Relativity and quantum looked as if they were going to clean out the whole problem between them. A theory of everything. But they only explained the very big and the very small. The universe, the elementary particles. The ordinary-sized stuff which is our lives, the things people write poetry about—clouds—daffodils—waterfalls—and what happens in a cup of coffee when the cream goes in—these things are full of mystery, as mysterious to us as the heavens were to the Greeks. We're better at predicting events at the edge of the galaxy or inside the nucleus of an atom than whether it will rain on auntie's garden party three Sundays from now. Because the problem turns out to be different. We can't even predict the next drip from a dripping tap when it gets irregular. Each drip sets up the conditions for the next, the smallest variation blows prediction apart, and the weather is unpredictable the same way, will always be unpredictable. When you push the numbers through the computer you can see it on the screen. The future is disorder. A door like this has cracked open five or six times since we got up on our hind legs. It's the best possible time to be alive, when almost everything you thought you knew is wrong. (48)

Wittingly or not, Valentine in this outburst invokes Wordsworth in several ways at the outset and closes with a surprising backward sort of affirmation that, with perhaps a little less gusto in its phrasing, could fit nicely into Wilde's preface.

Science for Valentine is the new Romantic poetry, celebrating life because it celebrates unsounded wonders all around and the excitement of not knowing—and the play celebrates him by pitting him against Bernard Nightingale, a don who knows (or thinks he knows) all the answers, about Byron, culture, women, fame, professional and personal ethics, everything. Thinking of himself as the modern literary mind, Bernard actually represents a variety of the entropy that Thomasina predicted—with his arrival this very room loses heat, and as he gets busy, the ghost of Byron gives way to "Bonking Byron Shot Poet" (the London tabloid report of Bernard's "discovery," which eventually turns out to be hilariously dead wrong). As the sort of academic parasite who also turns up in Stoppard's *Indian Ink*, Bernard has his professional and personal interests tidily united: "Sex and literature. Literature and sex," as Hannah describes them. But he also seeks a tawdry and transient sort of fame that pokes the contemporary world along from one day to the next. Bernard is a "wit" in the modern (or rather post-Romantic) and degraded sense of the word: mechanical and malicious, his little puns and jokes reveal only his arrogance. Opening and countenancing no mysteries, no refreshment of thought or of ordinary experience, they keep his world bordered and tractable. When Hannah returns fire early in scene 2, her own wit, in contrast, doesn't just derail his condescension; it also opens possibilities—about relationships past and present at Sidley Park and about where, playfully or otherwise, they might eventually lead:

HANNAH: How did you know I was here?

BERNARD: Oh, I didn't. I spoke to the son on the phone but he didn't mention you by name . . . and then he forgot to mention me.

HANNAH: Valentine: He's at Oxford, technically.

BERNARD: Yes, I met him. Brideshead Regurgitated.

HANNAH: My fiancé.

(She holds his look.)

BERNARD: *(Pause)* I'll take a chance. You're lying.

HANNAH: *(Pause)* Well done, Bernard.

BERNARD: Christ.

HANNAH: He calls me his fiancée.

BERNARD: Why?

HANNAH: It's a joke.

BERNARD: You turned him down?

HANNAH: Don't be silly, do I look like the next Countess of—

BERNARD: No, no—a freebie. The joke that consoles. My tortoise Lightning, my fiancée Hannah.

HANNAH: Oh. Yes. You have a way with you, Bernard. I'm not sure I like it. (23)

As an heir to Sidley Park and as a young man who values Hannah's "wanting to know" over self-serving one-upmanship, Valentine for the most part plays patient host to the obnoxious Bernard, who in the heat of one tirade to Hannah even addresses Valentine as a "fucking idiot." Replying occasionally with an elegant wit that Bernard never matches, Valentine embodies what his name suggests: selfless love—of his work, of great mysteries, of biology and mathematics and Hannah and his family and a world where everything is "back to the beginning again" and full of dark possibility. Bernard Nightingale's name is suggestive too—not his real one, but the name he chooses to operate under for a while when he arrives at Sidley Park—Mr. Peacock. It suits him admirably, for the Valentine-Peacock opposition is one of the perilously suggestive symmetries of *Arcadia*, a dangerous swing back to neat and amusing arrangements from Restoration comedies of wit, from lighter chapters in Jane Austen, from nostalgic golden moments in the stage comedies of Oscar Wilde. Nonetheless, parse the Bernard-Valentine rivalry for significations and a paradox will loom large. Glibness versus curiosity; smug ignorance versus genuine open-minded scholarship; claustrophobic self-love versus humility; complaisant latter-day "humanism" versus possibilities for real and fresh *humanitas*, and so on—this play, which seems at times defiantly antique in its tropes, its cleverness, its homage to old-style witty theater, seems to be satirizing a datedness in the postmodern, an obsolescence in what passes for au courant intellectual life. The flamboyant artifice of *Arcadia* seems to whiz blithely past nearly every established "ism" of modern serious theater, and the loving allusions to Wilde and Austen and a literature of wit continue right to the end. When she last appears, Chloë comes into the room dressed for a costume party—dressed up, she says, as Jane Austen, and in the final scene nobody is wearing twentieth-century clothing and every hint of the modern is gone from the room. Septimus has said to Thomasina that "time must needs run backward," to restore what we think we have lost, and that is a culminating theme of *Arcadia*: that literary time "must needs run backward," back to an idea of imagination and intellect that has been lost for too long, if theater and culture and literary thinking shall negotiate a future in which we are "back at the beginning," knowing less than we thought we knew when the all-covering, all-categorizing formulations closed in.

But *Arcadia* is about much more than Bernard and the kind of closed-mindedness and "modern" intellectual obsolescence that he represents. The child-woman Thomasina becomes the center of the play in its final, moving, and yet supremely artificial scene, in which the living and the dead of Sidley Park gather in that one room for a contemplation of the universe as Thomasina has blithely imagined it, as Bernard has dismissed it, and as Septimus, Hannah, and Valentine in their various and personal ways have taken it to heart. Ultimately, after the play's end, Septimus is destroyed by what he apprehends, looking at Thomasina's lesson books and seeing the world over her shoulder. We see an inkling of his own personal doom in his last meditation on the meaning of the girl's discovery, as Lady Crumb's new pianoforte is heard from elsewhere in the house. In that room two centuries later, yet nonetheless in the same instant, Valentine harmonizes for a moment with Septimus's brief ode in a minor key. But the discoverer herself, who will be seventeen tomorrow and wants to learn to waltz, will have none of their shared mood:

SEPTIMUS: So the Improved Newtonian Universe must cease and grow cold. Dear me.

VALENTINE: The heat goes into the mix.

(He gestures to indicate the air in the room, in the universe.)

THOMASINA: Yes, we must hurry if we are going to dance.

VALENTINE: And everything is mixing the same way, all the time, irreversibly . . .

SEPTIMUS: Oh, we have time, I think.

VALENTINE: . . . till there's no time left. That's what time means.

SEPTIMUS: When we have found all the mysteries and lost all the meaning, we will be alone, on an empty shore.

THOMASINA: Then we will dance. Is this a waltz?

SEPTIMUS: It will serve.

(He stands up.)

THOMASINA: *(Jumping up)* Goody! (93–94)

For art is only art, and even in a play about the human condition—or especially in such a play—something as far-off and abstract as the fate of the universe does not deny a brilliant, cheerful young woman the delights of her own seventeenth birthday. We are, as Arthur Symons lamented in the days of Wilde, "so admirably finite"—or perhaps it is wit (in the classic sense) that allows human beings to be wiser than their own reasoning, free of the confines and conclusions of their own relentless logic. One way or another, there will still be cakes and ale; Thomasina's joy can be ended by her death, even within the hour; but not by the end of the cosmos, not by anything so black and distant and therefore (to her own right reckoning) so absurd.

Dancing at the end of *Arcadia*, Thomasina is not a capricious child or an idiot-savant, refusing to look into a crystal ball that she herself has created; nor does she become a granddam of the little monsters in our postmodern mythology, the happy shallow nerds who clone the killer viruses and perfect the Bomb. In her wit and her insight, Thomasina has been a step ahead of her morose Byronic Septimus from the first lines of this play, and even after her death on this night she will stay ahead of him until the last day of his own dejected life. For Thomasina understands how Septimus's "empty shore" can and must be a place to dance—for the mind must keep free, unbounded by its own constructs and formulations or by anyone else's from the present or the past. She also understands, as Septimus apparently never does, that her own discoveries and models are liberating, even if they spell out portents of doom. "Till there's no time left. That's what time means," says Valentine to Hannah from within their quantum world, a world that is just now coming to understand what Thomasina intuited all by herself in a Byron-Austen golden age, that concepts like *time* and *place* and *being* are more mysterious than any Western culture has recognized before. The final scene of *Arcadia*, in which the pairs of Hannah and the never-speaking, possibly crazy, possibly brilliant Gus Coverly (twenty years her junior) and Septimus Hodge and Lady Thomasina waltz in the same room, in the same period-clothing, and two centuries apart, is exquisitely "clever," "neat," "well-made," and worthy of every other condescending compliment that critics toss out when they are suspicious of literary wit in a postmodern drama or a postmodern anything-else. A key premise of the scene, however, is that all of them are dancing now to Thomasina's waltz, caught up yet also liberated in the whirl of a universe that she has both dreamed up and rejoiced in. And this brilliantly and defiantly witty play, a play that opened as a celebration of language and talk, closes with music and movement—and no words at all.

The effect and the signification are not at all like the silence at the end of *Endgame* or *The Birthday Party* or *Krapp's Last Tape*. *Arcadia*'s closing waltz is in a sense about literary wit itself, the intellectual and psychological freedom to make or see and name the abyss and not fall into it, the freedom that Thomasina's kind of wit, and Valentine's, and Hannah's can make possible—the freedom to say, understand, affirm, and deny all in the same utterance, the same instant of complete and paradoxical apprehension. Thomasina's "Then we will dance," seems to say and do all these things at once; like the famous photon in the quantum-physics lesson books a century after her death, she can happily reside, psychologically and intellectually at least, in more than one place and condition at the same time. She dances too because human beings, banal or wise or whatever, always will dance, sooner or later—affirming their fate and ignoring, doubting, misprizing, or forgetting—all at once. As a postmodern culture we have become good at charting out inexorable pathways toward destruction while getting on with life, as if in a parallel world, an Arcadia of our own where varieties of death and doom do not figure at all. The waltz with Septimus is Thomasina Coverly's last consequential act on the last night of her life; yet if time itself is somehow a thing contingent, a thing that can end, or shift, or run backward, or behave in other unsettling ways suggested by Valentine and Septimus and the ingeniously woven fabric of this play, then Arcadia can express at the end both tragedy and joy. Thomasina Coverly is dead and she is here; she dances on the empty shore and does not know it, and yet she knows. In his own tragedy, Septimus will become almost Sophoclean; and on this night beyond time he is a handsome and contented young Darcy, dancing in the last scene of a costume comedy with his own Elizabeth Bennett.

This final scene, in other words, becomes an elegant, deeply moving cadenza on Erwin Schrödinger's signature story of multiplicity and uncertainty in a quantum universe. To complicate our thinking about matter and being and time, we can leave behind, at least for the moment, Schrödinger's generic cat and the fatal photon and the tedious box. Instead, imagine two pairs of dancers, fated pairs, in the same place, the same clothing, and moving to the same music. They are ages apart, yet together in temperament and intellect. Each pair is alone and yet joined with the other, across an ominous yet trivial expanse of centuries. As a possibility to imagine or even believe in, none of that would be a problem for Thomasina herself, for she can whirl psychologically and spiritually as well as physically and intellectually. Septimus's tragedy, or rather his impending tragedy, is that he cannot move like that. Though he can teach Thomasina to waltz, he cannot learn from her to dance through Romantic or modern darkness and whirl back into light again or to dwell in more than one imaginative and epistemological dimension at once.[8] Arcadia dances as well, ending wordlessly in a waltz of time and characters and emotions and literary modes, perhaps because the modes into which drama is parsed are insufficient to model or express our situation as we now apprehend it. Experience is hilarious and sad, ruled by fates and beyond their grasp; everything that happens or has happened or never happened is and isn't of the greatest consequence; literary texts and love and living are and are not a waste of everyone's time; and time itself, as an essence of tragedy and comedy and this whirling witty mixture of both, is a concept that means everything and nothing. A clever, witty play—a play, in other words, that takes amazing chances, achieving intellectual and emotional intensity that put it in a class by itself.

In life out beyond literary texts and their criticism, we seek a capacity for wit in one another because we value, from those we interact with every day, all signs of an ability to escape from psychological confinements, from dogma, from oppressive idea systems, which can hem in thinking and life. As *Arcadia* shows brilliantly, the notion that wit is coldly and inhumanely intellectual, that witty people and witty literary texts take no genuine or significant risks, is nonsense. Literary wit can affirm intensity; it can refuse, dangerously, to succumb even to rituals of desire, or grief, or any other emotion. In the time since wit was relegated to its current debased position in our critical discourse, strong suggestions have been made that the heart, like the intellect, takes cues and patterns from culture, that desire and even cosmic terror can be cultural constructs that are learned, at least to some extent, from living with others. In other words, as a Romantic, Septimus Hodge may be a Sidley Park hermit waiting to hatch, and Thomasina, not quite seventeen and raised literally in the Garden, can look placidly and penetratingly into the dark because she is prelapsarian, because her elders and her happy life have not taught her the psychological rituals of seeing things as others do. Can wit then be a species of innocence, and grief a kind of social conformity? Perhaps—but because wit, including of course the literary varieties, can also resist the psychological rituals of innocence, it will stay under no classification or valuation, except as resistance to classifications and valuations.

Wilbur's Wit

Early in his career, in a poem called "Ceremony" (the title poem in his 1950 collection), Richard Wilbur wrote a dangerous line. It works well enough in the poem, but in the aesthetic disruptions in poetry after the war, it gave some puzzled reviewers a lever for easing him into a category and keeping him there.

> Ho-hum. I am for wit and wakefulness, . . .

Aha—so Wilbur is witty, and wakeful, and ho-hum, and so much for him. For more than forty years after, Wilbur has been cheered, honored, lamented, and puzzled over for this wit, which he himself laid claim to here—perhaps too forthrightly for his own good—and which most critics affirm has distinguished his poetry from the start.[9] It would be well if we could describe what manner of literary wit this might be and what roles it plays in Wilbur's vision and work. In other words, it should be decided whether the term is appropriate or meaningful at all, as either praise or blame, or even as a clumsy stand-in name for qualities in Wilbur's poetry that commentary hasn't found words for yet. Modern American poetry at its best has tended to surprise, leaving readers at a loss for language to respond fully and convincingly. Some of Wilbur's poems seem to have that power, and this quality, which has regularly been called his "wit" or "elegance" or "cleverness," has much to do with the depth of his art—and not merely with dressing it up. I have suggested that Stoppard and Wilde and Mark Twain have all understood that there is much yet to learn about the scope and processes of the mind, that their texts can be thought of as breaking new ground, with regard to recognizing the complexity and multiplicity of utterance and cognition and the breadth of psychological activity in the instant of such utterance, such perception. I want to open several of Wilbur's ostentatiously or notoriously witty poems, in order to show that they have at their core this kind of insight, a similar surprising depth. Wilbur's verse provides plenty of additional and compelling evidence that literary wit can express much more than intellect, that it can resonate with deep intuitive powers of the mind.

We can start with his most famous, most-anthologized poem, "Love Calls Us to the Things of This World." This poem is saturated with wordplay and puns, and from the first line to the last it fits the disparaging glossary descriptions of wit. Though much has been written to decode this poem, little has been said about a large-scale conflict at its center. This is an exquisitely witty and performative Wilbur poem, a bravura display of what he can do with imaginative somersaults and the English language; and yet much of or even all this discourse, especially the pun-loaded six lines that close the poem, is supposedly spilling freely and spontaneously from the mind or the mouth of a sleepy man who is all alone, and just at this moment waking up, hallucinating for a moment, and climbing out of bed, and who is letting a Freudian-slip side of himself, and not his cocktail-party intellect, do the talking and connecting.

The soul descends once more in bitter love
To accept the waking body, saying now
In a changed voice as the man yawns and rises,
   "Bring them down from their ruddy gallows;
Let there be clean linen for the backs of thieves;
Let lovers go fresh and sweet to be undone,
And the heaviest nuns walk in a pure floating
Of dark habits,
              keeping their difficult balance." (233–34)

There are at least a half-dozen now-famous puns and word jokes here: *ruddy, fresh, sweet, undone, pure, dark habits, balance*—and hundreds of freshman English essays are written annually to unpack the meaning of these words and lines. They are, yes, clever and elegant and brilliant (again, all the loaded terms can be applied). But what is not usually noticed is that these words and lines also make psychological sense, and that this poem is at least as much about mysteries of the mind as it is about the external world, its hidden wonders, or epistemology as a poetic practice. The poem describes a hypnagogic state, a process of waking up, in which the mind, momentarily free, can make connections that could be either gone or impossible after the first cup of coffee and the first configuring interactions with others, when the ruts and patterns of cautious wakeful thought take over. If we don't want clinical explanations for this liberty and its implications, they aren't required for understanding the mental state that this poem is exploring and valorizing. It can be imagined in a general way, as any variety of psychological liberty from which powerful insights or good poems sometimes arise. "Love Calls Us" is ostentatiously witty, except that the wit it celebrates is not of the sort that wakeful, self-conscious intellects conjure up as performance. Rather, the poem delights in those radical, funny, and profound connections that can happen suddenly when supposedly higher faculties aren't quite on line. If "Love Calls Us to the Things of This World" is performance, what it performs is the poetry within, a way that the mind can freely and actually work. The poem doesn't just talk about a hypothetical morning and a hypothetical "man" in an entertainingly clever way.

This seems to me an important recognition from which to reread Richard Wilbur. If he really is what reviewers back in the 1950s called him— the maestro of our "Poetry of Wit"[10]—he is so because he understands that wit and cleverness and passionate intensity have deep connections, that intellect and emotion can be one, that science and knowledge and imagination have everything to do with one another. I have said elsewhere that wordplay and wit in Wilbur's poetry can create a kind of vortex in which perceptions and intentions combine in unexpected and profound ways.[11] But other kinds of wit, more suggestive of the Metaphysicals or the Restoration, turn up as well: perceptions ingeniously or miraculously conjoined, and even convincing—yet perhaps only so for the moment of the poem. In other words, Wilbur's literary wit often draws attention to the poem as a special and separate realm and to the contingency of imagining and reading. There is nothing radical about this: the insight of literary wit includes recognition of the limits of an insight. No reader is obligated, after all, to accept wisdom from a Donne poem because of its mental and linguistic acrobatics with a flea or with morning sunshine in the eyes of waking lovers. In a burst of epigrammatic eloquence, a character in a Molière play can whirl intellectually and linguistically in the air, yet create in us no requirement to carry such thinking home.

Thus, another strength and a guiltless pleasure of literary wit when it energizes a poem: it occurs, after all, within a poem, and not within a vehicle for instruction or argumentation. In "Love Calls Us," which is one of Wilbur's several returns to Donne's famous time of day, a waking man squints out a window at laundry on a clothesline. In "Shad-Time," a reverie set on a cold New England morning in early spring, someone takes a walk in a damp wood by a plunging stream. In "All That Is," an idler in a strange-sounding city lets his mind play with the citywide imaginative impact of a crossword puzzle in the evening newspaper. These poems are loaded with wordplay; the last one I mentioned is about the crazy words in the crossword and the mental cross-connections they trigger; and in the middle of this poem there is a giddy patch of lines that comprise a *son et lumière* display of literary wit:

> Is it a vision? Does the eye make out
> A flight of ernes, rising from aits or aeries,
> Whose shadows track across a harsh terrain
> Of esker and arête? At waterside,
> Does the shocked eeler lay his congers by,
> Sighting a Reo driven by an edile?
> And does the edile, from his running-board
> Step down to meet a ranee? (38–39)

Is this comic? Of course. Does something interesting come of it? Again, of course. Freewheeling associations are nonsense and wit and (sometimes) a breakthrough to insight, and we can never be sure what dizziness, or idle thought, or handsome verbal performance might reveal, as the speaker says later, about "the webwork of the world":

It is a puzzle which, as puzzles do,
Dreams that there is no puzzle. It is a rite
Of finitude, a picture in whose frame
Roc, oast, and Inca decompose at once
Into the ABCs of every day.
A door is rattled shut, a deadbolt thrown.
Under some clipped euonymus, a mushroom,
Bred of an old and deep mycelium
As hidden as the webwork of the world,
Strews on the shifty night-wind, rising now,
A cast of spores as many as the stars. (39)

Euonymus, mycelium—these are words from our crossword fugues, spores cast out like idle thoughts or lines of poetry, which may or may not map the universe. Modern poetic practice goes on under the "clipped euonymus" of everyday life, not in the wild and Byronized gardens of Sidley Park; for all their vaunted polish and craft, Wilbur's poems are among the most modestly proffered of any major poet since the Second World War. For they keep their place as poems and do not colonize into systematic philosophy or theology. Yet they are not "light" poems either. They seem uncommonly aware of varieties of human discourse and of the special and transforming place and role of verse amid the postmodern cacophony. What they celebrate is possibility and cautious, plausible hopes founded in the open-endedness and restorable freedom of thinking itself. The literary wit at their center is an agent in that project of restoration.

If a poem—and especially a Wilbur poem—can therefore be understood better as a moment than as a tract, then Wilbur's literary wit ought to be understood as having the time-sensitive qualities that I mentioned above with regard to Donne, qualities that no prolix description of wit, literary or otherwise, has countenanced. There may be crucial differences, in other words, between the instant that the mind perceives some small or immense incongruity, some unexpected and pleasurable connection or reconnection that knocks all down for a fresh seeing, and the moment after, when a culture-inflected consciousness recovers and sets limits to the disruptive outbreak. It may be that the smile or laugh does not signal merely that one "gets it," cracking the code of a Wilbur pun or a bit of his wordplay. It might also signify limitation, a moment when we decide intuitively, for our own psychological and cultural survival, how much and how far we are going to let ourselves "get it." Even so, with regard to Wilbur's poems, most of the published commentary has avoided this question about the reach and the perilous reverberations of his literary wit, though most of the published criticism has observed "wit" of some sort as a key characteristic of his work. Assigning seats in his hierarchical arrangement of postwar poets, Randall Jarrell located Richard Wilbur this way in 1951:

> Richard Wilbur is a delicate, charming, and skillful poet—his poems not only make you use, but make you eager to use, words like *attractive* and *appealing* and *engaging*. His poems are often gay and often elegiac—almost professionally elegiac, sometimes; funny or witty; individual; beautiful or at least pretty; accomplished in their rhymes and rhythms and language. Somebody said about Christopher Fry—and almost everybody must have felt it—"I don't think real poetry is ever as *poetic* as this." One feels this way about some of Mr. Wilbur's language (and about some of what he says, too: what poets say is often just part of their "language"); but generally his language has a slight incongruity or "offness," a skillful use of verbs and kinesthetic words, a relishable relishing texture, a sugar-coated-slap-in-the-face rhetoric, that produce a real though rather mild pleasure. The reader notices that the poet never gets so lost either in his subject or in his emotions that he forgets to mix in his usual judicious proportion of all these things: his manners and his manner never fail.[12]

Jarrell had a major influence on the reviewing and anthologizing of American poetry in the postwar years, and the same kind of language, and the assumptions that went with it, cropped up in many other reviews, laudatory and otherwise. A now-forgotten reviewer in *Poetry* from as early as 1948, writing of Wilbur's first collection, offers this, apparently triggered by recognition that literary wit, of some inconvenient kind, was underway: "Wit of the kind he is aiming at—the Swiftian or Elioteseque kind—demands more intellectual incisiveness and emotional 'blackness' than Mr. Wilbur is at present able to muster. His true domain is the borderland between natural and moral perception, his special gift for the genteel, non-metaphysical conceit which illuminates the hidden correspondences between natural and moral phenomena."[13]

The problem here is not just the assumption that poems should deal in uncontingent wisdom, but another unconsidered acceptance of an oppositional arrangement—that intellect is over here and the "stuff of the heart" is over there. If experience is organized into such dualisms, a poetry of wit, a poetry *with* wit, cannot speak. Michael Benedikt tried to move beyond this mentality in a 1970 review, again in *Poetry*. In a piece called "Witty and Eerie," Benedikt reviewed *Walking to Sleep* as a breakthrough, not for Wilbur but rather for ourselves in reading him. "The key to both poem and book," he said, "seems to me the poet's recommendation that we 'answer to our suppler self'—with all that implies, in earthly as well as extra-earthly terms."[14] This is better: suppleness of mind is what Wilbur's wit intends to recover or open up. Among both admirers and detractors of Wilbur's poetry, the pattern with regard to his use of literary wit continues into the 1990s. In one of Cleanth Brooks's last essays, an appreciation of Wilbur, Brooks offered this: "Wilbur is a poet of great wit, and the wit is interwoven with the very texture of his work. It appears steadily in his verse, but it takes various forms and serves diverse purposes."[15] Because that is as far as Brooks went in clarifying his observation, we might try taking it farther in its own direction. To do so, we can consider a Wilbur poem that is short, simple, and from several perspectives dangerous.

I have suggested that a fuller description of the power of literary wit—its power to open up realms of perception where the mind cannot venture by other means—can benefit from an expanded and transformed conception of the mind and how it moves. Again, we find ourselves in a transitional moment in which relevant sciences, engaged with problems of cognition and the nature of human intelligence and creativity, are moving rapidly away from certain assumptions still prevalent in literary analysis. Appropriating fresher and more effective paradigms from modern physics and computer engineering, investigators of the mind offer descriptions of consciousness as nonlinear, nondialectic, nonalgorithmic, and far more interesting.[16] Such propositions may be quickly superseded by others; but one way or another, conventions regarding the nature of thought are undergoing radical change, and discourse about poetry will need to respond. From *Things of This World*, Wilbur's brief poem "Mind" seems to speculate in such new directions, which may account in part for its popularity and frequent republication. "Mind" describes a faculty that Wilbur calls "senseless wit"—another highly compressed and, yes, a witty phrase, which can be decoded, sense by sense, in several ways. Or, as an alternative, "senseless wit" can be understood by applying the kind of wit that the poem is *about*, as a blind bat understands the cavern, in an instant of full yet inexpressible comprehension:

Mind in its purest play is like some bat
That beats about in caverns all alone,
Contriving by a kind of senseless wit
Not to conclude against a wall of stone.

It has no need to falter or explore;
Darkly it knows what obstacles are there,
And so may weave and flitter, dip and soar
In perfect courses through the blackest air. (240)

Senseless as stupid and mindless; *senseless* as without senses; *senseless* as freed from the senses—and *wit* bearing any and all of the significations reviewed at the beginning of this book. If they do not reconcile, if they do not add up, then the effect and the word choice are all the better: for this is a poem about how the mind can move, how experience is negotiated, how human beings apprehend what and where they are, or create or imaginatively "correct" what or where they are. We can organize reality rationally, intuitively, sensuously; we can do it slowly and deliberately or in a millisecond; we can bear in mind and verbalize mysteries and chaos around us, and yet also think—or is it feel? or imagine? or all of these and more?—as creatures in a knowable world. That capacity Wilbur refers to as *wit*, is wit in an older and richer sense: in other words, in a sense that has grown "senseless" because modern English has lost that sense (that definition) and has also lost the common sense to sense the importance of this faculty, which no longer has name or value—a capacity of the mind to move unpredictably and perilously and not become trapped within culturally prescribed patterns of motion. And what "wit" does at its best, or in its best and highest form, is caught in "Mind"'s brazenly neat and witty closing quatrain:

And has this simile a like perfection?
A mind is like a bat. Precisely. Save
That in the very happiest intellection
A graceful error may correct the cave. (240)

Happiest—meaning what? Lucky, blessed? Or is Wilbur being witty here also with *hap*, drawing on its meaning of fate, or sheer accident? Questions like that cannot be glibly answered—with regard to "Mind" the poem or the mind itself. And the puns within *graceful*: smooth and slick, like the movements of the blind bat? Or full of "grace" of some divine or transcendental sort, an inscrutable destiny that might shape our life flight and our imagination? In the last line, have we slipped into some Stoppard–Schrödinger–Heisenbergian contemplation, that imagination and physical universe and intellect and time are all "gracefully" (in all senses of the term) and sublimely intertwined? Summarized crudely, one theme of "Mind" seems to be that the mind, with "senseless wit" and other dark faculties, can go places where distinct or categorizable faculties of the mind (as our culture of the intellect has sorted and valorized them) cannot go alone. Systematic theology, philosophy, logic, and critical discourse, even poetry in its various schools and modes—these are all too encumbered to fly solo through "the blackest air," comprehending the dark and dancing through it like "some bat," or like Stoppard's Thomasina. The poem doesn't satirize or reject reason or any of its cultural applications; it doesn't valorize manic visions either. Instead, "Mind" seems to celebrate instants of imaginative escape from all the rules by which human "intellection"—which seems to be Wilbur's own coinage, signifying perhaps something like literary wit—is divided into the intellect, the intuitions, the rational, the emotional, or any other inadequate categories. And it is all done, performed, with rhymes, and quatrains, and epigrammatic lines, another exquisitely wakeful and self-conscious poem in praise of the unconscious self.

Another short poem—again, one of Wilbur's "light" ones, the kind that have convinced some critics that as a serious artist he is too damned jolly and sane—also opens ungainly questions about how the mind works, and how poems and consciousness can traffic in the rational, the irrational, the sublime and the banal, all at once. From *Ceremony*, Wilbur's 1950 collection, the poem "Epistemology"—which is not an epistemological mini-treatise at all but a poem about such treatises and about when and how they are believed—comprises just two rhymed couplets:

> I
> Kick at the rock, Sam Johnson, break your bones:
> But cloudy, cloudy is the stuff of stones.
> II
> We milk the cow of the world, and as we do
> We whisper in her ear, "You are not true." (288)

In "Epistemology" the "we" doesn't seem limited to academic philosophers, and it doesn't mean exclusively poets either. If the poem is urbanely and epigrammatically witty, then it is perhaps about wit of every sort. It is not just about cleverness and a Stoppard-like sense of the paradoxes of negotiating ordinary life—life after a college class, a church service, or an afternoon reading *American Poetry Review*—but also about the hardest and most important amalgams of reasoning and imagining: what these things are, how they blend, and what we can achieve in their company. To philosophize, fervently or otherwise, and in poems or out beyond them, may always be in some dimension a whisper in the ear of a cow. This is because poems are poems as plays are plays; and the cow of the world—which signifies here not just an external world but also the bovine side of the self—never truly listens or understands. This noumenal universe never pays attention, and in the more ordinary realms of human experience, perhaps nobody ever really hears what anyone else is saying. Bards may shout "No!" or "Yea!" in thunder as they please, but who or what difference does it really make whether he, or she, or we, accept worldly experience or not? The last couplet may sound Wildean, aesthetically Platonist, but it also broaches an idea about the status of such ideas in the mind—not an epistemological idea in itself, or some kind of manifesto about living in a world of contingency. Perhaps then every poem is always a whisper in the ear of damp, inattentive, ordinary experience and mundane consciousness; moreover, we may never quite (or entirely) listen to ourselves as we do the whispering, perhaps because we are busy and because every thought, even the most profound, remains contingent. There is always somewhere else to go, another waltz on an empty shore; another experience which intuitively, psychologically, rationally reshapes understanding of experience, understanding touched by, but not (if we are not despondent crazy Sidley Park hermits) utterly or simplistically transformed by this poem, this experience, this insight—or any other. The two epigrams that make up "Epistemology" are black holes, epigrams that implicitly devour all other epigrams, elegant, quotable wit-wisdom about the world and how we know it.

But, being epigrams themselves, they are also self-consuming, calling into doubt their own wisdom, whispering in the ear of the world that they, too, are "not true."

To sum up: to assume that cleverness means the opposite of intensity and seriousness is to miss not only interesting dimensions in Wilbur's short, quick, and ostensibly light poems but also what lies at the heart of longer and darker poems. A freewheeling intellect, a radical questioning of deep structures of language, of perception, of conventions of thought: these are powers Wilbur packs with him on many imaginative adventures. From the *New Poems* collection of 1987, "Lying," the longest poem in the set, has been drawing the most attention. It is a poem about seeing, and about the telling of lies and myths, and about the construction of history, belief, and poems. "Lying" is another risky poem. The lies that "Lying" relishes are the strict-sense lies of simile and metaphor, "the great lies told with the eyes half-shut / That have the truth in view" and the ordinary lies that bump conversation along and rise unbidden out of the imagination, allowing us to see experience as something both real and wonderful. "Odd that a thing is most itself when likened," says this speaker, and wit—senseless wit, cerebral wit, compulsive wit, and mother wit—is a capacity to "liken" out beyond the rules and borders. There are somersaults and wordplay in this poem too, proffered not as stunts of poem making but as refreshed ways of seeing everything, and even nothing. For an instant, and properly or not, the dry orderings and categorizings of experience into fact and fiction, truth and falsehood, and all other tidy, inadequate oppositions are knocked about roughly and rearranged. The showiest metaphor in this poem, the metaphor that comes closest to seeming like emptily cerebral wit or verbal parlor magic, is this meticulously constructed, ruminative, genial metaphor for Nothing.

> All these things
> Are there before us; there before we look
> Or fail to look; there to be seen or not
> By us, as by the bee's twelve thousand eyes,
> According to our means and purposes.
> So too with strangeness not to be ignored,
> Total eclipse or snow upon the rose,
> And so with that most rare conception, nothing.
> What is it, after all, but something missed?
> It is the water of a dried-up well
> Gone to assail the cliffs of Labrador.
> There is what galled the arch-negator, sprung
> From Hell to probe with intellectual sight
> The cells and heavens of a given world
> Which he could take but as another prison . . . (9–10)

As a bravura demonstration of literary wit of the grand Metaphysical variety, this passage includes what Clive James called "killer-diller" lines[17]— his Bush House way of saying that he found such lines both marvelous and suspicious. In Stoppard's *Rosenkrantz and Guildenstern are Dead*, the evasively witty Player King, who answers in riddles, says that his outrageous craft, of doing "on stage the things that are supposed to happen off," is really "a kind of integrity, if you look on every exit being an entrance somewhere else." That too is a killer-diller line: witty, possibly profound, and close in theme and tone to what Wilbur comes up with here. After we enjoy such lines as elegant, memorable imaginative leaps, what do such metaphors mean—or to put the question better, what do they do?

"Lying" seems to be about poetry—or rather ultimately it is about poetry as another thing that people do to make experience interesting, enliven the world, invent realities, and celebrate even when experience seems resistant to peace or joy. Echoing Wallace Stevens, "Lying" opens with a domestic scene and magisterial thoughts about fabrications and half-truths that keep discourse moving, for in the unstill voice lurk those faint chances for evasion, for renewal, for chance itself. After those opening lines, which I quoted above, a paradox deepens, having to do with perceiving, imagining, and knowing. Things are what they are: sights before the eye are really there, or so we are told, and not tricks in a phenomenological fun house; and yet one also sees what one wants to, or has to. And what we also need to do is tell lies, make up urbane and witty and dubious explanations for things we can never really understand. "The heart's wish for life" (as Wilbur calls it in "In the Field") may be what populates the world with belief, comforts, and poems, never leaving nothing alone.

And so, after the tour de force metaphor for Nothing, the water "Gone to assail the cliffs of Labrador," Satan next comes into mind, somehow—but signifying what? Some real Satan? A metaphor for an Everlasting No, a myth like Septimus's empty shore, which must be resisted by waltzing and wit and concocting other myths, and better? The unquenchable human need is to make connections, create meaning—which might include a need to create Satan, as the mythological archnegator of myth and meaning. Whatever he is this time around, the Satan of "Lying" is kept at bay with fictions; the great Liar is checked by other lies, for when we "liken" things, make metaphors and poems, we invent truth and falsehood in the same instant—because one "truth" known to the artist, if not to every philosopher, is that things are somehow most themselves when they are imaginatively "made" into something else:

> And in the barnyard near the sawdust-pile
> Some great thing is tormented. Either it is
> A tarp torn loose and in the groaning wind
> Now puffed, now flattened, or a hip-shot beast
> Which tries again, and once again, to rise.
> What, though for pain there is no other word,
> Finds pleasure in the cruellest simile? (10)

And having come back again to the smoke and mirrors of poetry, its contrived illusions and the inherent dubiousness of all that is "truly" out there, "Lying" molts into poetry of another sort, into lying in earnest and in the high old ways. The mind drifts outward to a fine spring day in the New England countryside, and the hypothetical grackle of the first line becomes (or *does* it?) a real catbird, and then a dove, which may or may not signify what poetic conventions tell that it should. After that, the poem is off into mythology—not as lies but as a species of truth—and then on to one crowning lie, the Song of Roland, invoked this time as a fabrication, a geste dreamed up from a sordid raid on a baggage train, which mysteriously becomes truer than unadorned truth. For one way or another, the world will be "dove-tailed," as Wilbur cleverly, wittily, dangerously calls it: endowed with shape and intention, even though that process, by which faith is reasoned out and told, is always inherently suspect, always a fabric of metaphors, and myths, and more lies.

Faith affirmed, then, or disparaged in "Lying"? Neither reading is quite right. Adrift between romantic belief and postmodern-style denial, "Lying" casts doubt on the craft and the agency of imagery, of verse making, of making sense of the world—*and* on poems, even as "Lying" affirms such false doing as obscurely true. We never know quite which way to go, for the free mind can head off in so many different directions.

From one perspective, then, "Lying" is about verbal and mental sleight of hand; our poet-host might be riddling like Stoppard's slippery Player King. But that interpretation will not satisfy, because we cannot be sure that these lines in "Lying" are elegant lies, or lies and also a kind of truth. Where does the dried-up water go? Not nowhere. Which is truer: the accumulated historical fact behind the Song of Roland . . . or the Song? Such questions are koanlike, dwelling in some tributary part of the consciousness, enlivening yet not transforming a sense of the way that water moves about this planet, the way poems work, the way things might really be.

With regard to scholastic discussion of contemporary verse, what suffers is sensitivity to the range of an individual voice, and psychological and philosophical possibilities in one writer's discourse. Rival-camp criticism hurts not just poems and poets but poetry, yet the pointless game still drags on.[18] Richard Wilbur cannot be construed as an artist on the complacent Right, as opposed to, say, Charles Olson's ostensibly Visigothic Left. There are monsters enough howling in Wilbur's own cellars; but those cellars are deep, and one has to listen hard. For this poet, reading strategies cannot be carried home from the mall and plugged in. Wilbur's

commitment to a totality of psychological experience is clearer in his poems than steadiness or comfort in a given belief system, and that totality
embraces a great deal of starless dark, or "pure cold" to borrow a phrase
from a short poem of Wilbur's called "Wyeth's Milk Cans," about a dry-
brush work by Andrew Wyeth, a small winter vignette in that unsettling
style that once experienced can be hard to get out of the mind:

> Beyond them, hill and field
> Harden, and summer's easy
> Wheel-ruts lie congealed.
>
> What if these two bells tolled?
> They'd make the bark-splintering
> Music of pure cold. (25)

Clever. The last verse is like others we can find in the Wilbur canon; with
a flourish suggesting haiku, or Pound, Frost, Dickinson, the French Sym-
bolists, or other voices that Wilbur has mastered—including of course
William Carlos Williams—the last line hovers beyond the reach of sure
interpretation. One can say yes, how like some of Wyeth's work, in atmosphere, in economy, in austere music, yet what does it signify, "music of
pure cold"?

If a reader insists on categorizing Wilbur as a latter-day Wordsworthian
or a tender-minded, restyled Robert Frost (who became Wilbur's mentor
and friend after the war) then this poem can be aligned with other, jollier
poems in the canon. Emersonian consolations might be heard here, variations perhaps on Emerson's premise that there is nothing on earth that
strong light cannot make beautiful; or whispers that things are right no
matter how cold it gets in the world or the mind, that there is no season
of nature or the self that doesn't rattle with immanence or transcendental
comforts. That can be done—if the object is to make a poet's work sound
all alike and deliver always to the same terminus. But if that isn't a motive
that lets poetry be interesting, and if an artist of experience can be allowed
other motions of the mind, then we can read this differently—as one
might gaze at a Wyeth landscape (like "Far from Needham" or one of the
vistas in the Kuerner series) and feel consoled, but look hard at it again a
moment later and be appalled. A pure cold might suggest terrible absolutes, recognitions that could splinter the bark of the psyche and break
life-conserving delusions, as readily as cold might hint of immanent pu-
rity or a dark sort of holiness.

The paradoxical beauty of these ice-cold cans and the winter landscape involves their perfect, pure resistance to human compulsions to find in everything reasons to love and feel summer-easy, to make nature comply to a human rage for order. If such a moral condition, or such a state between conditions, recalls moments in Robert Frost—"Design," for example, or "For Once, Then, Something," then well and good—provided other echoes are not thereby drowned out, echoes perhaps of William Carlos Williams; and provided this predicament can be understood as one to which contemporary artists—Left, Right, or off the map—may inevitably come when they look courageously at the natural world, never really knowing where they are, in contexts that none of us made and can never quite make out.

Wilbur's poetry can reply, refine, and quarrel outright with moods and themes in these other poets, just as it notoriously quarrels with the work of Poe—a quarrel that has been noticed much and abused at times to keep Wilbur in a category. "A Wall in the Woods," a fine poem in the new collection *Mayflies*, is not a simple dialogue with Frost or others in the Yankee pastoral tradition, though in some ways it seems to elegize that heritage—as a long effort worn toward oblivion by time, misuse, and misunderstanding—and to speculate darkly about the worth of whatever it is that poetry, and a life as a poet, leaves behind. Here is the first part of the two-part poem:

> What is it for, now that dividing neither
> Farm from farm nor field from field, it runs
> Through deep impartial woods, and is transgressed
> By boughs of pine or beech from either side?
> Under that woven tester, buried here
> Or there in laurel-patch or shrouding vine,
> It is for grief at what has come to nothing,
> What even in this hush is scarcely heard—
> Whipcrack, the ox's lunge, the stoneboat's grating,
> Work-shouts, of young men stooped before their time
> Who in their stubborn heads foresaw forever
> The rose of apples and blue of rye.
> It is for pride, as well, in pride that built
> With levers, tackle, and abraded hands
> What two whole centuries have not brought down.
> Look how with shims they made the stones weigh inward,
> Binding the water-rounded with the flat;
> How to a small ravine they somehow lugged

> A long, smooth girder of a rock, on which
> To launch their wall in air, and overpass
> The narrow stream that still slips under it.
> Rosettes of lichen decorate their toils,
> Who labored here like Pharaoh's Israelites;
> Whose grandsons left for Canaans in the west.
> Except to prompt a fit of elegy
> It is for us no more, or if it is,
> It is a sort of music for the eye,
> A rugged ground bass like the bagpipe's drone,
> On which the leaf-light like a chanter plays. (*Mayflies*, 45–46)

A somber poem, an elegy invoking Frost and Bryant and the entire tradition of the New England elegy, for this poem is also in a sense about
poetry. There is wordplay throughout, but fitted unobtrusively into the
crevices and cracks like the small stones that make the large contemplations of "A Wall in the Woods" hold together and "weigh inward." *Impar-
tial, transgressed, shrouding, tester, fit, chanter*—and yet the poem, or this first
part of it, meditates darkly on the futility of carefully constructing stone
walls and intricate poems. If Frost's "Mending Wall" resonates in "A Wall
in the Woods," then so does the Frost poem "The Woodpile," his uncon-
soled elegy for pastoral art and its dubious value in a grander indifferent
scheme of things. Somebody else built the woodpile that Frost contem-
plates in his poem; Wilbur's stone wall recalls the one that Frost mended
with his stolid neighbor—and that Frost implicitly likens to the labor and
stubborn formal beauty of his own poetry, its own uncertain worth and
staying power, and a perverse but necessary practice of holding something
back in the dark of the self, of conserving identity or sanity by means of
passionate reserve. At Cummington, where Wilbur's poem is set, and where
William Cullen Bryant, busy American Romantic poet and New York City
newspaperman, kept a family homestead, Wilbur seems to be looking
hard at an actual old wall as well as at Frost's poem, and at Frost's career,
and also perhaps at Bryant's, and Dickinson's and that of every other poet
who has lived and written and died in this neighborhood. Even so, at this
particular wall Wilbur seems both sharper eyed and colder minded than
Frost was in repiling his stones and making his poem. Marvelous as it
is, "Mending Wall" looks more intently at damage done by winter and
hunters than at the art of contriving stone walls (and poems) that don't
crumble in a few seasons. In Frost's eyes, the pointless repair work—his

own and his neighbor's—is amateur magic, not craft, and he talks of balancing stones with spells to keep them in place until the mender's back
is turned. Wilbur's eye is caught by what has held its place through human skill and stayed long, achieving an elegant futility. The mingled mood
of this part of "A Wall in the Woods," has to do with the private, forgotten heroics of doing that kind of work and with the anonymity and
fruitlessness not merely of stacking rocks artfully but of living hard and
stubbornly in a world that sooner or later buries all in moss, leaf mulch,
and oblivion. Here is an aging poet, wondering about fine artifice, which
endures yet which also in more than one sense comes to nothing. Much
more seems in doubt here than the worth of wall making or the long-term
worth of some other poet's "lover's quarrel with the world."

Even so, part 2 of "A Wall in the Woods" shifts not only meter but focus
and tone; yet whether it switches the poem into a major key and finds
Bryant-like consolations—which is to say consolations more musical than
reasoned—is a question that requires care to answer. After part 1, thick
and sonorous, and suggesting an obdurate (and possibly absurd) structure
of high-serious, old-style meditating, part 2 seems to leap and twist and
scamper like the chipmunk that it describes, the one thinking animate
presence observed in the scene, a little like the unspecified bird that flits
away in Frost's "The Woodpile."

> He will bear no guff
> About Jamshýd's court, this small
> Striped, duff-colored resident
> On top of the wall,
>
> Who, having given
> An apotropaic shriek
> Echoed by crows in heaven,
> Is off like a streak.
>
> There is no tracing
> The leaps and scurries with which
> He braids his long castle, ra-
> Cing, by gap, ledge, niche
>
> And Cyclopean
> Passages, to reappear
> Sentry-like on a rampart
> Thirty feet from here.

What is he saying
Now, in a steady chipping
Succinctly plucked and cadenced
As water dripping?

It is not drum-taps
For a lost race of giants,
But perhaps says something, here
In Mr. Bryant's

Homiletic woods,
Of the brave art of forage
And the good of a few nuts
In burrow-storage;

Of agility
That is not sorrow's captive,
Lost as it is in being
Briskly adaptive;

Of the plenum, charged
With one life through all changes,
And of how we are enlarged
By what estranges. (*Mayflies*, 46–47)

The small creature does not flee from the poet as Frost's bird does, leaving the elegist alone to deal with relics of human effort. Indeed, Wilbur's resident of his stone wall runs all through it, for the artifact belongs to him now and, commanding it to the end, he moves the watcher to thoughts about movement as some sort of end in itself, "agility / That is not sorrow's captive" and that promises refuge, a way of being "lost" in a world that seems too solid and inexorably glum. Like Wilbur's literary wit, the chipmunk runs for it, runs from history and tragedy and elegy and all such stone-fence constructions around the mind. Yet just how much lighter does the poem become here, looking at this chipmunk? The lines are quietly deft. The second and fourth lines of each stanza rhyme, and usually firmly, though sometimes with self-mocking magic, as in lines nine and eleven; the first and third verses rhyme too, but with rhymes popping up unexpectedly and in odd places, like this small quick animal popping up among these man-gathered rocks—or perhaps like a recognition that shows itself suddenly or like a fleeting illusion that seems hopeful because we make it so, not because it is surely there. There is a 1969 painting by

Andrew Wyeth called "End of Olsons," representing one end and much of the roof of that decrepit and haunted house on the Maine coast, on a blue-sky day in what appears to be autumn, at the end of Wyeth's long, intense, and darkly productive sojourn with the devastated family of the title. The house looks abandoned, as if the grim existence within it were itself over at last, leaving only a wrack behind: gray walls, a broken roof, a crumbling chimney. A small bird, possibly a barn swallow, is barely visible on the rooftop—and as a presence in Wyeth's acutely naturalistic yet treacherously symbolic universe, what can or should be surmised from that? Wyeth's small bird seems to float in that same between-world, between signification and rock-obdurate truth, which shelters the Cummington chipmunk. The question really isn't whether these details in painting or poem are modernized fragments of iconography, or do or don't have symbolic value. What we must see, first and last, is our own way of seeing, and the gorgeous, maddening resistance of the watchable world to mean for certain. Or to be certainly meaningless.

The effect of this closing section of "A Wall in the Woods" is not anagrammatic but dynamic: meaningful or not, there is movement, movement that dwells within the hunks and stasis of the wall itself; and an elegiac, comprehensive look at the wall also means a look at its denizen, this almost-concealed inner life. Yet as a poem that has looked mercilessly at the truth of walls and at the vanishing of their makers and purpose, "A Wall in the Woods" does not conclude with a bedtime story. If Bryant is invoked in a general way, then so of course is his "Thanatopsis," his own best known trip into these somber woods and out again. Yet "Thanatopsis" is here to be resisted, as another and perhaps obsolete way of achieving an end of such grim meditations. Bryant's poem, lurking here, looks as odd in the forgetful woods of time as this sinking wall. Bryant sings himself a lullaby of sorts to get "Thanatopsis" ended, about a human brotherhood of death, which makes the world one vast sepulchre, lovely and even convivial. In other words, Bryant's Romantic imagination gets him out of trouble, and he does not question the process either self-consciously or rigorously, perhaps because in that time and place you didn't have to. Times have changed. Wilbur has been all through the modern, ducked in foxholes from its incoming fire and gathered its dead; and depending on how one boundaries the postmodern, he has been through that show as well; and there is no going back to simpler days and easier modes of thinking and elegy making. These braiding rhymes and these agile lines suggest and emblematize not just moments of one small rodent but also quick, dubious, inevitable changes of the consciousness—and where Wilbur seems to arrive, in these closing stanzas, is one indefinite step short of nowhere at all.

These woods can say something only "perhaps," and that something seems to be about sheer motion, in perception, in imagining, in elegizing, a litheness that settles nothing perhaps, and reaches—perhaps—no consolation, yet that (perhaps, always perhaps!) keeps everything indeterminate, keeps the self some suspicious distance short of arrival at either faith or despair. In Wilbur's recent collections, there are several poems that affirm the provisional redemptions of not settling down and that seem to hope that the world's unsettledness is a cause for hope. "A Sketch" is a case in point, as is "In Limbo" and "The Catch" and even the haunting dream-poem "The Ride." In others there is deep uneasiness about becoming fixed—in identity, in artistic habit, even in belief of other sorts than this belief in the indeterminate. How conventional Christianity might figure into all this is a question we will have to turn to in a moment, not to settle it but rather to see it in something like its full complexity.

At readings in the 1990s, Wilbur favored another poem that brings together, in twelve handsome lines, many of those qualities that upset critics of the us-them school. Twirling on a single pun, "A Barred Owl," which opens *Mayflies*, is symmetrical, ironic, mannered, suggestive of Robert Frost and poetry-as-performance, a celebration (if you don't look too hard) of joys in seeing shapes and patterns in the natural world. The conspicuous twist in the poem recalls delightful turnarounds of words and meanings in his two children's books of "Opposites," playful short poems that delight in quirky arrangements in the English language and in the play of mind, the gratifying mother wit that allows us to see shapes and mirror images where without our mongrel lexicon there would be none. The familiar evening hoot of an American barred owl is conventionalized by ornithologists into a question for an English-trained ear, a question about cooking; but what a barred owl does is something handsomely and horribly "opposite":

> The warping night air having brought the boom
> Of an owl's voice into her darkened room,
> We tell the wakened child that all she heard
> Was an odd question from a forest bird,
> Asking of us, if rightly listened to,
> "Who cooks for you?" and then "Who cooks for you?"
>
> Words, which can make our terrors bravely clear
> Can also thus domesticate a fear,

And send a small child back to sleep at night
Not listening for the sound of stealthy flight
Or dreaming of some small thing in a claw
Borne up to some dark branch and eaten raw. (*Mayflies*, 3)

If we want to make familiar day noises about form and wit and craft as stays against confusion or celebrations of deep noumenal order out there, of symmetry, which reassures even in its fearfulness, we can go right ahead. The trouble for that approach here is that more seems to lurk in these woods, including a shadowed meditation about the making of such poems and, perhaps, about a life given over to finding words that illusorily "domesticate a fear." To listen "rightly" is to hear an owl self-servingly wrong. A barred owl says "Who cooks for you?" because we want him to, inflecting the noise of the woods with our own language; and the poem's irony, that this whimsical question from the night air really comes from a ruthless predator—is our irony, something dreamed up by us and our culture, not something half-perceived or even fractionally "out there." What is going on out there is pure nature, and pure nightmare, and with language and imagination we coerce those things into shapes that we can abide. "Who cooks for you?" is our own voice, not the owl's, just as in Wilbur's splendid and grim poem of nearly forty years ago, "Marginalia," unmediated shapes and patterns of nature give way to a somber recognition about the construction of faith, about mortality, and about the forever-dubious business of making poems:

Our riches are centrifugal; men compose
Daily, unwittingly, their final dreams,
And those are our own voices whose remote
Consummate chorus rides on the whirlpool's rim,
    Past which we flog our sails, toward which we drift,
    Plying our trades, in hopes of a good drowning. (266)

Not much cheer in that either, as an ending. The mood of a poem like "Mind" or "The Beacon" or "Walking to Sleep" seems more heartened, but those are different poems, and it is nonsense to make Wilbur's poetry arrive always in the same philosophical or psychological safe harbor. There are plenty of Wilbur poems, from the beginning of his career, in which hope, if it is present at all, doesn't have much to go on and in which consolations are entirely the work of the imagination and the English language (which of course is not the end of the road either, for recognizing that imagination and the English language are part of reality too, like those predator owls, leads to a fun house and a nightmare of regressions and mirrorings, a fun house and a nightmare of modern spiritual life).

And so this subject keeps coming up, this intertwined question about belief and Wilbur's matchless literary wit as a contemporary poet, the way that his lines and perceptions dodge and evade like the stone-wall chipmunk. Is this essentially a poetry of faith, or not? The matter cannot be settled easily, partly because words like belief and faith trigger peculiar reactions, and not just from some putative Left in current controversies. Though generalizing about how belief, if it can be called such, figures in Wilbur's art is a temptation and maybe even a necessity, it can hamper a reading of Wilbur's most interesting poems. His art rings with delight in Milton, Herbert, Traherne, and the Book of Common Prayer. But by the evidence, Wilbur also is drawn to Joseph Brodsky, Baudelaire, Wallace Stevens, Elizabeth Bishop, Voltaire, Jorge Luis Borges, and assorted other godless and near-godless folk; and a tour of his imaginative bookshelf, like a glance at his religious practices, tells nothing sure about a combat between darkness and light in the poetry, or about this artist's implicit relation to his own creed. A reading of the best modern poets, Judeo-Christian and otherwise, seems to teach clearer lessons about what belief is not, or rather about what belief need not be. In poems of Richard Wilbur, faith is patently not some variety of endorphin, pumping out biochemically to ease a psyche through spiritual trouble or disruptions in worldly experience. What I have tried to say elsewhere will perhaps hold: belief in Wilbur's poetry is more like a neighborhood that he calls home but that neither precludes nor limits psychological voyages as far from that home as anyone might go. Wilbur's civil surfaces deny him full regard for his range, his changefulness, and above all his capacity for darkness.

Wilbur's poems enact a reality where experience is what it is—sensory, psychological, spiritual—and where nothing is to be shunned by the mind. Is such experience mediated, critiqued, winnowed in mind and in poetry? Of course: Wilbur's three long and especially fine poems "Walking to Sleep," "The Mind Reader," and "Lying" are about that mediation and about what risky work the mind must do to see all and not go mad. Even so, things have to be seen before they can be mediated; the dark must be entered, and a way back is not always to be found; and the artifice of poetry and of faith as stays against undoing is a theme that runs through the work, not just the stuff like "Tywater," "Piccola Commedia," or "Year's End," or like "Another Voice," which is Wilbur's most mordant poem about life in the close company of madness. The poem ends with distinct nonac-

ceptance of consolations and with a recognition of the grieving self as
something rightly torn in two.

> Great martyrs mocked their pain
> And sang that wrong was right;
> Great doctors proved them sane
> By logic's drier light;
> Yet in those I love the most
> Some anger, love, or tact
> Hushes the giddy ghost
> Before atrocious fact.
>
> Forgive me, patient voice
> Whose word I little doubt,
> Who stubbornly rejoice
> When all but beaten out,
> If I equivocate,
> And will not yet unlearn
> Anxiety and hate,
> Sorrow and dear concern. (218)

If we have learned to countenance poets like Dickinson and Frost as figures of range and richness and contradiction rather than as writers of a
handful of themes sounded over and over, we should not miss such values
in a poet of our own time.

In 1991 Wilbur published a little book called *More Opposites*—more artifacts of a verse game Wilbur began, he says, when playing with his children back when they were very young (they are long since grown up). *More
Opposites* is dedicated to a grandchild. These are for fun, and readers, avid
or scrupulous ones, of Wilbur's whole achievement ought to be careful
with them and remember the fate of critics who try to make "McCavity
the Mystery Cat" into an outtake from "The Waste-Land." Nonetheless a
Wilbur temperament and special talent show here too—and with the
same humility that informs and controls the brio in the most challenging
verses he has written. What is interesting here is the skepticism, even
about skepticism, Wilbur's trusting doubt, if we can call it that, that any
human-concocted methodology, or refusal of methodology—even his
own concoctions and refusals—will get us safely out of the woods. Here
is "Opposite Number 33," the penultimate poem in the book:

> What is the opposite of Missouri?
> The answer's *California*, surely.

Missouri folk are *doubters* who
Won't take your word for two plus two
Until they add them up, by heck,
And then they like to double-check.
But people on our Western Coast
Believe in everything, almost.
The Californians think, I'm told,
That every river's full of gold,
That stars give good advice to men
On what they ought to do, and when,
And that we all had former lives
As Pharaohs or as Pharaoh's wives.

That's how those states are opposite.
I may exaggerate a bit,
But I have told you what we say
In *Massachusetts*, anyway. (*More Opposites*, n.p.)

Wilbur's *Massachusetts* is everywhere in between absolute credulousness
and confirmed skepticism; Wilbur's poetry occupies that vast mental territory between those two extremes. A lot of commentary about Richard Wilbur has cooped him up in the bottle he himself created when he published
"The Genie in the Bottle" in 1950 (an essay that grew out of the famous
Bard Conference) and "The Bottles Become New Too" in 1953. Those remarks are still hauled out as keys to his poetry, keys to an array of verse
that was just beginning to come out when these essays were written—as
if Wilbur were building a New England fabrication plant to turn out the
same product forever after. In 1986, Philip Dacey and David Jauss published *Strong Measures*, a collection of "Contemporary Poetry in Traditional
Forms," and they asked Wilbur, as a presiding elder among traditionalists,
to write the foreword. Compare what he says here, to what he said so long
ago in those "Bottle" essays, and hear a poet open to variety in consciousness and in mission:

> It does not seem to me that, at the present moment, the assignment
> of definite meaning or effect to poetic forms can be very persuasive.
> To be sure, there are people who associate meter and rhyme with
> order and good sense, or denounce them as affected and reactionary;
> there are those who regard free verse as sincere and forward-looking,
> and those who dismiss it as squalidly prosaic. But not much of that
> blather holds up if we look at what has actually been written in this

century, and at what is being written now. Was populism more at home in the jaunty measures of Vachel Lindsay, or in the loose chants of Carl Sandburg? One could readily think of twenty similar questions about modern and contemporary verse, questions which would destroy themselves in the asking. The fact is that no form belongs inevitably with any theme or attitude; no form is good or appropriate in itself, but any form can be *made* good by able hands. (xix)

Wilbur often writes highly formal verse; but neither verse nor a set belief-system write him. There are doctrine poets to be sure; the good poets are rarely to be counted in this number. From *Mayflies*, one brief elegy to end this chapter: "Zea" speaks with many voices, including many of the voices that Wilbur has learned from and fused into his own. There is Frost here, and Bishop looking at small natural objects, and the haiku tradition, Yeats singing as an aged man, and a touch of Keats in his own untimely autumnal season, and certainly Dickinson in late Indian Summer, and Eliot at Little Gidding, and William Carlos Williams celebrating small dry drab things in themselves. But if we were to diagram sources and voices in this brief poem, we must also countenance its theme about consciousness itself, its innate capacity to think and speak with many voices, both personal and overheard, consciousness that can operate deeply within its culture and also mysteriously beyond it:

Once their fruit is picked,
The cornstalks lighten, and though
Keeping to their strict

Rows, begin to be
The tall grasses that they are—
Lissom, now, and free

As canes that clatter
In island wind, or plumed reeds
Rocked by lake water.

Soon, if not cut down,
Their ranks grow whistling-dry, and
Blanch to lightest brown,

So that, one day, all
Their ribbon-like, down-arcing
Leaves rise up and fall

In tossed companies,
Like goose-wings beating southward
Over the changed trees.

Later, there are days
Full of bare expectancy,
Downcast hues, and haze,

Days of an utter
Calm, in which one white corn-leaf,
Oddly aflutter,

Its fabric sheathing
A gaunt stem, can seem to be
The sole thing breathing. (*Mayflies*, 7–8)

We can read this poem as verse from a poet who was approaching eighty when he wrote it, as one of the last survivors of that so-called Middle Generation of American poets, feeling perhaps that days of fruitfulness are behind, wondering what future there is and what it might bring, fearing yet relishing that moment of "bare expectancy" that the poem ends with. But if that is the key moment of the poem, then that moment is another vortex, a consecration of an instant in which nothing and everything is happening at once, in which an individual mind is alone and has vast company, is disconnected from others and from the world and yet caught deeply in a natural process. Relish the paradoxes here, not as binary or mechanical oppositions but as expressions of how we are. This is a poem that rejoices in the self as a diverse and unmappable world within; it is a gorgeous poem about artistic dryness, a life-filled poem about near exhaustion and being near the end. One gaunt stem can "seem" to be the sole thing breathing—and yes, in the tradition of Wilbur's literary wit, there is a crucial pun on "sole" here, as there is with "lighten" in the second line and "bare and downcast" in the seventh stanza—but beneath those surfaces of "seem," everything is going on: not "everything" in the sense of clever poet contrivance but "everything" in the sense of the motions of the unstoppable mind, which lights nowhere, and which is changefulness itself, and which gains heart and hope from the indeterminacy of itself and from the world as seen.

I do so loathe explanations.
—J. M. BARRIE

*Francis Bacon was right: the program
that began in doubt has produced
certainties beyond a medieval mind's
wildest dreams. But what was once a
certainty now drifts in a gulf of doubt
wider than the millennium itself.*
—RICHARD POWERS

IV

Wit, Wyt, and Modern Literary Predicaments

As 1999 began, an off-Broadway production of an austere drama with the
darkly witty title Wit, written by first-time playwright Margaret Edson, a
teacher from Atlanta, was causing a stir in literary New York. The excitement held, and in April of that year Wit won a Pulitzer Prize. Presenting
Vivian Bearing, a middle-aged English professor virtually alone in a battle
with ovarian cancer—she has spent her life as a rigorous, aloof expert on
John Donne and the literary wit of the Metaphysical poets—Wit has grueling stretches of realism, presenting the sort of struggle that goes on behind sound-deadening hospital doors everywhere in the Western world.
The play looks relentlessly at the cold ugliness of the medical practices

that Vivian must endure: dehumanizing wards and therapies and clinicians, the word wilderness of treatment for her dreaded disease, and prospects that professional affectations and exotic science can rarely brighten now. But contemporary clinical medicine, with its penchant for alienation, pretense, and euphemism, isn't a new subject in literary or popular culture. What sets *Wit* apart is the other half of the drama, its sustained interest in Professor Vivian Bearing's interest in *wit*—as a literary practice, a subject for study, a core of belief around which to organize a life, face catastrophe, and define professional and personal identity. At the opening of the play, Vivian enters an empty stage pushing an IV pole, introduces herself as "a professor of seventeenth-century poetry, specializing in the Holy Sonnets of John Donne," and about thirty seconds later, she tells her audience, "They've given me less than two hours"—which creates a blur of voices and significations, for no ovarian cancer patient given "less than two hours," to both tell her story and complete her time on earth, will be pushing her own IV pole in the ward hallways and orating in this ruefully chipper manner. Right away, *Wit* calls attention to its own ingenious and complex design: the artificial "less than two hours" signifies that Vivian is speaking here, and also the actress who plays her, and also the playwright who ventriloquizes for them both, who has to trim and pack this literary text into less than two hours of precious theater time. This virtuoso blending of voices and times keeps up until the final moments of a play that is all one act and scene, and Vivian soon appears to us as young graduate student, as teacher, as a mature and arrogant scholar, and as a variously defiant and vulnerable human being at moments in the course of her disease and its treatment. At the end we see that "less than two hours" refers not just to Vivian's account of herself, but to Vivian, who with absolute fidelity to Macbeth's last and darkest great speech, struts and frets her hour upon the stage and then dies silent before our eyes.

About four hundred years before Edson's *Wit*, a certain John Redford, who like Edson was a school teacher, was serving as master of a boy's choir at St. Paul's Cathedral in London. Sometime around 1530 he put together a short stage piece called *The Play of Wyt and Science,*[1] apparently to give his young charges an amusing fable about the value of learning their lessons and proper Anglican ways of growing up both virtuous and bright. Redford's play survives as a fragment. A portion of the opening scene or scenes is gone—exactly how much we cannot be sure. As Master Redford's hero, the allegorical Wyt is a breezy young innocent who after some mostly comic tribulation is happily married off to a blushing maiden called Science, with festive closing music and song, and with "Reson," as the bride's kindly, lordly father, presiding over the rites and paying the pipers. This is a lively innocent play from the infancy of English drama, an amateur entertainment that might have been a hit for pleasing and instructing Redford's corps of squirmy choirboys.

Young Wyt and his companions and foes carry the stock allegorical significations of the time, and if we want to frisk them for hidden profundities we will turn up little. There are no signs that Edson's *Wit* takes notice of John Redford, and on the subject of literary wit, neither play suggests any last word on interpretive problems described in the foregoing chapters. Even so, a glance into these two very different dramas—one of them a festive antique, the other new and sometimes excruciating—can bring together useful perspectives regarding ways in which literary wit is understood, negotiated, or resisted in today's interpretive communities. Together, the plays can clarify how certain understandings have been mislaid over a stretch of time, and at a cost—to the art of engaging with art.

Edson's play centers on a scholar who has sacrificed everything to one intellectual and professional quest, to have the interpretive "last word" on a supremely canonical body of English literary wit. Redford's play presents a promising barbarian who gets his head knocked and then weathers seizures of farcical stupidity, yet who ends up happily wedded to this young allegorical maiden called Science. With regard to understanding potentialities of literary wit, much can be gained from looking at each play in the reflected light of the other. Redford was not writing about wit as literary discourse; like his contemporaries, he took it for granted that wit meant intelligence, adaptability, cleverness, insight, mental variety of every useful sort. Nonetheless, like Margaret Edson, Redford brings "wyt" (no matter what human skill it means) through an epistemological barrier by moving it onto the stage, by situating it as a subject to be observed in a theater or chancel or some other place apart—in other words, as a subject in a distinctly literary arena. His boys were not watching "wyt"; they were watching a young man (one of their schoolmates perhaps, or someone else whom they knew in "real life") impersonating Wyt in a context that required extra measures of suspended disbelief. Allegories always require that—as do monologues and apostrophes from on-stage people like Vivian Bearing, who is presumably already dead when she speaks. When we go to hear Vivian's monologues, we go into a theater and hear an actress speak words from a playwright, words about a self and an illness and a culture and also about wit as a subject, and she speaks these words in a narrative context saturated not only with rituals of the clinic but also with rituals and sanctities of "serious" contemporary theater. In either case, an audience knows acutely where it is—or rather it understands certain rites and mysteries of where it is—and knows also that the subjects raised here for consideration are ultimately being raised by literary texts, or by writers of imaginative discourse, for an audience assumed to be open to that most peculiar kind of communication. John Redford was evidently not the Tom Stoppard or the Oscar Wilde of his day, and in the opening scenes of Wit Edson's graphic realism makes clear that we are a long way from the domestic gentility of Sidley Park. Nonetheless, the artifice of both Wit and Wyt and Science is strongly asserted, and that artifice has an important impact on the way that wit as a subject is presented. And because each play contains an imaginative critique of wit as cultural value in a particular historical moment, in each work we can consider both the idea and the critique: Redford's conception of wit in Tudor England; Margaret Edson's presentation of what literary wit was, and is, and finally becomes for a professional scholar who has given her life to that subject, and of what it might really count for, beyond the reach of old poems and tidy scholastic analysis. But more than that, we can glimpse what can happen when wit becomes a central subject in a literary text rather than a dimension of its discourse. If Redford's idea of wit is as quaint as his play, can it nonetheless suggest recognitions that a modern literary culture might usefully recognize? Does Edson's play achieve kinship of sorts with Redford's on this subject, an understanding that eludes the literary scholar who is Edson's protagonist? In considering such questions, we can revisit and extend some of the observations in the opening chapter of this book.

As was true for the Angels in America plays, Tony Kushner's Broadway triumph of a few years ago, much of the impact and signification of Wit depends on skillful and innovative direction and on how specific lines in Edson's text are delivered and situated. Much like Angels, Edson's essentially agnostic play about a death from cancer ends in a flash of mysticism, a moment of ambiguous spirituality. In Wit, however, no angel crashes at last through the clinic wall to lift Vivian from her deathbed. As a fruitless and mistaken "code blue" resuscitation riots around her, she rises silently and alone, shedding hospital gowns and IVs and all other medical and corporeal encumbrances, until finally she stands naked—and as isolated as always—reaching toward a bright light above, for an instant before the scene goes black and the drama ends, and we try to figure out what has happened.

Vivian seems to be free at last; yet of exactly what is she free? Of worldly and bodily suffering, surely, but also perhaps of the accumulated burden of her own identity, which is coextensive with her intellectual life. Is she also free now of the psychological encumbrance of literary wit (again, as she herself has defined it, and affirmed it, and lived with it, and perhaps lived behind it) and of studying and teaching it to waves of unappreciative students as intellectual calisthenics and an illusory stay against confusion? Has Vivian's intellectual life—again, equivalent to her entire adult life— turned out to be a fatal mistake? a blessing? Has that life-consuming liter- ary practice turned out to be a body of formulations that she finally out- grows? Or is it a valid body of faith that she finally and marvelously grows into? Early in the play and late, Vivian's attention focuses on Donne's Holy Sonnet Six, the sonnet beginning with "Death be not proud" and ending with "Death, thou shalt die!" We cannot be sure that this is the way things work out for Vivian, or that Vivian has been right or wrong about the truth of this sonnet. Amid the chaos of the rescue drill, Vivian ends the play, and her worldly existence, in pantomime. This person of words, words, words passes away from shouts and shocks and hubbub; or she transfig- ures perhaps, or ascends with perfect privacy and silence into the perfectly unknowable. There is no way to know exactly what is going on, except that silence has won out over talk and that the formulaic symmetries and certainties of Professor Bearing in her prime have given way to some ap- prehension that cannot be spoken or written. At the end, words have be- come useless; Vivian's avalanche of talk about her travail and her personal history gives way to distracting pain, then to the drowsiness of analgesics, and then to incoherence, and then to the end of talking. And the literary wit of Donne and the Metaphysicals—her one true subject and social and personal identity since her college days—this wit has perhaps ultimately failed Vivian Bearing too, not because of what it is or can be but rather because of how she has configured it, as an extension and expression of her own temperament. But regardless of what grand theme one does or doesn't find in it, Wit is wonderful in its quest to open and energize a conversation from which literary culture—except for a few (literally) die- hard academics like Vivian herself—and a larger world have largely turned away. An understanding of what might be at stake in this play and of the problems that seem to emerge within it, with regard to the scope, nu- ances, and powers of literary wit, can open a few un-final perceptions, with which to end.

Professor Vivian Bearing begins Wit as a patient in a chemotherapy clinic, giving her audience a perky "Hi. How are you feeling today? Great." Right away, however, she shifts to acerbic grammatical analysis of the contrived perkiness that she now has to endure and play along with, along with everything else in this chummy but essentially inhuman context.

Here and hereafter, the play takes care to establish Vivian as an isolated figure, a severely professional academic of a sort familiar enough in modern academe: a supposed humanist without family, without close friends, even without students who feel sufficient love or gratitude to visit her in her months of struggle against insidious disease. Professor Bearing's name says it all, and wittily—especially if one accepts an idea like hers, that literary wit amounts to handsome, cool, and psychologically serene contrivances of puns and clever turns of phrase and schematic ironies. Enduring her eight months of chemotherapy and the degradations of hospital existence, Vivian has been "bearing" these ills she has (more like a Brecht character than a Hamlet) rather than fly to others that we know not of. Dying from an insurrection of cells in organs that—more grim irony here—she has never used for "bearing" a child, Vivian has (on the evidence of flashback scenes) been bearing down for twenty years on the decoding of Renaissance English poetry; she has (as we see in other flashbacks) been overbearing in college classrooms, using her expertise about Donne, the Metaphysicals, the Renaissance, and English linguistics not to interest and educate young people so much as to confound them and to condescend to the vast witless world beyond her classroom.

Vivian's students are shown to be quite capable of wit themselves, but theirs is wit of another more spontaneous and serendipitous sort than Vivian can appreciate or indulge. They have dutifully borne the burden of her course; and then they have all gone away, bearing their textbooks to the buy-back counters and never bearing to look at a Metaphysical poet again. The Professor Bearing whom we are shown lacks human relationships, except for these awkward, coerced ones with a few doctors and later with a clinical researcher named Jason and a compassionate nurse (a "simple" woman, Vivian assures us) named Susie. It turns out that years before, Jason himself has endured Vivian's Metaphysical poetry class as a required course, a hurdle to jump on his way to medical school. He is the only exstudent of hers who turns up in this hospital, but professional duty and curiosity have brought him here, not any fondness for either Bearing or Donne. In an aside to Susie, Jason remembers his encounter with literary wit in those classes: "Listen, if there's one thing we learned in Seventeenth-Century Poetry, it's that you can forget about that sentimental stuff. Enzyme Kinetics was more poetic than Bearing's class. Besides, you can't think about that meaning-of-life garbage all the time or you'd go nuts" (77).[2]

Ultimately then, it is with Susie that Vivian creates her strongest relationship, in the last days of her life, yet to Vivian, Susie can never be more than a good-hearted bumpkin—"poor Susie," she calls her near the end, whose brain "was never very sharp to begin with." In one of their final conversations Vivian shatters an intimate moment, a little of the human kindness she has yearned for, by laughing uncontrollably at the young nurse's misunderstanding of the word *soporific*. Vivian's feelings for Susie never seem to ripen into more than a condescending affection, the sort of fondness that one might acquire for the pet in a hospice.

In the classroom yesterdays, Vivian's students don't seem to have ranked much higher in her regard. On one dangerous occasion, however, one particular class has almost spoken the words that might have changed everything, has almost named the inadequacy of Vivian Bearing's profession of literary wit—the limited, limiting analytic principles on which she has built a two-decade academic career. In this key flashback, a class of undergraduates stirs toward rebellion against a Donne sonnet—as Vivian has presented, prescribed, and circumscribed the poem:

> STUDENT 2: I think it's like he's hiding. I think he's really confused, I don't know, maybe he's scared, so he hides behind all the complicated stuff, behind this *wit*.
>
> VIVIAN: *Hides* behind *wit?*
>
> STUDENT 2: I mean, if it's really something he's sure of, he can say it more simple—simply. He doesn't have to be such a brain, or such a performer. It doesn't have to be such a big deal.
>
> *(The other* STUDENTS *encourage him.)*
>
> VIVIAN: Perhaps he is suspicious of simplicity.
>
> STUDENT 2: Perhaps, but that's pretty stupid. (60–61)

Suddenly Vivian finds herself in both professional and personal trouble with this class, and the implication is strong that down in some silenced corner of her own consciousness, she understands what they are suggesting—that she herself has been hiding behind literary wit for a long time. Her professional description of it cannot embrace uncertainty, or simplicity, or deep conflict in the psyche, or anything of a more personal nature than what she lists in her antiquated half-definition of her subject, which she offers midway through this play: "In his [Donne's] poems, metaphysical quandaries are addressed, but never resolved. Ingenuity, virtuosity, and a vigorous intellect that jousts with the most exalted concepts: these are the tools of wit" (48).

The "tools of wit"—Vivian never says "literary wit" because she never seems to notice any special circumstances in the literary context, no distinctions worth heeding between the kind of wit that informs poems and the wit that breaks out in negotiations with experience and people out beyond them. Vivian's failure, or refusal, to imagine such differences when dealing with Metaphysical verse or her own crisis is crucial to her professional identity, her personality, and her existential suffering. Her students have tried (and failed) to say that a polished Renaissance sonnet might be both a world apart and a foray into experience before and after the poetic interlude. In their bewilderment in Vivian's classes, they may have wanted to try reading Donne's poetry as an arena where a performance, a free play of words and surprising imaginative connections, might matter in the confrontation with mortality, with the darkness that surrounds—and at the same time might not matter at all, might in fact be an evasion of all that, favoring instead handsome resolutions that can satisfy and console only within the tidy rhymes and scansion of well-made sonnets or the safe slow-time surfaces of some Grecian urn. Twain, Wilde, Wilbur, and Stoppard can engage and evade within the same utterance; their literary wit can at once plunge into darkness and keep it at bay. Vivian Bearing never gives a hint of comprehending that possibility. For her, wit is wit; and because she cannot or will not countenance special and paradoxical dimensions of wit in the literary context, she evidently cannot make distinctions, which, to borrow one of Wilbur's phrases, give "Clearance to our human visions."

Briefly, Vivian tries again to explain her conception of what literary wit is really for, what sides and motions of the mind it can signify or betray. As white-coated technicians close in to transform her back to a dehumanized patient, she offers a hasty backward glance at her own scholarly zeal. The pause is Vivian's: "To the scholar, to the mind comprehensively trained in the subtleties of seventeenth-century vocabulary, versification, and theological, historical, geographical, political, and mythological allusions, Donne's wit is . . . a way to see how good you really are" (20).

Literary wit then as performance first and last—for the poet, for the scholar—and as pretext for self-congratulation and also perhaps for self-deception as to one's own insight and merits. Elsewhere in *Wit* we see that Vivian actually *hasn't* been trained to think this way or to be so self-congratulatory regarding her own analysis of texts and worldly experience. Using literary wit to avoid simplicity, to avoid encounter with the most unsettling paradoxes of both poetry and life: this has been her own project, and not that of her graduate school mentor Professor Evelyn (E. M.) Ashford, with whom Vivian first opened Donne and the Metaphysicals. Decades before (as seen in another flashback) Ashford has tried to convince Vivian not to go back to the library again to rewrite a clumsy, prescriptive paper about these poets but instead to walk out into the sunshine and "Enjoy yourself with your friends"—to experience a little unprogrammatic, unpredictable actual life and perhaps bring that real experience to bear on the reading of Renaissance verse, which Ashford considered as valuable as the Polonius sequence of "historical, geographical, political, and mythological allusions" Vivian commends to anyone who will or won't listen. When Ashford herself, an old woman now, appears unexpectedly in the clinic at the end of the drama to spend a few minutes with Vivian (who by this point is on "soporific" painkillers and well past wit of any variety), Ashford modestly appears as a scholar who nonetheless has lived, in ways that Vivian tragically has not. A greater academic than her protégé, E. M. Ashford has also filled her years with more than decoding poets and intimidating undergraduates. Eighty years old, the retired professor has come to the city to visit her grandchildren. Finding her former student in this terrible state, she has the "mother wit" (in the Shakespearean sense) to realize that at this moment in Vivian's life, more peace, consolation, and even more truth will be found in an intimate reading to her of an old children's book she has with her, The Runaway Bunny, than in those elaborate lyrics to which Vivian Bearing, when she had all her wits about her, has given over so much professional life.

Other than her own disease and the fixed professional habits of her own mind, Vivian Bearing does have a nemesis of sorts in Wit. The lead researcher in her experimental treatment program is the self-satisfied doctor named Jason, the former student who would rather forget all that he ever learned about Renaissance poetry. Not really menacing so much as egregiously unpoetic and unwitty (at least by Vivian's criteria) Jason seems preoccupied and callous in his role as mainstay (by default) in Vivian's life and as a center of her attention. The ironies here are of a sort that Vivian, as a connoisseur of literary irony, ought to appreciate but apparently doesn't. Below those situational ironies, however, there is a deeper and more troubling one: Professor Vivian Bearing has helped to create Jason. The grueling and (to Jason) gratuitous experience of her course in Metaphysical poetry has led him to his conclusions that enzyme kinetics is a subject more poetic than Donne, and that seventeenth-century poetry has no touch of "that sentimental stuff." As a mild try at wit, his remarks are a small whirlpool of significations, blending in a way that would put Professor Bearing on the defensive if this were an outbreak in one of her classes. Jason's wisecracks are facetious, yet they are also sincere; they are superficial yet perhaps accidentally profound. Personally, Jason really has found more "poetry" in hard science than in canonical English verse, because, as he tells Susie, hard science brings him the exhilaration of "looking at things in increasing levels of complexity" and "trying to quantify the complications of the puzzle."

There we have it: if these words don't describe satisfactorily the art of decoding literary wit—Metaphysical or otherwise—they are as good a description as Vivian Bearing offers. Her students have wanted to assert volatile perspectives and possibilities about Donne. They have wanted to suggest that in his verse one can sense fear and internal conflict and minglings of courage and cowardice, perspectives that would actually make the poetry more interesting, more intense—not at the expense of its literary wit but as a celebration of its eloquence. They have wanted to say that the "tricky stuff" in his verse might possibly be evasion as well as magisterial expression, a performance so exquisitely complex as to contain within it recognition that elegant literary performance may signify nothing and count for nothing and that simplicity, as a consummation to be feared, might also be a consummation to be wished.

As a teacher, Vivian Bearing has been closed to such possibilities. When her students have ventured into that uncharted territory, she has apparently waited them out or pushed them back into those readerly bypasses she herself prefers. Oblivious, through most of her life, to that need in others for the "simple human kindness" that she yearns for at the end, she ultimately loses the capacity not only for wit but also for coherent thought, becoming dependent on the professional judgment and kindness of near strangers. The ironies in her final predicament are obvious, frighteningly familiar, and in this context—again, a literary context as well as a life context—deeply provocative. For *Wit* is a narrated play, a story told, enacted (and mysteriously reenacted), and meditated on by a woman who in the final scene dies and transcends . . . perhaps. Drawing attention to its contrivance and reflexivity as well as to its verisimilitude, *Wit* plays the tech talk of the clinic as a chorus and orchestral background to Vivian's solo performances of her own past and present. An actress speaks to us, as a character speaking to us from the stage, the hospital, the classroom, and apparently also from beyond the grave—and the vertigo created by this blurring and blending of identities and conditions and voices is ingenious, clever—*witty*. What results, in fact, is a fuller expression of literary wit than Donne's poem "Death be not proud," not as that sonnet really is or could be, but as Vivian Bearing would control it. Margaret Edson's *Wit* has the wisdom to let the mysteries of experience remain mysterious, beyond the reach of either the professed old-school humanist or the contemporary scientist. In her "soporific" final hours, listening to *The Runaway Bunny* read by the now-old scholar whom she has revered, is Vivian closer to some truth than she was when her wakeful, laboriously clever and highly trained intelligence was humming along at full strength and (just possibly) obstructing the way? That question of course isn't answered. It is not answerable, except perhaps in formulaic literary discourse, the kind of discourse for which Vivian herself ultimately apologizes, offering a single, quiet "Sorry" to her audience after a burst of explication—of Holy Sonnet 6, of death, of her own life of reading. For Vivian, the consolation and triumph of the sonnet tethers to almost nothing, a use of a semicolon in the final verse. In the face of actual and personal death, that kind of intellectual lifeline will not hold. Life, death, poetry, and literary wit, as a lifelong subject of Vivian's concentration—these all slip back into the mystery. What is shuffled off and left behind, there on the gurney with the hospital gowns, the needles, bottles, and tubes, is Vivian Bearing's way of seeing, of reading—the cultural and psychological confinements that only her own death will allow her to escape.

So—a reading of one new play as a kind of morality play, with a theme that happens to correspond tidily with premises of this book, especially when this play is situated (again, with suspect neatness) alongside a certifiable morality play about wit from a golden age of such dramas. A caution: Margaret Edson's play can be understood as witty in a better, more literary, and more obstreperous way than Vivian Bearing in her classroom prime could appreciate. For no matter how many embedded ironies in this text can be totted up, this text mingles its own wit with humility, with a quiet, pervasive recognition that no arrangement of scenes and clever words and clever thoughts can evade for long the deeper mysteries about our experience: what it is for and whether any arrangement of modern life, or modern thinking, or modern drama can be surely other than a wasteful passing of time. In *Wit*, *The Runaway Bunny* does have the literary last word; not John Donne, and not Vivian—and not because *The Runaway Bunny* is inherently the wiser text, or because Donne's sonnets and modern books for children all amount to the same gibberish. On the contrary: this play is inherently gentle enough and skeptical enough about final formulations (literary or otherwise) to avoid such glibness in its final scenes. Vivian's silence at the end is the play's supreme moment of utterance, and also perhaps its supreme moment of literary wit, in which the self, aware at last of so much in a single instant, refuses to limit or profane with words and saying. Vivian's lifelong mistake has been her quest to have the last word—and only at the last does she discover that no word, last or otherwise, is ever sufficient as an expression of what we intend, and what we are.

But such an alternative reading of Wit should be as dubious as the one that it questions. One recognition that emerges here more surely, in Edson's play and even in John Redford's old moralizing farce, is that we do injury to texts, and ultimately to ourselves as readers and reasoners, when we reduce literary wit to irony or cleverness, or when we understand the intellect as an entity distinct or disconnected from the whole self. Donne, Ben Jonson, Robert Herrick, Anne Bradstreet—these poets understood much about literary wit; and they also evidently understood something about love and about "the touch of simple human kindness" that Vivian comes to appreciate at the last. Vivian's tragedy, or at least a part of it, is not that she has dismissed literary wit as superficial and trivial but that she has loved it too much and too narrowly, reading it as a personal refuge and a world elsewhere. In Wit, we never see that Vivian has seen the psychological complexity of Metaphysical poetic discourse or found in it anything larger and richer than this virtuoso aloofness she has loved too much, and around which she has constructed her ethos. Literary wit has not failed Vivian Bearing. Her way of reading it has. She cannot countenance a possibility that literary wit can signify not knowing, or psychological and moral conditions in which serene cleverness does not enthrall and pacify the mind.

In Vivian's reality—meaning reality as imaginatively shaped and defended by this professor in a modern research English department—science is the enemy of poetry, literary wit, and the self. The science she encounters and endures is frightening, insensitive, deficient in beauty, mechanical in its intelligence, verbally pretentious yet inarticulate, and hostile to Vivian's personal and professional ways of seeing. And if John Redford's text brings Wyt and Science together in matrimonial bliss at the end, what of that? Because Science has grown and changed so immensely since Redford's day, could modern literary wit (as controlled by Professor Bearing or described in any other way) have anything in common with whatever "wit" it is that Redford's Wyt represents? In The Play of Wyt and Science, Wyt is only a loosely defined assemblage of virtues that Shakespeare might have taken for granted. Reason, Instruction, Honest Recreation, Diligence—these wiser elders who roll across the stage in The Play of Wyt and Science are not Wyt's rivals or adversaries. They come to him as kin, friends, teachers. Wyt's enemies are only three: Idleness seduces him into a drowsy trance; Ignorance garbs him in a fool's coat and a coxcomb; and Tediousness, appearing out of nowhere in armor and with a visored face, attacks without a quarrel and clubs Wyt so hard that "Wyt fallyth downe and dyeth." The good lad does get on his feet again, as allegorized virtues in old simple plays are wont to do, and armed Tediousness makes no return appearance. We could bring Tediousness back quickly, of course, by bearing down too hard on this light-hearted play from another age. But even a glance at *Wyt and Science*, with Edson's *Wit* fresh in mind, raises the inkling that John Redford might have been on to something. Isn't it possible, for instance, that the worst enemy of wit (literary or otherwise) is neither sentiment nor learning, nor reason, nor any other human quality or practice that from Tudor times to modern ones has been upheld as a virtue? This club-swinging Tediousness doesn't explain himself. He comes crashing out of the wings and puts out the light, knocking silly the human capacity to connect, to think, to speak with the kind of freedom and curiosity that can keep the self and the world interesting, open, and young. What might this signify, if indeed it signifies anything at all?

An answer requires only a little coercion. Road test *The Play of Wyt and Science* as a modern sort of morality play, if only to arrive at relevant speculations. If science has been a happy companion of wit from the days of Bacon through Franklin and the philosphes and straight ahead through Huxley and Einstein and Feynman, is literary wit blackballed from the party? Only perhaps by a scattering of academics like Vivian Bearing, who may have forgotten something that John Redford apparently knew. A constrictive modern scholastic idea of literary wit—which really isn't modern at all but a lingering Romantic and Victorian prejudice—must reacquire empowering notions taken for granted by writers in the English Renaissance. A young Cambridge mathematician in *Arcadia* loves an age of hyperscience for the invigorating uncertainty it brings to the contemplation of life and the self, a wonderfully unstable context in which "everything you thought you knew is wrong." John Redford's Lady Science, who (or which) marries Wyt at the end, bears at least a family resemblance to Valentine's kind of science. The virtue of Wyt's new wife is her festive curiosity and her delight in both knowing and not knowing. But Redford's play can help us open richer possibilities, especially if we can avoid doing a Professor Bearing interpretive job on this gentle allegory. Wit, science, reason, instruction, honest recreation—these values and practices are taken for granted in the play rather than defined, but together they suggest an overarching concept of the self, a paradigm of consciousness in which such virtues and dimensions are assumed to be neither static nor antithetical. In such a consciousness, wit can embrace science without losing that *humanitas* that makes literary wit powerful and appealing as an engagement with experience. In Redford's time, reason is not construed as dulling wit, or formulating it, or setting it at odds with intuition, empathy, piety, or any other psychological or moral value. If Redford's conception of wit seems naïve, at least it is not constricted by prejudice or reduced to fit some model of consciousness that contemporary "science" has already left behind.

Though wit and humor may not be inherently reflexive, literary wit characteristically is. For in disrupting the dramatic circumstance, the intellectual and emotional flow, the textual moment, and the patterns and habits of thought and literary ritual that sustain the moment, literary wit unmasks the contingency of literary utterance, the multiplicity of the dimensions in which the text and its disruption (which is also the text) can resound. In the same instant, Vivian Bearing's rueful wisecracks echo in a hospital ward, in her classroom, in a theater, in some realm beyond worldly life, and also in the mood and manner of the actress who gives Vivian being and voice, and even in an implied printed text, for in the collective rituals of drama, a crafted script, a page with words—and in this case, semicolons—arranged just so, is always there in the backstage shadows. When Vivian quotes and ponders John Donne's wit, Donne's clever lines are also a printed text; and they are also Donne's psychological crisis, and Vivian's crisis of professional and theological faith, and a crisis in the plot and dramatic structure of the play. When Wyt rises from the dead in Redford's play, the literary wit of the drama blossoms, for young men rise from the dead only if they are gods, messiahs, or allegories, and allegories are contrivances that flaunt the freedom of an author's imagination, a freedom so great that it can ignore even rules of life and death.

A recurring assertion in this book has been that literary wit is a much more interesting variety of discourse than our critical strategies, vocabularies, and prejudices have allowed. In the opening chapter, I also proposed that prevailing descriptions of literary wit are outmoded because they depend implicitly on outmoded models of consciousness and Victorian-era theories of literary discourse. When she thinks about Donne, Vivian resists the speculations of her own students because she cannot accept a model of the mind as being serendipitous and methodical in the same moment, or bold and fearful, or direct and evasive, or capable of combinations of thought that embarrass such dualisms as these. The significations of Redford's Wyt are at once too innocent and too disheveled for a modern literary audience schooled on illusory distinctions with which nineteenth-century thinkers organized thinking itself. The exciting uncertainty in Valentine's quantum-theory and chaos-theory universe has its parallel in the worlds of cognitive science and artificial intelligence,[3] and it would be absurd to configure some new theory of literary wit to suit one or another specific, and probably transient, new body of thought about thought itself, some evolving and vigorously debated model of consciousness and the various capacities and agilities of the mind. In a sense, anyone who considers the problematics of literary wit runs a risk of Jason's mistake, and Vivian's as well, for with taxonomies and methodologies replacing each other so rapidly, nobody's hard-won expertise about the structure and activity of human thought can be assumed to remain valid for long. Cognitive-science-based explications for literary wit should spoil overnight, and disciplines in the humanities already have trouble enough of this sort, valorizing and laboring under formulations that have lost credibility in other venues. We need to keep in mind that literary wit can both express and thrive on that kind of instability, that uncertainty about what thinking is and what we consciously and unconsciously intend by our own literary utterance; and we must remember as well that literary wit can be a variety of utterance that rejoices in multiplicity and mystery, reconciling or obliterating in amazing moments the distinctions between the flippant and the profound, the light and the heavy heart, the whim and the credo, the affirmation, the hesitation, the negation.

When we do not know, or do not assume we know, answers about the motions of the mind, literary wit can excite our attention. Happily, we find ourselves in a time of enormous uncertainty with regard to what goes on within the brain, as well as out there in the cosmos. As Richard Powers tells us rather cheerfully, we are now afloat in a gulf of doubt "wider than the millennium itself."[4] In some of the better newspapers, section 3 stories offer a column or two on the latest from the astrophysicists. Stephen Hawking, Andrei Linde, Wendy Freedman, Alan Guth—these surfers of the vast unknown raise possibilities that creation might be perpetual, infinite, with parallel universes, "eternal inflation," and countless new ones (not galaxies, *universes*) arising out of nothing every second. The contemplations grow wilder from there. To think steadily about such a reality, or realities, or whatever they are would seem to require some unimaginably perfect suppleness of mind—or perhaps an admirably *finite* imagination, a salutary obtuseness, so as not to lose grip on whatever it is that passes for sanity in this (perhaps luckily) deluded historical moment. Jason seems admirably and happily finite: his comfort with the rush and flux of scientific inquiry and expertise allows him to wander amid the uncertainties and maintain an ability to function. As a supporting character in *Wit*, he isn't developed clearly enough for us to tell whether he has considered the implications of what he thinks he knows. Though his research does not heal, it does keep moving along; and change and movement for Jason are evidently comfort enough—so long as he doesn't find himself on the other side of a doctor-patient relationship, a victim of the terrible diseases that, in his youth and his health, he regards as a curiosity. Perhaps this is why he is only a clumsy ironist. His imagination cannot bring him to face the moral and psychological consequences of accepting a world without values. Jason is an incarnation of method. Modern literary wit requires, and nurtures, an openness of mind which methods, interpretive and otherwise, inherently resist.

Literary wit explores, exploits, and celebrates differences between conventions of textuality and the broader possibilities inherent in language and the mind. It marks an exhilarating open space between culturally defined processes and constructions relating to the expression and interpretation of written thought and wisdom, and those leaps of the literary imagination that those processes and constructions cannot anticipate, situate, or adequately describe. To put it simply, literary wit signifies distinction between thinking and the rules, habits, and norms for the written representation of thinking. As modern readers and critics, we are confined and coaxed by texts and interpretive strategies into powerful but limited patterns of logic, rituals of subject and verb, of paragraphs, and chapter 1's and chapter 2's, and conclusions and last words and supposedly authoritative citations. It's all valuable; or at least it is what we do. But obviously no imaginable sequence of such stuff could achieve representation, in language and print, of the mental motions and complications of even one sentient human being. Language and grammars make trouble enough; but we have plenty of cultural habits to make the situation worse. Dogmas and agendas are used to reduce the minds of other humans, and the mind of God, to our own deplorable level, flattening and diminishing possibilities of thought and expression. When ideology is on the move—as perhaps it always is—literary wit is devalued, and mechanized ridicule is substituted for the real thing. The culture of the humanities is still a long way from outgrowing its long-standing obsessions with dyads, dialectics, agonistic structures. Though taxonomies and interpretive strategies proliferate and quarrel, the larger patterns of literary discourse have still not made their escape, for it is in the nature of professional scholars to prefer simple contrasts and oppositions. Ideology and agency, love and will, exteriority and interiority, consciousness and false consciousness, humor and seriousness, the diachronic and the synchronic, comedy and tragedy, discours and histoire, genotext and phenotext, hypertext and hypotext, meaning and significance, the readerly and the writerly, the ego and the id, reason and understanding, education and training, sanity and madness, base and superstructure, fancy and imagination, orthodoxy and heterodoxy, art and science, the human and the machine, and life and death, and so on from three hundred years ago until this moment. A modern liberal arts education, especially with a concentration in the humanities or the social sciences, still seems inherently a tour through sequences of paired words, arranged in supposedly meaningful oppositions, as insight into literary and human experience. In some graduate programs, where bright students spend so many additional years acquiring their expertise, the curriculum can be dyads, dualisms, and binaries all the way down.

It is no surprise, then, that the interpretive environment remains perilous for literary wit. It can be paradoxical, dangerous, like Thomasina Coverly's final dream-dance, which accepts, and denies, and fears, and welcomes all in an instant the possibility of an empty shore, or Oscar Wilde's elegantly artful lessons that literary art teaches nothing, or Richard Wilbur's darkly playful camaraderie on the edge of his own abyss, or Mark Twain's world-jarring, text-jarring hodgepodge of agnostic proverbs from Nobody and Nowhere. Literary wit can take us into the core of a text, into its deepest and broadest intensity, its consequence as a human document. To reach that core, one simple-sounding first order of business is to assume, or at least countenance as a possibility, that with regard to the dynamics and interpretation of modern literary wit, almost everything we thought we knew is wrong.

About this undervalued discourse—undervalued because of its subversive powers and its celebration of the mind's freedom from the constructs of culture, of intellectual and literary culture, and of the mind itself— nothing final can or should be said. A last word on literary wit is grotesquely out of the question, except perhaps for this: literary wit anathematizes the ideology of the last word. This short book has been a call to reopen a necessary general conversation not to settle its major issues. There is so much to be done. There is as yet no strong body of commentary about literary wit in the African American experience,[5] or in the Native American or Hispanic American experience, or about its importance in gay and lesbian literary culture or in the postcolonial literary renaissance, or in other literary discourses that now flourish. I have been writing predominantly about a few white English-speaking males. If that provokes or incenses others to take the discussion in very different directions, then so much the better. With that purpose in view, a few larger propositions, or provocations, can be summarized, and a few more added to those with which the book began.

Modern literary wit is resistance to conclusiveness and resistance to the confining powers of language, syntax, grammar, and literary discourse. Literary wit worthy of our attention is resistance to QEDs and complete answers and finality in any sort of human inquiry or narrative. Like the four characters on stage, together and yet two centuries apart, who wordlessly end *Arcadia*, the mind dances onward after the last word, the last scene, in faith and in faithlessness, unbounded by time, or logic, or even one's own utterance, or the ingenious contrivances of one playwright working (alas, or thank heavens) in the English language. Richard Wilbur's brilliant poem "Walking to Sleep" is a skein of words, puns, paradoxes, quick "clever" allusions and associations—the characteristics of the Wilbur voice that some readers value and others patronize. But it is also a poem about a quest to get away from all that, to escape into the dangerous, wordless, unbounded seeing that comes with sleep and deep dreams. The psychological strategy of the poem is to make the mind word-dizzy, so thoroughly hypnotized that talk and similes and likenings and flashes of logic and poems will not matter anymore. The closing lines of "Walking to Sleep" are a bravura performance of literary wit but also an incantation, casting a spell, which, if it works, leaves witty performance behind:

> As for what turn your travels then will take,
> I cannot guess. Long errantry perhaps
> Will arm you to be gentle, or the claws
> Of nightmare flap you pathless God knows where,
> As the crow flies, to meet your dearest horror.
> Still, if you are in luck, you may be granted,
> As, inland, one can sometimes smell the sea,
> A moment's perfect carelessness, in which
> To stumble a few steps and sink to sleep
> In the same clearing where, in the old story,
> A holy man discovered Vishnu sleeping,
> Wrapped in his maya, dreaming by a pool
> On whose calm face all images whatever
> Lay clear, unfathomed, taken as they came. (161)

A breakthrough into a contemplation of everything and nothing, a condition of consciousness in which readiness is truly all, a readiness whose essence is its own liberation from all conventions of conditioning and preparation? After the last line of the loquacious Oscar Wilde's laconic preface, "All art is quite useless," there is a paper-white space of silence; and then with a page turned, thick artful paragraphs start whirling and cranking again, contriving a novel from which we may receive much that is not useless, much because we have been instructed to expect nothing—which does not mean that nothing or uselessness follow but rather that useless expectations should be left at the portal. The welter of epigrams in Pudd'n-head Wilson and atop the chapters of Following the Equator are proverbs out of the dark, a miscellaneous, dubious wisdom of a man who does not exist—not even as a plausible or even consistently visible character in a novel that bears his name—and from an author whose own equatorial ocean of printed words teaches over and over the absurdity of receiving printed words as having anything to do with wisdom or truth.

Literary wit is not only moments of carefree adventure in thought but also celebration of thinking, of a possibility that, like Schrödinger's famous photon, human consciousness can occupy more than one "state" and "place" in a given instant, that it can move with immeasurable speed and multiplicity, that it can operate free of restrictions and limits inherent in any culture or description of thinking. Literary life and the discourse of critics are marred by elaborate attempts to achieve superiority not only to other readings and readers but also to the interrogated text. This is a commonplace fact that sometimes triggers delusions of superiority to all critical discourse. In such an interpretive landscape, literary wit can be misvalued and ignored because it is volatile and troublesome to such rituals of interpretive aggression. If a text, or specific moments within a text, can break away in unpredictable directions, embarrassing the one-two-three dance steps of interpretive methodology, then a natural inclination is to steer clear of that kind of art, as if it were some enemy position too strong to engage head-on. In opening a better discussion of modern literary wit, the primary interpretive need is to cease trying to avoid it or reduce it. When it is read with lively humility, and with a renewed wonder not only for possibilities within the work but also within ourselves, then literary wit can open to us as a source of intensity, insight, and pleasure.

Though it is a serious mistake to undervalue or circumscribe the importance of wit in a literary text, it is also wrong to overvalue its cultural or moral impact, for such overvaluation is likewise a circumscription. The evidence is clear in countless essays, accumulating for most of a century, about how Shakespeare's wit, or Wycherley's, or Fuller's, or Dickinson's, or Wilde's, or Swift's destroyed or devastated or otherwise palpably affected some great wrong, corrupt social institution, or malign cultural practice. This kind of evangelizing for the moral power of literary wit or literary satire saps credibility from the reading. The returns are in: those Armados and Tartuffes confounded on stage did little against pedantry and affectation; Congreve's Witwoud and Lady Wishfort had no measurable effect on the way of the world; Swift's proposal has not perceptibly lightened the miseries of poor children. In fact, to make such claims for the social or moral importance of literary wit is to indulge in a pretense that some of that literary wit may be about. Worse, this way of reading can degrade wit into mechanism, into a presumptuous simple "tactic" or a distraction in a literary text. The pleasure and power of that text might be apprehended better if literary wit is allowed to be anything, and not merely simple and tactical.

The richest kind of literary wit destabilizes and refreshes not just perceptions of social ills and moral hypocrisies but also habits of thought, ingrained patterns of the mind—not ways of seeing *something*, but ways of *seeing*. The delight is a delight of sheer escape—from confinements of culturally inflected identity, even from patterns and values that are revered as transcendent, at least most of the time. In literary criticism, we seem to have learned, by a sequence of painful steps, to free ourselves from reducing every dimension of literary discourse, every rhetorical device, to a means; we have learned the pleasures of discovering or rediscovering poetics as an end. Few varieties of discourse are left behind in the old place, still treated as devices and strategies and tools of the craftsman rather than as strengths of the literary art. Literary wit has unfortunately been one of these castaways—and the harm to criticism and to our conversation with the modern literary heritage has been severe.

Nonetheless, a misvaluation or dismissal of literary wit is a commonplace tactic in interpretive struggles with difficult texts. Professional readers can achieve short-term advantages by keeping such works confined within an aesthetic or thematic category. Outbreaks of literary wit, however, can allow a text to slip loose, playing havoc with such categories and with narratives of cultural and literary history. If the ulterior motive is dominion over texts, then literary wit can be a nuisance, allowing texts to stay wild and have the last laugh.

Valentine's haunting summation echoes as I try to sum up the situation myself, with regard to the potential importance of literary wit in a new century. In a time in which almost everything we thought we knew is wrong, our literary culture seems to cling to deep misapprehensions and complacent assumptions, to cling so tightly that our fingers have grown numb and we no longer know what we are grasping. The incongruity seems enormous, between the kind of reality that an informed public is beginning to apprehend—a universe of universes where possibilities seem endless, where absolutes crumble, and where all theoretical bets, as it were, are off—and a preference, in too many corners of the imperiled humanities, for reductive formulations and interpretive strategies, many of which derive from paradigms concocted when the world had barely ceased being flat and when Valentine's "nearly everything" could still be modeled with crystal spheres. This lag, this resistance, is not quaint, nor is it even intelligently contrarian. As humanistic disciplines strive to catch up with the larger culture—which means to respond to a scientific, technological, commercial culture and regain a measure of plausibility as a locus for expression of culture—the real problems may not lie in specific interpretive idea systems that pass in and out of vogue but rather in the aura of certainty with which they are advanced, the implicit message that some given strategy might settle any literary or cultural question worth thinking about, beyond reclassifying a few texts which may have lost relevance, for the time being, in an endless conversation about who and what we are. Literary wit is a nemesis of certainty. It is free sacrifice to the water gods in Richard Powers's gulf of doubt. It is life-saving affirmation of the certainty that we know nothing for certain. If the millennial gulf really is to be our habitat for the foreseeable future, then literary wit is one of those human achievements that can keep us awake, afloat, moving, and spiritually alive.

But if any part of the above polemic is even partially true, What then of this presumptuous little book—the one you are now done with? Does it end up caught in its own springe? Certainly. Any meditation about possibilities of modern literary wit must recognize the importance of escape from its own descriptions. The varieties of literary wit that we have been sampling, if they are as interesting as I have urged, must ultimately outface all such interpretive assaults. The best that we can achieve is a rediscovery of this neglected dimension of our literary legacy, a reawakening to possibilities, and a questioning of outmoded assumptions that have kept our thinking and our reading closed.

Notes

1. A Description of Literary Wit

1. This book seeks to remedy the misunderstanding and misvaluation of literary wit and to demonstrate its possibilities as a distinct kind of literary discourse, which is quite different from disparaging or dismissing excellent work done in recent decades to engage broader and kindred subjects, such as humor (literary and otherwise), satire, the comic spirit and mode, and the general importance of laughter in cultural and psychological life. To those many and various efforts any new book on a related subject owes much. In reviewing strengths and weaknesses of formulations that have influenced discussion of Anglo-American comic tradition, there are several good places to begin. Chapter 1 of Paul Lewis's *Comic Effects* summarizes twentieth-century studies and pronouncements on

the psychology, aesthetics, and literary significance of humor and laments the continuing restrictive influence of Henri Bergson and Sigmund Freud on literary studies of comic discourse. Though Lewis faults Neil Shaeffer's *The Art of Laughter* for not recognizing the importance of distinctions between humor and laughter and for paying insufficient attention to research in psychology and anthropology, neither Shaeffer's nor Lewis's book emphasizes the peculiarities of the literary context, explores the dynamics of the epigram, or observes differences among literary wit and other varieties of comic discourse. But the omission is common; in fact, throughout the vast body of publication about laughter, comedy, humor, wit, and similar subjects, these distinctions rarely appear and are never sustained. Lewis and Shaeffer both achieve a measure of clarity after a hundred-year jumble of commentary from many theoretical and untheorized perspectives. Among recent works of literary and cultural criticism, Gregg Camfield's *Necessary Madness: The Humor of Domesticity in Nineteenth-Century American Literature* opens up new and important speculative connections between theories of humor, laughter, and wit and transformed models of the cognitive processes (see note 30 below). Camfield, at the moment, is almost alone in trying to modernize discussion of literary humor in light of such new descriptions of consciousness.

With regard to humor and comic discourse as art, some older twentieth-century works retain special value. In *The Act of Creation* Arthur Koestler has difficulties organizing literary art into an array of interconnected categories while also recognizing that "laughter" (which he does not distinguish effectively from humor or wit) need serve no other purpose than to "provide temporary relief from utilitarian pressures" (31), pressures that could include a hypertrophy of literary categories. Susanne Langer's *Feeling and Form: A Theory of Art* made durable connections between the aesthetics of comic discourse and early modern psychological theory. Harry Levin's *Playboys and Killjoys* talks almost exclusively about stage comedies and relies heavily on Bergson and Freud; it describes comedy and humor persuasively as acts of resistance against puritan oppression, that is, against an American cultural habit of requiring a moral dimension in all discourse.

Though Norman Holland's *Laughing: A Psychology of Humor* remains important as a critique of totalizing formulations in circulation in the 1980s with regard to humor and the comic, its own perspectives are for the most part as broad as the commentary that Holland undermines. To review the evolution of modern theoretical and philosophical traditions that Holland challenges, see John Morreall, ed., *The Philosophy of Laughter and Humor*, Nancy Somers and Paul P. Somers, "Literary Humor," and Paul Lauter, ed., *Theories of Comedy*.

With regard to the history of humor and comic discourse and the contributions of individual artists to this tradition, the excellent commentary is vast. In opening up the American comic tradition, Constance Rourke, Kenneth S. Lynn, Henry Louis Gates, Hennig Cohen, M. Thomas Inge, Lawrence Buell, David E. E. Sloane, John Seelye, James Cox, Cameron Nickels, Judith Fetterley, Michael Kiskis, Henry Nash Smith, and a host of others have established the dignity and cultural importance of this legacy, and no useful reopening of Mark Twain or any other American comic genius could go far without them.

2. Readers looking into the modern behavioral sciences for discussions of literary wit will find extensive and diverse arrays of publications that tend to mingle subjects together: humor, laughter, wit, jokes, physiological responses, and models of social contexts and dynamics relating to all of the above. In sorting this out, a good starting point is Antony J. Chapman and Hugh C. Foot's 1976 edited collection, *Humor and Laughter: Theory, Research, and Applications.* Though recent developments in the cognitive sciences and artificial intelligence are not, of course, discussed in a book this old, the essays here represent the sort of interdisciplinary connections that are still favored in opening literary texts from the perspectives of psychology and cultural and physical anthropology. Also helpful in providing an overview is Mahadev L. Apte, *Humor and Laughter: An Anthropological Approach.* Apte lists forty-six different English terms which are commonly used to express varieties and qualities of what he calls the "culturally defined domain of humor" (207).

3. With regard to wit as a distinct variety or dimension of modern Anglo-American literary discourse, the bibliography of useful commentary is brief, though the subject is raised in passing in countless discussions of comedy, humor, farce, and satire and of texts that express any of these genres or modes. Carl Hill's *The Soul of Wit: Joke Theory from Grimm to Freud* is predominantly about wit as a presence in the German cultural landscape and about ways in which *Witz* (meaning wit and jokes of any variety) were theorized and configured from the Renaissance through the end of the nineteenth century. For students of Anglo-American literature and culture, however, Hill's book offers a good history of an English and Continental golden age of wit (in literature and as a philosophical subject) and of the subsequent evolution of thinking about *Witz* as an aesthetic principle and matter of scholarly interest in the German-speaking world: Christian Wolff, Friedrich Schlegel, Christian Wernicke, Friedrich Vischer, Jacob and Wilhelm Grimm, and of course Freud. George Williamson's *The Proper Wit of Poetry* centers on English poetry from about 1603 through the Augustans. However, Williamson nicely describes the cultural shift (the misapprehension, in his view) that drove wit out of poetic and intellectual favor: "For Hazlitt the object of imagination is to magnify, of wit to diminish; and the purposes of wit are served by superficial resemblances between things generally unlike. The end of this course is reached in the doctrine of high seriousness, where Arnold, like Addison, separates force and wit in poetry. The seventeenth century made no such distinctions between wit and imagination, or their suggested rhetorical functions, but rather assimilated them to a perception of unexpected resemblances" (11–12).

4. The modern permutations of *esprit* as a potentially relevant term in theoretical discourse illustrate problems inherent in the adaptation of expressions or categories of analysis from a different language and cultural context. When Bergson made repeated use of *esprit* in *Le Rire,* he signified practices much like those intended by *wit* in Edwardian English parlance: performative mental agility, cleverness, exuberance of mind. The term seems stable, clear, and instructive in Bergson's inquiry, and the translation of his *esprit* into *wit* was sensible and easy. However, Derrida, in his textual analysis of what Heidegger came to intend, over a twenty-year period, by the German word *Geist* renders *Geist* into French (perhaps inevitably) as *esprit*—and in his ruminations both words carry the

weight of humanist teleology, suggesting something more akin to the modern English *spirit* or even *soul*. Derrida notes how interpretive troubles compound in a chronological progression through kindred expressions, from *pneuma* to *spiritus* to *Geist*, disruptions attributable to changes in language, culture, and historical moment, and his own complication here of *esprit* is a case in point. Moreover, in the published English translation of Derrida's lecture, *esprit* is indeed rendered as *spirit*, which probably does not carry the precise (or elegantly imprecise) meanings that Derrida intended and which therefore adds yet another layer of confusion (Derrida, *Of Spirit: Heidegger and the Question*).

5. Barthes is often credited with putting *jouissance* into the vocabulary of postmodern literary criticism. In his own explanations of the meaning of the term, however, *jouissance* denotes an inescapable cognitive and interpretive dissonance, emanating from all directions— text, author (or author-function), context, readerly prejudice, experience, imagination, and so forth. If *jouissance* amuses the textual or cultural critic, that is a side effect of the cacophony of discourse in which the text and reader inevitably participate. The witty utterance is only part of this grander and permanent uncertainty:

> Je vis dans une société d'émetteurs (en étant un moi-même): chaque personne que je rencontre ou qui m'écrit, m'adresse un livre, un texte, un bilan, un prospectus, une protestation, une invitation à un spectacle, à une exposition, etc. La jouissance d'é-crire, de produire, presse de toutes parts; mais le circuit étant commercial, la produc-tion libre reste engorgée, affolée et comme éperdue; la plupart du temps, les textes, les spectacles vont là où on ne les demande pas; ils rencontrent, pour leur malheur, des "relations," non des amis, encore moins des partenaires; ce qui fait que cette sorte d'éjaculation collective de l'écriture, dans laquelle on pourrait voir la scène utopique d'une société libre (où la jouissance circulerait sans passer par l'argent), tourne au-jourd'hui à l'apocalypse. (*Roland Barthes par Roland Barthes*, 84)

> I live in a world of word-senders (while being one myself): everyone I meet or who writes to me or who sends me a book, a text, a leaflet, a protest, an invitation to a show, or an exposition or whatever. The *jouissance* of writing, of producing language, comes at us from all sides. But because this process is essentially commercial, free production remains swollen, crazed, unrelieved. Most of the time, texts and distrac-tions come without our asking; and fare the worse because they collide with one an-other like shirt-tail relations, not like friends, and even less like partners; what results today is a sort of mass ejaculation of *écriture*, in which the possibility of a free and utopian society (where *jouissance* would flourish without commercial exchange), turns instead into apocalypse. (My translation)

6. Kristeva's interest in *jouissance* as a semiotic, psychosexual, and literary construct figures in many of her works. One sustained and perhaps definitive description of Kristevan *jouissance* can be found in *About Chinese Women*, where it represents a primordial and con-tinuing female revolt against the tyranny of the male—a tyranny that extends to lan-guage, conventions of reason, and nearly every other aspect of culture: "let us reject the development of a 'homologous' woman, who is finally capable and virile; and let us

rather act on the socio-politico-historical stage as her negative; that is, act first with all those who refuse and 'swim against the tide'—all who rebel against the existing relations of production and reproduction. . . . let us on the contrary refuse all roles to summon this 'truth' situated outside time, a truth that is neither true nor false, that cannot be fitted in to the order of speech and social symbolism, that is an echo of our jouissance, of our mad words, of our pregnancies" (The Kristeva Reader, 156).

7. Jouissance is a term that Lacan, as both a post-Freudian psychologist and a philosopher, returns to repeatedly, and with a variety of significations, over half a century of writing. The discussion that perhaps comes closest to the subject of the current study is to be found in "Dieu et la Jouissance de la Femme," in Encore, 1972–1973.

Like his erstwhile student Kristeva, Lacan associates jouissance with sexual rebellion and proposes that it is centered in "jouissance clitoridienne" against traditions of courtly love and all other rituals and styles of sexual repression. About women, jouissance, and language, he paternalistically, and paradoxically, comments that the verbal rebellion of modern (French) women is inadequate, lacking the self-awareness of which he is the master:

Il n'y a de femme qu'exclue par la nature des choses qui est la nature des mots, et il faut bien dire que s'il y a quelque chose dont elle-mêmes se plaignent assez pour l'instant, c'est bien de ça—simplement, elles ne savent pas ce qu'elles disent, c'est toute la différence entre elles et moi. (68)

All women are excluded by the nature of things, which is the same thing as the nature of words; and it must be said that if there's one thing which they themselves complain about, it is this—simply put, they don't know the content of what they are saying, and that is the difference between them and me. (My translation)

8. Most of the interpretive models that characterized literary criticism throughout the twentieth century—including field theories of many sorts, oppositional and dialectical arrangements, symmetrical models of action and response and intervention, of class struggle, of gender, of the conscious and unconscious self, and of the mind as essentially linear or (at most) dualistic in its motions and processes—have emanated from paradigms of the nineteenth century or earlier cultural periods. Conventional modern descriptions of verbal irony are a case in point, eliminating the phrase as another possible way of signifying literary wit. If jouissance is too broad to serve, then verbal irony is too narrow. In the glossaries, guidebooks, and literary encyclopedias, verbal irony is described as a discourse of contradiction, of saying one thing and intending the opposite, of "double meaning" (see for example Beckson and Ganz, Literary Terms: A Dictionary, 119, and Holman and Harmon, A Handbook to Literature, 264–65). Construed as a discourse of duality, not multiplicity, verbal irony cannot signify more than one or two intentions in the same utterance or a mind operating in some other pattern than linear or serial action and reaction.

Meanwhile, in other corners of the modern college campus, the best thinking about nearly everything—including about thinking itself—has changed radically, freeing itself from confinement within such structures. We have evolved nonlinear, nondialectical descriptions of thought; classical physics has lost dominance as an explanation of the most interesting dimensions of external reality. If literary wit can overturn conventions and categories, freeing and exhilarating the mind, and if it is, in some way, an empowering escape from culture-based patterns and confinements of thought, then we must avoid scuttling alternative descriptions before they can leave the dock. In other words, we do need to repress, at least for a while, an urge to be categorical straight away, applying once again a dubious array of prenineteenth-century static structures and universals.

9. Camfield, *Necessary Madness*, xii.

10. *Oxford English Dictionary*, 2nd ed., s.v. "wit."

11. Johnson, *A Dictionary of the English Language*, s.v. "wit."

12. For a provocative summary history of the word *wit* as used from the English Renaissance to modern times, see C. S. Lewis, *Studies in Words*, 86–110.

13. *The New Princeton Encyclopedia of Poetry and Poetics*, 1,375.

14. The recent *Encyclopedia of Literature and Criticism* handles wit and humor by ignoring them altogether. There are no index listings for either humor or wit and in Peter Thomson's included brief overview of *comedy*, the cited modern authorities are Bergson and Freud—in other words, nothing at all after 1925. Jeremy Hawthorn's *Glossary of Contemporary Literary Theory* also includes no entries or cross-listings for *wit* or *humor*, and there is nothing on *comedy*, but an introductory note explains that the intention of the book is to define "the more common specialist terms used by recent literary critics or theorists which cannot be found in more general dictionaries or glossaries of literary terms" (ix). Literary-term glossaries seem to be deferred to, on these subjects, by guides to "criticism" and "theory." The latest edition of *The Harper Handbook to Literature* follows another common strategy, collapsing *wit* and *humor* into the same entry and relying on the Victorian heart-head dualism to negotiate both terms:

> Wit is intellectual acuity; humor, an amused indulgence of human deficiencies. Wit now denotes the acuity that produces laughter. It originally meant mere understanding, then quickness of understanding, then, beginning in the seventeenth century, quick perception coupled with creative fancy. Humor . . . was simply a disposition, usually eccentric. In the eighteenth century, which, with the seventeenth century, had debated the terms, *humour* came to mean a laughable eccentricity and then a kindly amusement at such eccentricity. Ben Jonson's comic satires on fixated eccentricities . . . show the way in which early *humor* indicated the laughable. (487)

That is the complete description. Humor became "kindly" (Mark Twain, Alfred Jarry, Dorothy Parker, Christopher Hitchens, Eddie Murphy, Chris Rock, Matt Groening, Maureen Dowd, Pat Oliphant, Jerry Seinfeld, etc., etc. take notice) and wit, as a modern practice, became a cold-hearted intellectual laugh worth two sentences and no more. The *Harper Handbook* is a respected guide, edited by major scholars in the field, including Northrop Frye, Sheridan Baker, and George Perkins, all of whom focus professionally on a literary history that begins around the year 1500 and closes with the death of Wordsworth. If we "*q.v.*" here to the entry for *fancy*, which was historically and culturally coupled with *wit* somehow before *wit* ceased to be interesting, we find this definition: "Day-dreaming wish fulfillment; building castles in air. As William Shakespeare's love-sick Orsino says in *Twelfth Night*: 'So full of shapes is fancy / That it alone is high fantastical.' Samuel Taylor Coleridge saw fancy as a 'mechanical' associative function 'emancipated from the order of time and space' as contrasted with the IMAGINATION, which penetrates sensory images to an essential reality" (188).

If Coleridge organized literary and worldly experience into memorable binaries and clean oppositions, *Harper Handbook*'s descriptions of *fancy* and *wit and humor* operate on similar assumptions. And those descriptions would be valid if modern literary wit, as expressed by powerful artists, offered cool, tidy, cerebral paradoxes that produce only laughter and have nothing to do with other human potentialities, perceptions, or aspirations. But at least this is thoughtful and sensitive to long-term changes in literary culture and intellectual habit.

15. M. H. Abrams's classic *Glossary of Literary Terms*, currently in its seventh edition, handles *wit* under the heading "Wit, Humor, and the Comic." Quoting Pope's great epigram about epigrams, "What oft was thought, but ne'er so well expressed" (*Essay on Criticism* [1711]), the excellent but Freud-favoring *Glossary* talks about *wit* in terms of aggression, frustration, and displaced or sublimated gratification. It recognizes, however, the importance of the epigram to literary wit and pleasures of *détournement* in one's thinking: "'Wit,' that is, now denotes a kind of verbal expression which is brief, deft, and intentionally contrived to produce a shock of comic surprise; its typical form is that of the epigram. . . . The surprise is usually the result of a connection or distinction between words or concepts which frustrates the listener's expectation, only to satisfy it in an unexpected way" (330).

The modern authority featured for this entry is of course *Jokes and Their Relation to the Unconscious*, and Freud's century-old distinction between "harmless wit" and "tendency wit" or "aggressive wit," a distinction addressed to interpersonal behavior rather than to literary discourse, if offered again without question.

16. Harry Shaw, *Concise Dictionary of Literary Terms*, 289–90.

17. Babette Deutsch, *Poetry Handbook*, 194–95.

18. In one forgotten imprint, *The Edinburgh Encyclopedia of Wit*, the anonymous author-compiler, in a time when prescriptions for wit were being laid down firmly, wrote with a graceful humility that took him farther than many of his peers: "The various definitions which have been given of *wit*, do not elucidate the idea, or sensation, we have of it. This property, like that of common sense, is one of which we have the clearest conception, and in rendering the sentiment into language, the sense is lost in the translation. As Cicero finely remarks, 'One may write with more wit upon any subject than upon Wit itself'" (iii).

19. In 1937 *Webster's New International Dictionary* was still appending cautionary glosses to the definition of *wit*. In literary discourse, the Depression-era *Webster's*, perhaps with an eye toward the wisecracking that was already growing dated at the Algonquin, still finds wit

disruptive and a waste of intellect, if hierarchies of value and culturally prescribed habits of thought are to be conserved: "Wit consists typically in a neat turn of speech by which disconnected ideas are unexpectedly associated. It may take the form, as in poetical or whimsical composition, of association of the trivial and sublime, the literal and figurative, the corporeal and abstract, or of things between which there is apparent contrariety or of various senses of the same word (cf. PARONOMASIA); it may consist of deft and spontaneous play with unperceived or artificial analogies, often with a severely critical or satirical or maliciously personal application, always expressed in a way to give mental stimulation and entertainment."

It's easy enough to understand why comic outbreaks would be regarded so in the days of Wordsworth, Tennyson, and a stubbornly morose English monarch and why such formulations would have such durability even as Modernism overswept the Anglo-American literary scene.

20. *The Spectator*, 1:265.

21. "Self-Reliance," *Collected Works of Ralph Waldo Emerson*, 3:24.

22. Though "The Poet" is at times a hymn to liberation, by means of language, from stifling habits of culture and thought, it ends in a cadenza that celebrates dominion, a vision of some still-to-appear Great Poet casting his lordly shadow (as always in Emerson, the poet and the artist are men) over the landscape and all who dwell there: "And this is the reward: that the ideal shall be real to thee, and the impressions of the actual world shall fall like summer rain, copious, but not troublesome, to thy invulnerable essence. Thou shalt have the whole land for thy park and manor, the sea for thy bath and navigation, without tax and without envy; the woods and the rivers thou shalt own; and thou shalt possess that wherein others are only tenants and borders. Thou true land-lord! sea-lord! air-lord!" (Ibid., 2:30).

23. One of the best expositions of this premise is Joanne Feit Diehl, *Women Poets and the American Sublime*.

24. The familiar excerpt comes from Hunt's "Illustrative Essay," which served as an introduction to his collection *Wit and Humour Selected from the English Poets*. But just after the famous remark about the "*Arbitrary Juxtaposition of Dissimilar Ideas for some lively purpose of Assimulation or Contrast*" [Hunt's emphasis], his observations broaden and move toward a perception that wit in the literary context can intend the liberation of thought. Wishing however to cover wit of every sort (in prose, in poetry, in literature, and out beyond it), Hunt dilutes distinctions that he seems on the verge of articulating:

> Wit does not contemplate its ideas for their own sakes in any light apart from their ordinary prosaical one, but solely for the purpose of producing an effect by their combination. Poetry may take up the combination and improve it, but it then divests it of its arbitrary character, and converts it into something better. Wit is the clash and reconcilement of incongruities; the meeting of extremes round a corner; the flashing of an artificial light from one object to another, disclosing some unexpected resemblance or connection. It is the detection of likeness in unlikeness, of sympathy in

antipathy, or of the extreme points of antipathies themselves, made friends by the very merriment of their introduction. (8–9)

25. "On the Combination of Grave and Gay," in *Leigh Hunt's Literary Criticism*, 562.

26. Charles Lamb, "On the Artificial Comedy of the Last Century," in *The Works of Charles and Mary Lamb*, 2:142.

27. "Lectures on the English Comic Writers" (1818), in *Selected Essays of William Hazlitt*, 425–26.

Camfield observes that Kierkegaard and Schopenhauer, the two great nineteenth-century Continental philosophers who engaged with wit, humor, and the comic, kept faith with the rules of the dialectic as they did so (*Necessary Madness*, 31, 158). Accordingly, in their major publications they offer models that are clear, linear, useful, and limited. For Schopenhauer, the ludicrous results from a perception of the incongruity between the intellectual construct and the actuality: the greater the incongruity, the "more violent will be [the] laughter" (*The World as Will and Idea*, 2:271). "The opposite of laughing and joking," he says, "is *seriousness*. Accordingly it consists in the consciousness of the perfect agreement and congruity of the conception, or thought, with what is perceived, or the reality. The serious man is convinced that he thinks the things as they are, and that they are as he thinks them. This is just why the transition from profound seriousness to laughter is so easy, and can be effected by trifles. For the most perfect that agreement assumed by seriousness may seem to be, the more easily is it destroyed by the unexpected discovery of even a slight incongruity. Therefore the more a man is capable of entire seriousness, the more heartily can he laugh" (280–81). Readers now may see such a model as more suggestive of a quirk in nineteenth-century Teutonic culture than of the motions of the modern mind. Schopenhauer offers no distinctions between the literary and the nonliterary context and has little to say about wit; but true to the dialectic, he offers humor as "the double counterpoint of irony" (282).

In *The Concept of Irony*, Kierkegaard is more persistent in arguing for an adversarial relationship between wit and humor, and his famous premise that humor is a gateway to faith and that irony leads to nihilism underlies the widespread modern assumption that wit is characteristically cold and intellectual and hopeless (174–76). Kierkegaard is writing about strategies of theological and philosophical inquiry, not about literary texts, contexts, and imagination. Moreover, critics who continue to cite Kierkegaard as a source on the problem of literary wit and humor should also consider observations in his journals, moments in which he describes wit and irony as more conducive to a higher and broader insight than to a descent into the dark. From entries of 1837:

If I have conceived . . . of the romantic position as a see-saw, the ends of which are characterized by irony and humor, then it follows naturally that the path of this oscilla-tion is extremely varied, all the way from the most heaven-storming humor to the most desperate bowing-down in irony, as if there were a certain rest and equilibrium in this position . . . for irony is first surmounted when the individual, elevated above every-thing and looking down from this position, is finally elevated beyond himself and from this dizzy height sees himself in his nothingness, and thereby he finds his true elevation.

This self-overcoming of irony is the crisis of the higher spiritual life; the individual is now acclimatized—the bourgeois mentality, which essentially only hides in the other position, is conquered, and the individual is reconciled.

The ironical position is essentially: nil admirari; but irony, when it slays itself, has disdained everything with humor, itself included—. (Journals and Papers, 2:254–55)

28. Early in the twentieth century, Georges Bataille was bothered by the narrowness of Bergson's prescriptions and his disinclination to see humor, laughter, or wit as psychologically and intellectually restorative:

I was in London (in 1920) and I was to have dinner with Bergson; . . . I had this curiosity—while at the British Museum I asked for Laughter (the shortest of his books); reading it irritated me—the theory seemed to me to fall short (for this reason, the public figure disappointed me: this careful little man, philosopher!) but the question—the meaning of laughter which remained hidden—was from then on in my eyes the key question (linked to happy, infinite laughter, by which I saw right away that I was possessed), was the puzzle which at all costs I will solve (which, solved, would itself solve everything). For a long time I knew nothing other than a chaotic euphoria. (Inner Experience, 66; Bataille's italics)

Bataille eventually arrives at perceptions that, like Bergson's, are not specific to literary discourse but are more acutely aware of the psychological and intellectual revolution that humor and laughter can intend: "But laughter does not reach merely the peripheral regions of existence—it does not have as its object only fools or children . . . ; by a necessary reversal, it returns from the child to the father, from the periphery to the center, each time that the father or the center betray, in their turn, their insufficiency. . . . The necessity for reversal is so important that it had, at one time, its consecration; there is no constitution of society which does not have, on the other hand, the challenging of its foundations; rituals show it: the saturnalias or festivals of madmen reversed the roles" (90).

In Bergson, A. R. Lacey provides a very useful overview of the strengths and weaknesses of Le Rire, and of its grounding in premodern dialectical paradigms and in now-dubious models of consciousness:

Bergson criticises other views because they only give necessary conditions for the comic and not sufficient conditions which could provide a recipe. Laughter is often explained, for instance, in terms of surprise or contrast; we laugh at things because they are unexpected or not as they should be. But this clearly won't do because there are so many surprises or contrasts that we don't laugh at. But does Bergson escape the same criticism? We laugh at human automata—but we don't if our emotions are aroused or if we are not in company. If Bergson's theory can be tidied up by exception clauses, why couldn't other theories too? (192–93)

29. One helpful recent evaluation of Bergson on the subject of laughter and wit is Louisa

Jones's, "The Comic as Poetry: Bergson Revisited." Jones observes a core problem with the Bergson formulations: "Bergson cannot foresee that the emerging twentieth century, with all its diversities, will tend to reject the body/soul dualism" (78–79) on which his theory depends and that his separation of the literary artist from the wit is problematic because "the modern aesthetic, in all genres, frequently follows Baudelaire rather than Bergson, playing on the laughter that hurts, mixing the farcical and the lyrical ironically" (82). Also see Thomas Pugh, "Why Is Everybody Laughing? Roth, Coover, and Meta-Comic Narrative." Pugh observes that the contemporary comic narrative can subvert "Bergson's view of the comic as a social narrative because it subverts the opposition between 'life' and 'art' couched in terms of 'reality' and 'fiction'" (76).

30. A succinct recent summary of the problems of relying on Freud as a guide to humor, wit, and the comic in literary discourse can be found in Camfield's fine closing essay, "Humorneutics":

> What seems to me the ultimate inadequacy of Freud's interpretation of humor lies in his insistence that we are compelled to suffer. Freud's system of psychology, even though it changed over the course of his career, is based on a mechanical model of mind and, even as he increasingly renounced the neurological systems on which he originally based his theories, he never renounced the mechanical, Newtonian determinism of his scientific predisposition. Recognizing his deterministic bias, then, I wonder, when I see him insist that we are "compelled to suffer," about the agency behind that compulsion. Who or what compels us? What arrows of reality strike all of us? . . . To call one emotional reaction to the world truth and the other illusion is a neurotic compulsion to find the world meaningful in one dimension only. Pleasure is as real as pain, and the humorist, even when using the abstract reality of pleasure's existence to compensate for immediate and actual pain, is not "repudiating reality" but instead insisting that meaning can be larger than the moment, that there is more than one meaning available to humanity. Humor in this sense is a defiant assertion of the contingent and plural nature of truth. (155)

Influential objections (from the perspective of literary discourse and criticism) to Freud's way of seeing human psychology, utterance, and most of worldly experience in terms of binary oppositions, also turn up in Derrida's essay "*Différance*": "According to a schema that never ceased to guide Freud's thought, the movement of the trace is described as an effort of life to protect itself by *deferring* the dangerous investment, by constituting a reserve. . . . And all the oppositions that furrow Freudian thought relate each of his concepts one to another as moments of a detour in the economy of *différance*. One is but the other different and deferred, one differing and deferring the other. One is the other in *différance*, one is the *différance* of the other. This is why every apparently rigorous and irreducible *opposition* . . . comes to be qualified, at one moment or another, as a 'theoretical fiction'" (121).

31. For instance, Martin Grotjahn's *Beyond Laughter* offers minor extensions and distinctions with regard to Freud's theorization of humor but presents Freud's writings on the subject as definitive. Max Eastman's oft-cited, anecdotal *Enjoyment of Laughter* is generally Freud-

ian in its premises; more recently, Marcel Gutwirth's *Laughing Matter: An Essay on the Comic* presents a fine overview of Freud and his subsequent detractors on the subject of humor, but acquiesces to Freud's principles, except that of "psychic economy," and likewise declines to see crucial distinctions between the literary context and any other.

32. Cultural historians often challenge the factuality of Bakhtin's concept of carnival as a transnational, transcultural presence though centuries of medieval life and his description of the relationship of carnival to literary discourse. For example, Terry Castle's *Masquerade and Civilization: The Carnivalesque in Eighteenth-Century English Culture and Fiction* is a study that breaks significantly with several of Bakhtin's generalizations. A good overview of the controversy can be found in Caryl Emerson's *The First Hundred Years of Bakhtin* (162–205). About carnival, Emerson concludes that by the 1990s no one "doubted that Bakhtin's image of carnival was utopian fantasy. It had long been a matter of record, stressed by cultural historians both East and West, that real-life carnival rituals—although perhaps great drunken fun for the short term—were not necessarily cheerful or carefree." Defending the concept by narrowing it, however, Emerson proposes that "since Bakhtin . . . reads so much of Rabelais's novel through the lens of preliterate (and arguably Slavic) folklore and thereby de-historicizes the literary text, French medieval society appears rigidly, artificially stratified. Bakhtin functions here more as a mythographer than as a literary scholar or social historian" (164). Emerson's perspective here seems similar to Richard Berrong's in *Rabelais and Bakhtin: Popular Culture in* Gargantua and Pantagruel that with regard to Rabelais and carnival, Bakhtin offers courageous anti-Stalinist political allegory but naive or misguided social history. "Popular culture does figure in *Gargantua and Pantagruel*," says Berrong, "but in a way far more complex than the one Bakhtin proposed" (13). A useful evaluation of the impact of *Rabelais and His World* on postmodern literary studies is Simon Dentith, "Bakhtin's Carnival" (65–87) in his volume *Bakhtinian Thought*.

33. Kristeva has attempted to expand and gender the Bakhtinian concept of the carnivalesque, accommodating the term to her translinguistic conceptions of "text," intertextuality, orthodoxy, resistance, and codes of discourse. See *Desire in Language: A Semiotic Approach to Literature and Art*, 67–80.

34. For a summary of objections to Bakhtin's use of medieval history, see Dentith, *Bakhtinian Thought*, 70–71, 73–76, and note 32 above.

35. Nancy A. Walker's *A Very Serious Thing: Women's Humor and American Culture*, a social history of humor by women from the middle of the nineteenth century through Ellen Goodman and Erma Bombeck, observes some fundamental differences between the genders with regard to comic discourse and between "women's humor" and feminist humor. The wit and humor engaged with here are interpreted as social criticism, as strategies in a power struggle and as a subversion of stereotypes related to an oppressed social, domestic, and intellectual status. Though she pays no attention to the special potentialities of wit in the literary context, Walker does point out limitations of Freud's findings when applied to wit and humor by women (25–26). She also quite rightly observes that most twentieth-century academic and belles lettres overviews of "American humor" have ignored humor by American women.

One exception, as Walker notes, is Alfred Habegger's *Gender, Fantasy, and Realism in American Literature*. Habegger was one of the first American critics to observe that the wit and humor that have been valorized in our literary and cultural histories exemplify a masculinist aesthetic and that as humorists men have been allowed to play the "bad boy" because the culture has required women to embody gentility (see 117, 124–25).

36. Two recent examples are Sherman Alexi's *The Lone Ranger and Tonto Fistfight in Heaven* and Simon J. Ortiz's *Men on the Moon: Collected Short Stories*.

37. About the modern epigram as a variety of literary discourse, the commentary is scarce and unsystematic. The most sustained and helpful discussions of the art of the epigram deal with classical texts, with poetry of the Renaissance, or with literature of the seventeenth and eighteenth centuries. For a useful discussion of the English Renaissance response to the classical epigram, see Ann Baynes Coiro, *Robert Herrick's Hesperides and the Epigram Book Tradition*, esp. 47–69. Coiro is especially helpful on the subject of Thomas More and the special philosophical, theological, and political power that the epigram, in the right historical moment, can sometimes achieve (61–69). Though Hoyt H. Hudson died before he could complete what promised to be a masterwork, *The Epigram in the English Renaissance*, the small volume that appeared posthumously, offers a fine description of the epigram (as both utterance and brief poem) as it was understood and emulated by English writers of the sixteenth and seventeenth century, and of the classical models that they adapted.

2. A Calendar and a Preface

1. The two writers had scattered direct encounters and many mutual acquaintances. Constance Wilde's autograph book shows that Twain visited the Wildes at one of their residences in London; Clara Clemens reported that her father and Wilde encountered each other in a hotel in Bad Nauheim in the summer of 1892. In *Century Magazine* in 1887, Wilde published a friendly review of Twain's sketch "English as She Is Taught." See Rodney Shewan, *Oscar Wilde: Art and Egotism*, 38–39; J. R. LeMaster and James D. Wilson, eds., *The Mark Twain Encyclopedia*, 792.

2. There are several fine accounts of Mark Twain's efforts to create and sustain his worldwide celebrity. The most detailed is Louis J. Budd, *Our Mark Twain*. See also Andrew J. Hoffman, *Inventing Mark Twain*, esp. xii–xiv, 152–67, 312–43; Justin Kaplan, *Mr. Clemens and Mark Twain*, 228–38. For the story of Wilde's courtship of the press and the Anglo-American public after 1885, see Richard Ellmann, *Oscar Wilde*, 261–310, 346–70, 380–83.

3. See Ellmann, *Oscar Wilde*, 78–79, 157–58, 164, 206, 220. See also Gary Schmidgall, *The Stranger Wilde*, 65–70.

4. Ellmann, *Oscar Wilde*, 151–52, 186–92.

5. Although Twain's biographers report that the white suit did not become his regular public attire until the final three years of his life, Twain was dressing in unconventional lighter hues frequently as he reached middle age and as his red hair lightened toward gray and white. Earlier in his career, long before he had ever heard of Wilde, there had been a sealskin coat and, of course, a Hartford house designed to break the rules of

taste, astonish visitors, and create a stir and a landmark. See Budd, *Our Mark Twain*, 206–12; Kaplan, *Mr. Clemens*, 181–85.

6. See Everett Emerson, *The Authentic Mark Twain*, 151–74; Hoffman, *Inventing*, 351–77; Kaplan, *Mr. Clemens*, 277–331.

7. See Ellmann, *Oscar Wilde*, 292–94, 305–10.

8. See, for example, Twain's famous 22 September 1889 letter to William Dean Howells about needing a "pen warmed up in hell" to do the kind of writing that he contemplated after the completion of *Connecticut Yankee*. (*Selected Mark Twain–Howells Letters*, 286–87).

9. For recent commentary on *Pudd'nhead Wilson* as a moral and political document, see Susan Gillman and Forrest Robinson, eds., *Mark Twain's Pudd'nhead Wilson: Race, Conflict, and Culture*. Also see Brook Thomas, "Tragedies of Race, Training, Birth, and Communities of Competent Pudd'nheads," 754–85, and Shelly Fisher Fishkin, "Race and Culture at the Century's End: A Social Context for *Pudd'nhead Wilson*," 1–27. See also Henry Nash Smith, *Mark Twain: The Development of a Writer*, 171–84.

10. *Pudd'nhead Wilson* is a popular focus of commentary, yet surprisingly little has been said about *Calendar* as a text in its own right or as a consequential presence in the narratives in which it appears. For a brief but provocative discussion of *Calendar*'s importance in developing David Wilson as a character, see David E. E. Sloane, *Mark Twain as a Literary Comedian*, 179–81. Also see Lawrence Howe's *Mark Twain and the Novel*, 202–3.

11. Even so, and in the midst of a storm of fine publication about Wilde's aesthetics, his martyrdom, and his impact on modern and postmodern culture, there is very little in the way of sustained commentary on the preface as a discrete text, a manifesto, or (as I shall suggest) a poem. For useful commentary on what was at stake in the battle over the novel in the year of its publication, see Lawrence Danson, *Wilde's Intentions: The Artist in His Criticism*, 128–39. Much of the recent commentary on *Dorian Gray* favors the perspectives of gender studies and Queer Theory. For a summary of how the novel can be approached from such perspectives, see Elaine Showalter, *Sexual Anarchy*, 173–77. Melissa Knox's *Oscar Wilde: A Long and Lovely Suicide* offers a refreshed psychoanalytic reading of the novel but makes scant mention of the preface. Michael Patrick Gillespie's *Oscar Wilde and the Poetics of Ambiguity* offers a detailed account of the publication of the novel, the critical furor, and the general circumstances that surrounded the writing of the preface but little about its content, except that it "seeks to reply directly to many of the specific criticisms of the moral atmosphere that characterized the serialized version. In its attempts to facilitate full understanding, it draws sharp attention to a number of the controlling creative assumptions that emerge only implicitly over the course of the novel's narrative" (55).

12. See R. Kent Rasmussen, *Mark Twain A–Z*, 379–80.

13. Budd, *Our Mark Twain*, 140.

14. Donald L. Lawler describes the early versions of the novel and its preface in his excellent critical edition of *The Picture of Dorian Gray*, x–xiii. All quotations from the preface are taken from this edition (3–4).

15. For example, in the widely used college edition of *Dorian Gray* in *The Portable Oscar Wilde*, the complete novel is reprinted, but without Wilde's signature on the preface.

16. Marcus Aurelius, *Meditations*, 22.

17. In a footnote in the Norton Critical Edition of *Dorian Gray*, Lawler comments that Wilde's preface repeats "rather sententiously the major points of his aesthetic creed at the time," and reveals that "Wilde could be every bit as pompous as those he ridiculed . . . " (3n).

18. For an acerbic, detailed account of the novel's composition, see Hershel Parker, "Pudd'nhead Wilson: Jack-leg Author, Unreadable Text, and Sense-Making Critics," in his *Flawed Texts and Verbal Icons: Literary Authority in American Fiction*, 147–80.

19. All citations from *The Tragedy of Pudd'nhead Wilson* are taken from the 1894 edition.

20. *The Collected Writings of Ambrose Bierce*, 193.

21. *Webster's New Universal Unabridged Dictionary*, s.v. "calendar."

22. Norman Page, *An Oscar Wilde Chronology*, 39, 41.

23. "A Few Maxims for the Instruction of the Over-Educated," in Wilde, *Plays, Prose Writings, and Poems*, 519.

24. "Phrases and Philosophies for the Use of the Young," ibid., 521.

25. Ibid.

3. Witty Plays, Witty Poems

1. Patricia Wallace, introduction to "American Poetry since World War II" in *The Norton Anthology of American Literature*, 2:2405–6.

2. Linda Wagner-Martin, in *The Heath Anthology of American Literature*, ed. Paul Lauter et al., 2:2021.

3. Wilbur, *New and Collected Poems*, 9. Unless otherwise stated, the poetry of Richard Wilbur is quoted from *New and Collected Poems*, and page numbers will be given in the text.

4. Rich, *Collected Early Poems: 1950–1970*, 119.

5. *Arcadia* premiered at the Royal National Theatre in April 1993, and the only published edition to date is the Faber and Faber imprint of the same year (page numbers in the text refer to that edition). Because the play is so recent, useful commentary about it (other than reviews in newspapers and magazines) is scarce. Articles about *Arcadia* have focused on unpacking its complex plot and laying out its "serious" themes and allusions. In "The Arts, the Sciences, and the Making of Meaning: Tom Stoppard's *Arcadia* as a Post-Structuralist Play," Heinz Antor extensively summarizes the play and its philosophical and scientific content, but without noticing its wit or its comic dimensions. Peter W. Graham does observe that *Arcadia* is "a comedy centering on a country family," but reads the play as a handsome piece of mechanical structure and order, rather than as an exuberant questioning of all such paradigms: "*Arcadia*'s genius exerts itself through juxtapositions, intellectual theatrics, and the pattern of performance. The shape of the play might be seen as a dramatic analogue to the palimpsest of garden styles at Sidley Park, or as the blend of pattern and unpredictability that is the province of nonlinear mathematics" ("Et in *Arcadia* Nos," 314). Another basic explication of major intellectual subjects in the play is Jeffrey Kramer and Prapassaree Kramer, "Stoppard's *Arcadia*: Research, Time, Loss."

There are many useful studies of Stoppard's work through the end of the 1980s. See, for example, Anthony Jenkins, *The Theatre of Tom Stoppard*, Paul Delaney, *Tom Stoppard: The Moral Vision of the Major Plays*, Katherine Kelly, *Tom Stoppard and the Craft of Comedy: Medium and Genre at Play*, and Neil Sammells, *Tom Stoppard, the Artist as Critic*.

6. It turns out that Chater and Co. were expelled from the house just before the duel (Mrs. Chater having been caught in a tryst with Captain Brice) and that all of them had subsequently gone to the Caribbean as a ménage. To keep Chater occupied, Brice secured a job for him as a botanist, and he died in Martinique from a monkey bite—not from a bullet from Septimus or Byron. After Thomasina's death in the fire, Septimus has evidently (we can't be sure) moved into the new-old hermitage on the park grounds, dying there in 1834 at the age of forty-seven, having spent decades and reams of paper trying to work out what Thomas Love Peacock (as quoted by Hannah) calls "the restitution of hope through good English algebra," and living in despair overcome by "the melancholy certitude of a world without light or life," and by the loss of Thomasina.

7. All quotations from *The Importance of Being Earnest* are from Wilde, *Plays, Prose Writings, and Poems*. Page references to this edition will be given in the text.

8. Septimus might become the hermit of Sidley Park, or he might not, or he might both be *and* not be the hermit, because in *Arcadia* history and personal identity, like quantum mechanics, have such maddening and heartening multiplicities and mysteries. When Gus Coverly, in the last scene, brings Hannah the sketch by Thomasina of "Septimus holding Plautus," Hannah believes that she knows the answer—that Septimus has spent years in the hermitage destroying himself in grief for the lost girl and the lost safe universe. But a young and happy Septimus is dancing in that same room and moment, with a living Thomasina. When are we most genuinely what we are?

9. On Wilbur's poetry, many of the interesting reviews and critical studies published before 1982 were collected by Wendy Salinger in *Richard Wilbur's Creation*. More recent appraisals of his work include Peter Harris, "Forty Years of Richard Wilbur: The Loving Work of an Equilibrist," Anthony Hecht, "The Pathetic Fallacy," and Ben Howard, "Incarnate Lights," and a special issue of *Christianity and Literature* on Richard Wilbur which included essays by Clara Claiborne Park, Jewel Spears Brooker, Cleanth Brooks, Marjory Scheidt Payne, and Bruce Michelson. The book-length studies of Wilbur are Donald Hill, *Richard Wilbur* (New York: Twayne, 1967), Bruce Michelson, *Wilbur's Poetry: Music in a Scattering Time*, John B. Hougen, *Ecstasy within Discipline: The Poetry of Richard Wilbur*, and Rodney Stenning Edgecombe, *A Reader's Guide to the Poetry of Richard Wilbur*.

10. As early as 1948, both Babette Deutsch and Allan Swallow were reviewing Wilbur's first collections as "clever" and "witty"; in a thoughtful 1951 essay in the *Harvard Advocate*, Donald Hall tried to distinguish between two schools of poets that were developing in postwar years: the "Wurlitzer wits" and the "School of Elegance." Counting John Ciardi, John Frederick Nims, and Karl Shapiro as "Wurlitzer wits," poets whose wit was cerebral, satirical, and ironic, Hall singled out Wilbur, James Merrill, and William Jay Smith as members of a School of Elegance, and saw Wilbur as having the "widest range of emotion and subject matter." Hall was on to the fact that Wilbur's literary wit was of a different character from other witty poets of his time, and he remained steadfast in his belief in Wilbur's importance; but in subsequent years his distinctions about varieties of wit in

modern verse were lost on other reviewers. For example, Ian Hamilton, championing the Lowell–Plath confessional mode, was evidently incensed by Wilbur's poem "Cottage Street, 1953" (a poem in part about Sylvia Plath's "brilliant negative") and in retaliation harped on Wilbur's literary wit as grounds for calling the *New and Collected Poems* the work of a poet who, because of his lifelong interest in literary wit, "cultivation," and "subtlety," "underextended his considerable talent" ("A Talent of the Shallows," 999). See also Deutsch, review of *The Beautiful Changes*, Swallow, "Some Current Poetry," and Hall, "Richard Wilbur and Others."

11. Michelson, *Wilbur's Poetry*, see esp. pp. 36–83.
12. Randall Jarrell, "A View of Three Poets," in Salinger, *Wilbur's Creation*, 47.
13. F. C. Golffing, "A Remarkable New Talent," in Salinger, *Wilbur's Creation*, 32.
14. Michael Benedikt, "Witty and Eerie," in Salinger, *Wilbur's Creation*, 104.
15. Cleanth Brooks, "This World and More: The Poetry of Richard Wilbur," *Christianity and Literature* 42, no. 4 (1993): 544.
16. For example: in the highly influential *Consciousness Explained*, David Dennett offers an appendix "For Philosophers" who remain allegiant to classical, Cartesian, or dialectical models of thinking:

> The closer you get, the more the disunity, multiplicity, and competitiveness stand out as important. The chief source of the myth of the Cartesian Theater, after all, is the lazy extrapolation of the intentional stance *all the way in*. Treating a complex, moving entity as a single-minded agent is a magnificent way of seeing pattern in all the activity: the tactic comes naturally to us, and is probably even genetically favored as a way of perceiving and thinking. But when we aspire to a science of the mind, we must learn to restrain and redirect those habits of thought, breaking the single-minded agent down into miniagents and microagents (with no single Boss). Then we can see that many of the *apparent* phenomena of conscious experience are misdescribed by the traditional, unitary tactic. The shock-absorbers that deal with the tension are the strained identifications of heterophenomenological items (as conceived under the traditional perspective) with events of content-fixation in the brain (as conceived under the new perspective). (458)

A century before Dennett, William James's heretical thinking about thinking was taking James in a similar direction, though at the dawn of modern psychology James's prose was necessarily more impressionistic:

> Instead of thoughts of concrete things patiently following one another in a beaten track of habitual suggestion, we have the most abrupt cross-cuts and transitions from one idea to another, the most rarefied abstractions and discriminations, the most unheard-of combinations of elements, the subtlest associations of analogy; in a word, we seem suddenly introduced into a seething cauldron of ideas, where everything is fizzling and bobbing about in a state of bewildering activity, where partnerships can be joined or loosened in an instant, treadmill routine is unknown, and the unexpected seems the only law. According to the idiosyncrasy of the individual, the scintillations

will have one character or another. They will be sallies of wit and humor; they will be flashes of poetry and eloquence; they will be constructions of dramatic fiction or of mechanical devices, logical or philosophic abstractions, business projects, or scientific hypotheses. . . . But, whatever their differences may be, they will all agree in this—that their genesis is sudden and, as it were, spontaneous. ("Great Men, Great Thoughts, and the Environment," *Atlantic Monthly* 46, [October 1880], quoted in William H. Calvin, *The Cerebral Code: Thinking a Thought in the Mosaics of the Mind*, 98)

17. Clive James, "When the Gloves Are Off," in Salinger, *Wilbur's Creation*, 106–17.

18. In a 1992 essay, "From Left to Right: Olson and Wilbur," Edward Butscher reheated the cliché that Charles Olson was "a howling cellar monster, part crank, part martyr" (Olson in fact was domesticated enough to serve as president of a college) and located Wilbur, once again, as a figure on the genteel, cautious Right, with antiformalist, anticomposure Olson thundering on the heretical Left. If Olson bellows on the page, then Olson is fierce and bold; and as for bothersome poets who do not bellow, who scan and do wordplay and sometimes rhyme . . . what to say of them? "Wilbur's inordinate fear of evoking the terror that births beauty (to borrow a Rilkean trope) tokens a compulsive reflex that can be artistically self-defeating, impelled, for example, to convert anxiety into sermonizing allegories" (66).

When all else fails, there is always mail-order psychoanalysis: Wilbur's literary wit and artifice are a "compulsive reflex." With such anxious simplisms refusing to give way, small wonder that even sharp graduate students flinch from engagement with poetry after Stevens, and that for a broader American public the genre counts for nothing as a cultural practice. In the work of such an artist, isn't it possible that finesse and indirection might not be symptoms of "emotional retardation" or evasion of truth but rather the heart of a drama unfolding from poem to poem, a drama of the self struggling to keep certain horrors and passions uncertainly at bay—and of the psyche safe for the moment perhaps yet never truly saved by its relentless thinking?

4. Wit, Wyt, and Modern Literary Predicaments

1. A standard edition of *Wyt* is in Joseph Quincy Adams's anthology, *Chief Pre-Shakespearean Dramas*.

2. All quotations from *Wit* are from the 1999 edition. Page numbers are given in the text.

3. Cognitive neuroscience and related disciplines focused on consciousness, intentionality, and processes of thought are energized by controversy, research from psychology and biological sciences, technological leaps in artificial intelligence (AI), and gifted outsiders saying subversive things about the nature of the mind. For interested nonspecialists, a prudent strategy is to try to let go of discredited models without cleaving to any particular new ones—at least not yet. To understand how far such disciplines have moved from assumptions that supported Victorian-era psychology and literary analysis, one good place to begin is with connectionism, a loose heading for a dynamic array of theoretical models and investigative strategies that accept a hypothesis that thinking is essentially a

nonlinear process. Though connectionism can seem a locus of controversy rather than a new model of the mind, connectionism's various schools firmly reject Cartesian and Freudian models of consciousness and twentieth-century descriptions inspired by the structure and operations of serial computers. In *Bright Air, Brilliant Fire*, Gerald Edelman, a Nobel Prize–winning physiologist and leading advocate for new directions in the cognitive sciences, catalogs a range of outworn ideas that a modern public, and many fellow scientists, must finally move beyond:

> One is that human beings are born with a language acquisition device containing the rules for syntax and constituting a universal grammar. Another is the idea, called objectivism, that an unequivocal description of reality can be given by science (most ideally by physics). This description helps justify the relations between syntactical processes or rules and things or events—the relations that constitute semantic representations. Yet another idea is that the brain orders objects in the "real" world according to classical categories, which are categories defined by sets of singly necessary and jointly sufficient conditions.
>
> I cannot overemphasize the degree to which these ideas or their variants pervade modern science. They are global and endemic. But I must also add that the cognitivist enterprise rests on a set of unexamined assumptions. One of its most curious deficiencies is that it makes only marginal reference to the biological foundations that underlie the mechanisms it purports to explain. The result is a scientific deviation as great as that of the behaviorism it has attempted to supplant. The critical errors underlying this deviation are as unperceived by most cognitive scientists as relativity was before Einstein and heliocentrism was before Copernicus.
>
> What is it these scholars are missing, and why is it critical? They are missing the idea that a description of the mind cannot proceed "liberally"—that is, in the absence of a detailed biological description of the brain. They are disregarding a large body of evidence that undermines the view that the brain is a kind of computer. They are ignoring evidence showing that the way in which the categorization of objects and events occurs in animals and in humans does not at all resemble logic or computation. And they are confusing the formal power of physics as created by human observers with the presumption that the ideas of physics can deal with biological systems that have evolved in historical ways. (14)

Concerned that such constrictive models of consciousness (e.g., low-speed serial computers) will be supplanted by dubious models borrowed from elsewhere, Edelman is hostile to the spread of quantum paradigms by anyone, whether credentialed physicists or enthusiastic amateurs. "Quantum this, quantum that, quantum everything," he grumbles (263), and he gives special attention to refuting propositions of Roger Penrose, the British mathematician and astrophysicist who has called for quantumizing cognitive theory. In AI circles and among biological neuroscientists, Penrose's well-known 1989 book, *The Emperor's New Mind*, finds little favor, perhaps because it denies the possibility that AI, which Penrose describes as still operating from an assumption that the brain is essentially algorithmic in its functions, will achieve understanding of "all mental qualities—thinking, feeling, intelligence, understanding, consciousness" (17), and be-cause Penrose evangelizes for a quantum paradigm with little solid research to support his propositions.

The rift between Penrose and Edelman is one of many such in the contemporary de-bates about consciousness, intelligence, and the nature of thought, and no lay person can presume to enter a matter of this complexity and consequence. With relevance to wit, however, Penrose and Edelman do seem to share one premise that would have seemed outlandish in 1900, when theories of humor, laughter, and wit were taking a form that still persists. They begin from a proposition that consciousness is much more complex and much less serial, or linear, than nineteenth-century psychology, neuroscience, and academic humanism could conceive. Penrose's proposal of consciousness as a quantum computer might show more fervor than precision—but when it is considered alongside other new formulations, including connectionism, fin de siècle ideas of mind, still domi-nant in humanist disciplines, seem all the more quaint:

> "oneness" of conscious perception seems to me to be quite at variance with the picture of a parallel computer. That picture might, on the other hand, be more appropriate as a model for the *unconscious* action of the brain. Various independent movements—walking, fastening a button, breathing, or even talking—can be carried on simulta-neously and more or less autonomously, without one being consciously aware of *any* of them!
>
> On the other hand, it seems to me that there could conceivably be some relation between this "oneness" of consciousness and *quantum parallelism*. Recall that, ac-cording to quantum theory, different alternatives at the quantum level are allowed to coexist in linear superposition! Thus, a *single quantum state* could in principle consist of a large number of different activities, all occurring simultaneously. This is what is meant by quantum parallelism, and we shall shortly be considering the theoretical idea of a "quantum computer," whereby such quantum parallelism might in principle be made use of in order to perform large numbers of simultaneous calculations. If a conscious "mental state" might in some way be akin to a quantum state, then some form of "oneness" or globality of thought might seem more appropriate than would be the case for an ordinary parallel computer. (399)

An inclusive overview of "the new cognitive neuroscience" is Stephen M. Kosslyn and Olivier Koenig's *Wet Mind*, which attempts to find points of reconciliation between AI and biological and psychological studies of cognitive process. Conserving a hypothesis that the brain operates in some way like a computer, Kosslyn and Koenig alter the Neu-mann model to allow for a higher level of liberation and free connection than the digital-computer metaphor usually permits. "In an actual network model," they say, "each input unit is connected to many hidden units, and each hidden unit is connected to many output units" (24). Computation, therefore, is

> . . . nothing more than a rule-based association game; given an input, a particular output is required by the rules. The inputs and outputs have interpretations in the

context of the larger system, which includes other components that produce the inputs and act on the outputs. Note that a computational system need not actually involve rules that are explicitly specified ("mentioned") and followed; the system need not include a cookbook that specifies recipes, which in turn are read and followed a step at a time. Rather, . . . the system may not specify rules at all, but rather is "wired" in such a way that the relations between its inputs and outputs can be *described* using rules. (31)

Another useful overview is Howard E. Gardner, *The Mind's New Science: A History of the Cognitive Revolution.* For an informed consideration of the applicability of all this to a refreshed theorizing of humor in American literature, see Gregg Camfield's fine chapter "Humorneutics," in *Necessary Madness,* 150–86.

4. Richard Powers, "Eyes Wide Open," 83.

5. Though not specifically about literary wit, or even about humor as a literary mode, Henry Louis Gates Jr.'s *The Signifying Monkey: A Theory of Afro-American Literary Criticism* provides strong foundations on which to build discussions of literary wit in African American discourse. Establishing the special situation of African American texts—West African folk-narrative traditions and their powerful applicability to slave culture and postslavery underclass predicaments—Gates emphasizes the importance of wit and wordplay in the black American speaker-author's Fabian struggle for survival and self-expression against "The Lion" and "The Elephant," representing powerful Others that cannot be resisted head-on. Gates offers unprecedented insight into the complexity of this discourse:

The ironic reversal of a received racist image of the black as simianlike, the Signifying Monkey, he who dwells at the margins of discourse, ever punning, ever troping, ever embodying the ambiguities of language, is our trope for repetition and revision, indeed our trope of chiasmus, repeating and reversing simultaneously as he does in one deft discursive act. If Vico and Burke, or Nietzsche, de Man, and Bloom, are correct in identifying four and six "master tropes," then we might think of those as the "master's tropes," and of Signifyin(g) as the slave's trope, the trope of tropes, as Bloom characterizes metalepsis, "a trope-reversing trope, a figure of a figure." Signifyin(g) is a trope in which are subsumed several other rhetorical tropes, including metaphor, metonymy, synecdoche, and irony (the master tropes) and also hyperbole, litotes, and metalepsis (Bloom's supplement to Burke). To this list we could easily add aporia, chiasmus, and catechresis, all of which are used in the ritual of Signifyin(g). (52)

Gates's project here is to describe the strength and profundity of the connection between an African–African American oral tradition, the "speakerly text," and a more distinctly and self-consciously literary variety of "Signifyin(g)": "the play of tradition, the play on the tradition, the sheer play of indeterminacy itself" (227). Especially with regard to Ishmael Reed and Alice Walker, Gates begins to establish the importance and complexity of wit in the contemporary African American novel. Gates is a pioneer: there are many other such novels by black American writers that can be effectively recognized and discussed in similar ways.

Works Cited

Abrams, M. H. *A Glossary of Literary Terms.* 7th ed. New York: Harcourt Brace, 1999.

Addison, Joseph. *The Spectator.* Edited by Donald F. Bond. 2 vols. Oxford: Clarendon, 1965.

Adams, Joseph Quincy, ed. *Chief Pre-Shakespearean Dramas: A Selection of Plays Illustrating the History of the English Drama from Its Origins down to the Present.* Boston: Houghton Mifflin, 1952.

Alexi, Sherman. *The Lone Ranger and Tonto Fistfight in Heaven.* New York: Harperennial, 1994.

Antor, Heinz. "The Arts, the Sciences, and the Making of Meaning: Tom Stoppard's *Arcadia* as a Post-Structuralist Play." *Anglia: Zeitschrift fur Englische Philologie* 116, no. 3 (1998): 326–54.

Apte, Mahadev L. *Humor and Laughter: An Anthropological Approach.* Ithaca: Cornell University Press, 1985.

Bakhtin, Mikhail Mikhailovich. *The Dialogic Imagination*. Edited by Michael Holquist. Translated by Caryl Emerson and Holquist. Austin: University of Texas Press, 1981.

———. *Rabelais and His World*. Translated by Hélène Iswolsky. Bloomington: Indiana University Press, 1984.

Barthes, Roland. *Roland Barthes par Roland Barthes*. Paris: Editions du Seuil, 1979.

Bataille, Georges. *Inner Experience*. Translated with an introduction by Leslie Anne Boldt. Albany: SUNY Press, 1988.

Beckson, Carl, and Arthur Ganz. *Literary Terms: A Dictionary*. New York: Farrar, Straus, and Giroux, 1983.

Benedikt, Michael. "Witty and Eerie." In Salinger, 101–5. First published in *Poetry* 115 (March 1970): 422–45.

Bergson, Henri. *The Creative Mind*. Translated by Mabelle L. Andison. New York: Citadel Press, 1992.

———. *Laughter: An Essay on the Meaning of the Comic*. Translated by Cloudesley Brereton and Fred Rothwell. New York: Macmillan, 1913.

Berrong, Richard. *Rabelais and Bakhtin: Popular Culture in Gargantua and Pantagruel*. Lincoln: University of Nebraska Press, 1986.

Bierce, Ambrose. *The Collected Writings of Ambrose Bierce*. New York: Citadel Press, 1996.

Blair, Walter. *Native American Humor*. San Francisco: Chandler, 1960.

Brooker, Jewel Spears. "A Conversation with Richard Wilbur." *Christianity and Literature* 42, no. 4 (1993): 517–40.

Brooks, Cleanth. "This World and More: The Poetry of Richard Wilbur." *Christianity and Literature* 42, no. 4 (1993): 541–50.

Budd, Louis J. *Our Mark Twain*. Philadelphia: University of Pennsylvania Press, 1983.

Butscher, Edward. "From Left to Right: Olson and Wilbur." *Poet Lore* 87, no. 1 (1992): 61–66.

Calvin, William H. *The Cerebral Code: Thinking a Thought in the Mosaics of the Mind*. Cambridge: MIT Press, 1996.

Camfield, Gregg. *Necessary Madness: The Humor of Domesticity in Nineteenth-Century American Literature*. New York: Oxford University Press, 1997.

Castle, Terry. *Masquerade and Civilization: The Carnivalesque in Eighteenth-Century English Culture and Fiction*. Stanford: Stanford University Press, 1986.

Chapman, Antony J., and Hugh C. Foot, eds. *Humor and Laughter: Theory, Research, and Applications*. New York: John Wiley and Sons, 1976.

Clemens, Samuel L. "The Belated Russian Passport." *Harper's Weekly* 46 (6 December 1902): 4–5, 8–9.

———. *Following the Equator and Anti-Imperialist Essays*. New York: Oxford University Press, 1996.

———. *Pudd'nhead Wilson's Calendar for 1894*. New York: Century Company, 1893.

———. *Selected Mark Twain–Howells Letters*. Edited by Frederick Anderson, William M. Gibson, and Henry Nash Smith. New York: Athenaeum, 1968.

———. *The Tragedy of Pudd'nhead Wilson and The Comedy Those Extraordinary Twins*. Hartford: American Publishing Company, 1894.

——. *The Writings of Mark Twain*. Author's National Edition. 24 vols. New York: Harper and Brothers, n.d.

Coiro, Ann Baynes. *Robert Herrick's Hesperides and the Epigram Book Tradition*. Baltimore: Johns Hopkins University Press, 1988.

Cox, James M. *Mark Twain: The Fate of Humor*. Princeton: Princeton University Press, 1966.

Dacey, Philip, and David Jauss, eds. *Strong Measures: Contemporary American Poetry in Traditional Forms*. New York: Harper and Row, 1986.

Danson, Lawrence. *Wilde's Intentions: The Artist in His Criticism*. Oxford: Clarendon, 1997.

Delaney, Paul. *Tom Stoppard: The Moral Vision of the Major Plays*. New York: Macmillan, 1990.

Dennett, Daniel C. *Consciousness Explained*. Boston: Little, Brown, 1991.

Dentith, Simon. *Bakhtinian Thought*. New York: Routledge, 1995.

Derrida, Jacques. *De l'esprit: Heidegger et La Question*. Paris: Editions Galilee, 1987.

——. "Différance." In *A Critical and Cultural Theory Reader*, edited by Antony Easthope and Kate McGowan. Buckingham: Open University Press, 1992. First published in *Speech and Phenomena and Other Essays on Husserl's Theory of Signs*, trans. David B. Allison. Evanston: Northwestern University Press, 1973.

——. *Of Spirit: Heidegger and the Question*. Translated by Geoffrey Bennington and Rachel Bowlby. Chicago: University of Chicago Press, 1989.

Deutsch, Babette. *Poetry Handbook*. 4th ed. New York: Barnes and Noble, 1981.

——. Review of *The Beautiful Changes*, by Richard Wilbur. *Tomorrow* 8, no. 2 (1948): 58–59.

Diehl, Joanne Feit. *Women Poets and the American Sublime*. Bloomington: Indiana University Press, 1990.

Easthope, Antony, and Kate McGowan. *A Critical and Cultural Theory Reader*. Buckingham: Open University Press, 1992.

Eastman, Max. *Enjoyment of Laughter*. New York: Simon and Schuster, 1936.

Edelman, Gerald M. *Bright Air, Brilliant Fire*. New York: Basic Books, 1992.

Edgecombe, Rodney Stenning. *A Reader's Guide to the Poetry of Richard Wilbur*. Tuscaloosa: University of Alabama Press, 1995.

The Edinburgh Encyclopedia of Wit. Edinburgh: Denham and Dick, 1802.

Edson, Margaret. *Wit*. New York: Faber and Faber, 1999.

Ellmann, Richard. *Oscar Wilde*. New York: Knopf, 1987.

Emerson, Caryl. *The First Hundred Years of Bakhtin*. Princeton: Princeton University Press, 1997.

Emerson, Everett. *The Authentic Mark Twain*. Philadelphia: University of Pennsylvania Press, 1984.

Emerson, Ralph Waldo. *The Collected Works of Ralph Waldo Emerson*. 5 vols. Cambridge, Harvard University Press, Belknap Press, 1983.

Encyclopedia of Literature and Criticism. Edited by Martin Coyle and Peter Garside. New York: Routledge, 1990.

Fetterley, Judith. *The Resisting Reader: A Feminist Approach to American Fiction*. Bloomington: Indiana University Press, 1978.

Fishkin, Shelly Fisher. "Race and Culture at the Century's End: A Social Context for *Pudd'nhead Wilson*." *Essays in Arts and Sciences* 19 (1990): 1–27.

Freud, Sigmund. "Humour." *International Journal of Psychoanalysis* 9 (1928): 1–6.

———. *Jokes and Their Relation to the Unconscious*. Translated and edited by James Strachey, with a biographical introduction by Peter Gay. New York: Norton, 1960.

Gardner, Howard E. *The Mind's New Science: A History of the Cognitive Revolution*. New York: Basic Books, 1987.

Gates, Henry Louis, Jr. *The Signifying Monkey: A Theory of Afro-American Literary Criticism*. New York: Oxford University Press, 1988.

Gillespie, Michael Patrick. *Oscar Wilde and the Poetics of Ambiguity*. Gainesville: University Press of Florida, 1996.

Gillman, Susan, and Forrest Robinson, eds. *Mark Twain's Pudd'nhead Wilson: Race, Conflict, and Culture*. Durham: Duke University Press, 1990.

Golffing, F. C. "A Remarkable New Talent." In Salinger, 32–33. First published in *Poetry* 71 (January 1948): 221–23.

Graham, Peter W. "Et in Arcadia Nos." *Nineteenth-Century Contexts* 18, no. 4 (1995): 311–19.

Grotjahn, Martin. *Beyond Laughter*. New York: McGraw-Hill, 1957.

Gutwirth, Marcel. *Laughing Matter: An Essay on the Comic*. Ithaca: Cornell University Press, 1993.

Habegger, Alfred. *Gender, Fantasy, and Realism in American Literature*. New York: Columbia University Press, 1982.

Hall, Donald. "Richard Wilbur and Others." *Harvard Advocate* 134, no. 5 (1951): 2–4, 10–12.

Hamilton, Ian. "A Talent of the Shallows." *TLS*, 15–21 September 1989: 999.

The Harper Handbook to Literature. Edited by Northrup Frye, Sheridan Baker, George Perkins, and Barbara Perkins. New York: Longman, 1997.

Harris, Peter. "Forty Years of Richard Wilbur: The Loving Work of an Equilibrist." *Virginia Quarterly Review* 66 (Summer 1990): 412–25.

Hawthorn, Jeremy. *A Glossary of Contemporary Literary Theory*. London: Edward Arnold, 1992.

Hazlitt, William. *Selected Essays of William Hazlitt*. Edited by Geoffrey Keynes. New York: Random House, 1934.

Hecht, Anthony. "The Pathetic Fallacy." *Yale Review* 74, no. 4 (1985): 481–99.

Hill, Carl. *The Soul of Wit: Joke Theory from Grimm to Freud*. Lincoln: University of Nebraska Press, 1993.

Hill, Donald. *Richard Wilbur*. New York: Twayne, 1967.

Hoffman, Andrew J. *Inventing Mark Twain*. New York: Morrow, 1997.

Holland, Norman. *Laughing: A Psychology of Humor*. Ithaca: Cornell University Press, 1982.

Holman, C. Hugh, and William Harmon. *A Handbook to Literature*. 5th ed. New York: Macmillan, 1986.

Hougen, John B. *Ecstasy within Discipline: The Poetry of Richard Wilbur*. Atlanta: Scholars Press, 1995.

Howard, Ben. "Incarnate Lights." *Poetry* 154, no. 2 (1989): 99–112.

Howe, Lawrence. *Mark Twain and the Novel*. Cambridge: Cambridge University Press, 1998.

Hudson, Hoyt H. *The Epigram in the English Renaissance*. Princeton: Princeton University Press, 1947.

Hunt, Leigh. *Leigh Hunt's Literary Criticism*. Edited by Lawrence Huston Houtchens and Carolyn Washburn Houtchens. New York: Columbia University Press, 1956.

———. *Wit and Humour Selected from the English Poets*. 1846. Reprint, London: Smith, Elder and Co., 1893.

The Imperial Dictionary, English, Technological, and Scientific Applied to the Present State of Literature, Science, and Art; on the Basis of Webster's English Dictionary. Edited by John Ogilvie. London: Blackie and Son, 1853.

James, Clive. "When the Gloves are Off." In Salinger, 106–17. First published in *The Review* (London), no. 26 (Summer 1971): 35–44.

Jarrell, Randall. "A View of Three Poets." In Salinger, 46–49. First published in *Partisan Review* 18 (Nov.–Dec. 1951): 691–700.

Jenkins, Anthony. *The Theatre of Tom Stoppard*. Cambridge: Cambridge University Press, 1987.

Johnson, Samuel. *A Dictionary of the English Language*. London: W. Strahan, 1755. Facsimile reprint. London: Longman, n.d.

Jones, Louisa. "The Comic as Poetry: Bergson Revisited." *Nineteenth-Century French Studies* 2, nos. 1–2 (1974): 75–85.

Kaplan, Justin. *Mr. Clemens and Mark Twain*. New York: Simon and Schuster, 1966.

Kelly, Katherine. *Tom Stoppard and the Craft of Comedy: Medium and Genre at Play*. Ann Arbor: University of Michigan Press, 1991.

Kierkegaard, Søren. *The Concept of Irony*. Translated by Lee M. Capel. Bloomington: Indiana University Press, 1965.

———. *Søren Kierkegaard's Journals and Papers*. Edited and translated by Howard V. Hong and Edna H. Hong. 7 vols. Bloomington: Indiana University Press, 1970.

Knox, Melissa. *Oscar Wilde: A Long and Lovely Suicide*. New Haven: Yale University Press, 1994.

Koestler, Arthur. *The Act of Creation*. New York: Macmillan, 1964.

Kosslyn, Stephen M., and Olivier Koenig. *Wet Mind*. New York: Free Press, 1992.

Kramer, Jeffrey, and Prapassaree Kramer. "Stoppard's *Arcadia*: Research, Time, Loss." *Modern Drama* 40, no. 1 (1997): 1–10.

Kristeva, Julia. *Desire in Language: A Semiotic Approach to Literature and Art*. Edited by Leon S. Roudiez. Translated by Alice A. Jardine and Thomas Gora. New York: Columbia University Press, 1990.

———. *The Kristeva Reader*. Edited by Toril Moi. Oxford: Blackwell, 1986.

Lacan, Jacques. *Encore, 1972–1973. Le Seminaire de Jacques Lacan*, vol. 20. Edited by Jacques-Alain Miller. Paris: Editions du Seuil, 1975.

Lacey, A. R. *Bergson*. New York: Routledge, 1989.

Lamb, Charles, and Mary Lamb. *The Works of Charles and Mary Lamb*. Edited by E. V. Lucas. 7 vols. London: Methuen and Co., 1903.

Langer, Susanne. *Feeling and Form: A Theory of Art*. New York: Scribner's, 1953.

Lauter, Paul, ed. *Theories of Comedy*. Garden City: Doubleday Anchor, 1964.

Lauter, Paul, et al., eds. *The Heath Anthology of American Literature*. 3rd ed. 2 vols. Lexington, Mass.: D.C. Heath, 1997.

LeMaster, J. R., and James D. Wilson, eds. *The Mark Twain Encyclopedia*. New York: Garland, 1993.

Levin, Harry. *Playboys and Killjoys*. New York: Oxford University Press, 1987.

Lewis, C. S. *Studies in Words*. Cambridge: Cambridge University Press, 1967.

Lewis, Paul. *Comic Effects.* Albany: SUNY Press, 1989.

Lynn, Kenneth S. *Mark Twain and Southwestern Humor.* Boston: Little, Brown, 1959.

Marcus Aurelius. *Meditations.* Translated by George Long. Edited by William Kaufman. 1886. Reprint. New York: Dover, 1997.

Meredith, George. *An Essay on Comedy and the Uses of the Comic Spirit.* New York: Scribner's, 1923.

Michelson, Bruce. "Richard Wilbur's Music of Pure Cold." *Christianity and Literature* 42, no. 4 (1993): 585–600.

———. *Wilbur's Poetry: Music in a Scattering Time.* Amherst: University of Massachusetts Press, 1991.

Morreall, John, ed. *The Philosophy of Laughter and Humor.* Albany: SUNY Press, 1987.

Nickels, Cameron C. *New England Humor: From the Revolutionary War to the Civil War.* Knoxville: University of Tennessee Press, 1993.

Ortiz, Simon J. *Men on the Moon: Collected Short Stories.* Tucson: University of Arizona Press, 1999.

Oxford English Dictionary. 2nd ed. Prepared by J. A. Simpson and E. S. C. Weiner. New York: Oxford-Clarendon, 1989.

Page, Norman. *An Oscar Wilde Chronology.* Boston: G. K. Hall, 1991.

Park, Clara Claiborne. "Called to Praise: Richard Wilbur's Brilliant Positive." *Christianity and Literature* 42, no. 4 (1993): 551–68.

Parker, Hershel. *Flawed Texts and Verbal Icons: Literary Authority in American Fiction.* Evanston: Northwestern University Press, 1984.

Payne, Marjory Scheidt. "Doubt and Redeeming Gaiety: Religious and Philosophical Strands in Richard Wilbur's Poetry." *Christianity and Literature* 42, no. 4 (1993): 569–84.

Penrose, Roger. *The Emperor's New Mind.* New York: Oxford University Press, 1989.

Powers, Richard. "Eyes Wide Open." *New York Times Magazine,* 18 April 1999, 83.

The New Princeton Encyclopedia of Poetry and Poetics. Edited by Alex Preminger and T. V. F. Brogan. Princeton: Princeton University Press, 1993.

Pugh, Thomas. "Why Is Everybody Laughing? Roth, Coover, and Meta-Comic Narrative." *Critique* 35, no. 2 (1994): 67–80.

Rasmussen, R. Kent. *Mark Twain A to Z.* Oxford: Oxford University Press, 1995.

Rich, Adrienne. *Collected Early Poems: 1950–1970.* New York: Norton, 1995.

Rourke, Constance. *American Humor: A Study of the National Character.* Garden City: Doubleday, 1953.

Salinger, Wendy, ed. *Richard Wilbur's Creation.* Ann Arbor: University of Michigan Press, 1983.

Sammells, Neil. *Tom Stoppard, the Artist as Critic.* New York: St. Martin's, 1988.

Schaeffer, Neil. *The Art of Laughter.* New York: Columbia University Press, 1981.

Schmidgall, Gary. *The Stranger Wilde.* New York: Dutton, 1994.

Schopenhauer, Arthur. *The World as Will and Idea.* 3 vols. Translated by R. B. Haldane and J. Kemp. London: Routledge, 1883.

Searle, John. *Intentionality: An Essay in the Philosophy of Mind.* Cambridge: Cambridge University Press, 1983.

Shaw, Harry. *Concise Dictionary of Literary Terms.* New York: McGraw-Hill, 1976.

Shewan, Rodney. *Oscar Wilde: Art and Egotism.* New York: Harper and Row, 1977.

Showalter, Elaine. *Sexual Anarchy*. New York: Viking, 1990.

Sloane, David E. E. *Mark Twain as a Literary Comedian*. Baton Rouge: Louisiana State University Press, 1979.

Smith, Henry Nash. *Mark Twain: The Development of a Writer*. Cambridge: Harvard University Press, Belknap Press, 1962.

Somers, Nancy, and Paul P. Somers. "Literary Humor." In *Humor in America*, edited by Lawrence E. Mintz. New York: Greenwood, 1988.

Stoppard, Tom. *Arcadia*. London: Faber and Faber, 1993.

Swallow, Allan. "Some Current Poetry." *New Mexico Quarterly* 18 (Winter 1948): 455–62.

Thomas, Brook. "Tragedies of Race, Training, Birth, and Communities of Competent Pudd'nheads." *American Literary History* 1 (Winter 1989): 754–85.

Walker, Nancy A. *A Very Serious Thing: Women's Humor and American Culture*. Minneapolis: University of Minnesota Press, 1988.

Wallace, Patricia. Introduction to "American Poetry since World War II," in *The Norton Anthology of American Literature*, ed. Nina Baym et al. 5th ed. 2 vols. New York: Norton, 1998.

Webster, William G., and William A. Wheeler, eds. *A Dictionary of the English Language, Explanatory, Pronouncing, Etymological, and Synonymous*. Academic Edition. New York: Ivison, Blakeman, Taylor, and Co., 1867.

Webster's New International Dictionary. 2nd ed. Springfield: G. and C. Merriam, 1937.

Webster's New Universal Unabridged Dictionary. New York: New World Dictionaries, Simon and Schuster, 1983.

Wilbur, Richard. *Mayflies*. New York: Harcourt Brace and Co., 2000.

———. *More Opposites*. New York: Harcourt Brace Jovanovich, 1991.

———. *New and Collected Poems*. New York: Harcourt Brace and Co., 1988.

Wilde, Oscar. *The Epigrams of Oscar Wilde*. Edited by Alvin Redman, with an introduction by Vyvyan Holland. Twickenham: Senate, 1996.

———. *Oscar Wilde: A Critical Edition of the Major Works*. Edited by Isobel Murray. Oxford: Oxford University Press, 1989.

———. *The Picture of Dorian Gray*. Edited by Donald L. Lawler. New York: Norton, 1988.

———. *Plays, Prose Writings, and Poems*. Edited by Anthony Fothergill. London: J. M. Dent, 1996.

———. *The Portable Oscar Wilde*. Rev. ed. Edited by Richard Aldington and Stanley Weintraub. New York: Viking Penguin, 1981.

Williams, Raymond. *Keywords: A Vocabulary of Culture and Society*. Rev. edition. New York: Oxford University Press, 1983.

Williamson, George. *The Proper Wit of Poetry*. Chicago: University of Chicago Press, 1961.

Index